Personal Identity

The Problems of Philosophy:
Their Past and Present

General Editor: Ted Honderich
Professor of Philosophy
University College
London

Each book in this series brings into clear view and deals with a great, persistent, or significant problem of philosophy. The first part of each book presents the history of the problem. The second part, of an analytical kind, develops and defends the author's preferred solution.

PRIVATE OWNERSHIP
James O. Grunebaum

RELIGIOUS BELIEF AND THE WILL
Louis P. Pojman

RATIONALITY
Harold I. Brown

THE RATIONAL FOUNDATIONS OF ETHICS
T.L.S. Sprigge

MORAL KNOWLEDGE
Alan H. Goldman

PRACTICAL REASONING
Robert Audi

Forthcoming:

MIND–BODY IDENTITY THEORIES
Cynthia Macdonald

IF P THEN Q
THE FOUNDATIONS OF LOGIC AND ARGUMENT
David H. Sanford

Personal Identity

Harold W. Noonan

Routledge
London and New York

First published 1989
by Routledge
11 New Fetter Lane, London EC4P 4EE
29 West 35th Street, New York, NY 10001

Printed in Great Britain
by TJ Press (Padstow), Padstow, Cornwall

British Library Cataloguing in Publication Data

Noonan, Harold W.
    Personal identity.
    1. Man. Identity. Philosophical perspectives
    I. Title
    126

    ISBN 0 415 03365 9

Library of Congress Cataloging in Publication Data

Noonan, Harold W.
    Personal identity.

    (The Problems of philosophy : their past and present)
    Bibliography: p.
    Includes index.
    1. Identity. 2. Mind and body. 3. Self. I. Title.
II. Series: Problems of philosophy.
BD450.N635   1989   126   88–26422
ISBN 0 415 03365 9

Contents

Preface

I am grateful to my colleagues at the University of Birmingham for the patience with which they have read and commented on successive redraftings of this material. I am also grateful for their comments to Nicholas Measor of the University of Leicester and Greg McCulloch of the University of Nottingham. Drafts of various chapters have been read to the philosophy societies of St Andrews, Durham, Edinburgh, Lancaster, Leeds, Sheffield and Stirling. I am grateful to the audiences on those occasions for their helpful comments, and particularly to Crispin Wright, Vinit Haksar, Geoffrey Madell, Jonathan Lowe, Andrew Brennan and Bob Hale.

Material used from my article 'The closest continuer theory of identity' was previously published in *Inquiry*, vol. 28, 195–229, and appears here by kind permission of Universitetsforlaget, Oslo.

H.W.N.

CHAPTER 1
An Initial Survey

1.1 Introduction

What am I? And what is my relationship to the thing I call 'my body'? Thus each of us can pose for himself the philosophical problems of the nature of the self and the relationship between a person and his body. The nature of personal identity over time, and the link, if any, between personal identity and bodily identity are aspects of these problems and it is this, of course, that accounts for the immense philosophical interest in the concept of personal identity. But, perhaps unlike some other philosophical problems, the nature of personal identity is not merely of interest to professional philosophers, but also a matter of great practical concern to all of us, philosophers and non-philosophers alike. Man has always hoped to survive his bodily death, and it is a central tenet of many religions that such survival is a reality. But, of course, whether such survival is possible, and what forms, if any, it might take, are matters which depend crucially on the nature of personal identity over time. For to survive, in the sense that concerns us, means to *continue to exist* as persons identifiable as those here and now. Again, our concept of personal identity is intimately linked with our concept of responsibility for past actions and with our practices of praise and blame; whilst our own pasts and futures are the primary focus of many of our central emotions and attitudes. Were we to give up the idea of a person as a unitary continuing entity, it is hard to imagine the drastic impact this would have on our picture of the world and our emotional and moral responses to it.

In what follows we will be looking closely both at the history of the problem of personal identity and at the main solutions to the problem defended in contemporary debate. But it will be useful, before getting too involved in details, to begin with a survey of these solutions and a sketch of the main arguments put forward in their favour.

1.2 Constitutive and evidential criteria

The problem of personal identity over time is the problem of giving an account of the logically necessary and sufficient conditions for a person identified at one time being the same person as a person identified at another. Otherwise put, it is the problem of giving an account of what personal identity over time necessarily consists in, or, as many philosophers phrase it, the problem of specifying the criterion of personal identity over time. On an alternative use of the term 'criterion', to specify a criterion of personal identity over time would be to say something about what could count as evidence for personal identity. It is important to be aware at the outset that this is *not* what philosophers are interested in when they debate the problem of personal identity. Their concern is with the constitutive, the metaphysical-cum-semantic, not the evidential, criterion of personal identity. Of course, this is not to say that a philosophical account of personal identity can just put aside as a mere irrelevance what actually counts as evidence for personal identity. For both our own identity over time and that of others is, we ordinarily think, something of which we can have knowledge. Conceivably this common opinion may be mistaken, but the onus of proof must be on the philosopher who says so. In the absence of such proof then it must be regarded as a condition of adequacy on any account of what personal identity consists in that it not entail that personal identity is unknowable, or not knowable in the ways we ordinarily take it to be, or leave it completely mysterious how it *can* be known in these ways.

I shall have more to say later in elucidation of these points; but that will suffice for the moment as a specification of our problem. Let us now turn to its possible solutions.

1.3 The bodily criterion

The most natural theory of personal identity, which would be almost anyone's first thought, is that personal identity is constituted by bodily identity: $P2$ at time $t2$ is the same person as $P1$ at time $t1$ if and only if $P2$ has the same body as $P1$ had. I shall call this *the Bodily Criterion* of personal identity. According to this view personal identity is essentially no different from the identity of material objects in general. An artefact, like a ship, or a living thing, like an oak tree or a horse, persists through time. Its persistence does not consist in its retention of the same matter – for artefacts can be repaired and patched up and living things are necessarily involved in a constant exchange of matter with their environment – but in its retention of the same form as its matter undergoes gradual replacement. Likewise, according to the Bodily Criterion of personal identity, what is required for the identity of person $P2$ at time $t2$ and person $P1$ at time $t1$ is not that $P2$ and $P1$ are materially identical but merely that the matter constituting $P2$ has resulted from that constituting $P1$ by a series of more or less gradual replacements in such a way that it is correct to say that the body of $P2$ at $t2$ is identical with the body of $P1$ at $t1$.

According to this view, as I said, personal identity is essentially no different from the identity of such things as oak trees or horses. And this conforms to our ordinary experience. We do not in the normal run of things in fact ever regard it as an open question whether someone who, by the Bodily Criterion of personal identity, is identical with some earlier person, *is* that person, or whether someone who, by the Bodily Criterion of personal identity, is not identical with some earlier person, is *not* that person. Personal identity, as we know it in our everyday lives, is in fact constituted by bodily identity.

Nor can it be made an objection against the Bodily Criterion of personal identity that it excludes any hope of an after-life. For it does not. What it does exclude, however, is any possibility of an after-life otherwise than by resurrection. But that can hardly be regarded as a conclusive objection to it.

1.4 The brain criterion

Nevertheless the Bodily Criterion of personal identity has not proved popular with philosophers. For though it is undeniable that in our everyday experience personal identity is constituted by bodily identity, it seems all too easy to imagine possible cases in which this is not so. But if such cases are indeed possible then personal identity cannot, *as a matter of logical or conceptual necessity*, consist in bodily identity.

The sort of case which has led most modern philosophers to think that the Bodily Criterion of personal identity must be rejected is the following.

One part of the body – the brain – seems to be of crucial importance in determining the psychology of the person whose body it inhabits. Damage to someone's brain can cause amnesia or radical changes in personality or character. Not so for damage to, say, one's left knee. Imagine, then, that in the twenty-first century it is possible to transplant brains, as it is now possible to transplant hearts, and let us suppose that the brain of a Mr Brown is transplanted into the skull of a Mr Robinson. This could be done even with existing techniques. Just as my brain could be extracted, and kept alive by a connection with an artificial heart-lung machine, it could be kept alive by a connection with the heart and lungs in someone else's body. The drawback, today, is that the nerves from my brain could not be connected with the nerves in the other's body. My brain could survive if transplanted into his body, but the resulting person would be paralysed. Even so, he could be enabled to communicate with others. One crude method would be some device, attached to the nerve that would have controlled this person's right thumb, enabling him to send messages in Morse Code. Another device, attached to some sensory nerve, could enable him to receive messages. Many people would welcome surviving, even if totally paralysed, if they could still communicate with others.

Let us suppose, however, that the surgeons in the twenty-first century are able to connect the nerves from Brown's brain to the nerves in Robinson's body. The result of the operation, call him Brownson, will then be a completely healthy person, without any paralysis, with Robinson's body, but in character, memories and personality quite indistinguishable from Brown, and this not as a consequence of some freak accident, but because of his possession of Brown's brain (there might be a problem about how Brown's personality can express itself in the Robinson body if we imagine that the two bodies are very dissimilar in appearance, so, for the sake of the example, let us imagine that this is not so; let us imagine in fact that Robinson is Brown's double). Now who will this person be?

Most modern philosophers who have reflected on this case (which I have taken from Shoemaker 1963, with elaborations due to Parfit 1984) have not found this a difficult question to answer. They have found that they could not honestly deny that Brownson, in the case imagined, was Brown, and so they have been led to reject the Bodily Criterion of personal identity. As Parfit puts it (1984:253), they have been led to accept that 'receiving a new skull and a new body is just the limiting case of receiving a new heart, new lungs, and so on'.

But a fairly simple modification of the Bodily Criterion can accommodate the Brown/Brownson case, whilst retaining the assumption that personal identity consists in nothing other than the persistence of a certain physical entity. The obvious response to the case is to say that it shows only that what is required for personal identity is not identity of the whole body but, merely, identity of that part of the body – which, contingently, is the brain – which is the central organ controlling memory, character and personality. According to this suggestion $P2$ at $t2$ will be the same person as $P1$ at $t1$ just in case $P2$ at $t2$ has the same brain as $P1$ at $t1$. Let us call this *the Brain Criterion* of personal identity.

1.5 The physical criterion

But in fact this modification of the original Bodily Criterion of personal identity is not sufficiently radical. For if one accepts the Brown/Brownson case as a case of personal identity one is bound to find compelling also other cases in which identity of brain is not preserved, but the later person is psychologically identical with the earlier person, as Brownson is with Brown, in a way that is quite as scientifically comprehensible as in the Brown/Brownson case.

The human brain has two very similar hemispheres – a left hemisphere and a right hemisphere. The left hemisphere plays a major role in the control of the limbs on the right side of the body and in the processing of information from the right side of the body and the right sides of the eyes. The right hemisphere plays a major role in the control of the limbs on the left side of the body and in the processing of information from the left side of the body and the left sides of the eyes. The left hemisphere typically has the linguistic and mathematical abilities of an adult, while the right hemisphere has these abilities at the level of a young child. But the right hemisphere, though less advanced in these respects, has greater abilities of other kinds, such as those involved in pattern recognition or musicality. After the age of 3 or 4 the two hemispheres follow a 'division of labour' with each developing certain abilities. The lesser linguistic abilities of the right hemisphere are not intrinsic or permanent. People who have had strokes in the left hemisphere often regress to the linguistic ability of a young child, but with their remaining right hemisphere many can relearn adult speech. It is also believed that, in a minority of people, there may be no difference between the abilities of the two hemispheres.

In a normal adult the two hemispheres are connected and communicate by a bundle of fibres – the corpus callosum. But in the treatment of some epileptics these fibres were cut. It was this that led to the discovery of the independent functioning and (typically) different roles of the two hemispheres. For when these patients were tested in specially designed experimental situations the effect, in the words of one surgeon (Sperry 1968b: 724), was to appear to reveal 'two independent spheres of conscious awareness, one in each hemisphere, each of which is cut off from the mental experience of the other . . . each hemisphere seems to have its own sensations, perceptions, concepts, impulses to act. . . . Following the surgery each hemisphere has its own memories.' The facts which prompted this description are set out in Nagel (1971). For example, in the case of these patients,

> what is flashed to the right half of the visual field, or felt unseen by the right hand can be reported verbally. What is flashed to the left half field or felt by the left hand cannot be reported, though if the word 'hat' is flashed on the left the left hand will retrieve a hat from a group of concealed objects if the person is told to pick out what he has seen. At the same time he will insist verbally that he saw nothing. Or, if two different words are flashed to the two half fields (e.g. 'pencil' and 'toothbrush') and the individual is told to retrieve the corresponding object from beneath a screen with both hands, then the hands will search the collection of objects independently, the right hand picking up the pencil and discarding it while the left hand searches for it, and the left hand similarly rejecting the toothbrush which the right hand lights upon with satisfaction.

Now as indicated above, both hemispheres are not in fact necessary for survival. People have survived when one hemisphere has been put out of action by a stroke or injury, the other hemisphere then combining the functions of both. And if parts of a hemisphere are removed, at any rate early in life, the roles of these parts are often taken over by parts of the other hemisphere. Brain operations which remove substantial parts of the brain are not infrequent. It might be possible one day to remove a whole hemisphere without killing the patient, the other hemisphere taking over its functions as sometimes happens when one hemisphere is incapacitated by a stroke. But then we must reject the Brain Criterion of personal identity, for in such a case there will be personal identity without brain identity, the survivor only having *part* of the brain of the original person.

Admittedly in this case we have the rest of the body to hang on to, so we could appeal to the original Bodily Criterion of personal identity to justify our judgement. But an obvious extension of the case shows that this manoeuvre gets us nowhere.

Let us suppose that half of a man's brain is destroyed and then the remaining half transplanted into another body with consequent transference of memories, personality and character traits. Here we can neither appeal to the original Bodily Criterion of personal identity nor to the Brain Criterion to justify the judgement that the surviving person is the brain hemisphere donor. Yet it seems quite clear that if we accept that Brownson is Brown in the original Brown/Brownson case we cannot deny that in this case also the survivor is the original brain hemisphere donor. For if we accept that a person goes where his brain goes it cannot make any difference if his brain in fact consists of only one brain hemisphere combining the functions usually divided between two.

This line of thought thus leads us away from both the original Bodily Criterion of personal identity and its too simple modification, the Brain Criterion. But it does not yet force us to accept that personal identity does not consist in the persistence of any physical entity. Rather, we are led to what I shall call *the Physical Criterion* of personal identity, a version of which is put forward in Wiggins (1967), and discussed in Parfit (1984). The simplest formulation of this suggestion is that what is necessary for personal identity is not identity of the whole of the brain, but identity of enough of the brain to be the brain of a living person: person $P2$ at $t2$ is the same person as person $P1$ at $t1$ if and only if enough of the brain of *P*1 at *t*1 survives in *P*2 at *t*2 to be the brain of a living person.

1.6 Objections to the physical criterion

The Physical Criterion of personal identity does not provide an easy stopping place, however, for someone who has been persuaded by the Brown/Brownson case and the brain hemisphere transplant case to reject the Bodily and Brain Criteria of personal identity. For if one is persuaded by these cases yet another piece of science fiction leaves one with no convincing defence of the Physical Criterion.

The piece of science fiction in question is one employed by Bernard Williams (see Williams (1970) and 'Are persons bodies?' in Williams 1973). Williams is in fact one of the few modern writers on personal identity who have resisted the conclusion that Brownson is Brown, and his argument in these papers is directed against those who accept this conclusion.

We can imagine, he says, the removal of the information from a brain into some storage device (the device, that is, is put into a state information-theoretically equivalent to the total state of the brain), whence it is then put back into the same or another brain. It seems clear, he says, and in this he seems to be correct, that if this were done to one man, information being removed from his brain (for purposes of brain repair, for instance) and then put back – then, supposing that he recovered all his dispositions, with regard to memory and so forth, that he had had before – we should not dream of saying that he did not, at the later stage, really remember. The passage of the information *via* the device would not count as the kind of causal route to his later knowledge which was incompatible with that later knowledge's being memory. As things are, the sorts of causal route that go outside the body do not count for memory: if a man learns anew of his past experiences by reading what he earlier wrote about them in his diary, then he does not remember his earlier experiences. But the imagined passage of the information *via* the device is obviously not a case which would fall under this ban: the replacement of the information is not as such 'learning again'; it is not, then, in itself incompatible with the later knowledge being memory.

Moreover, Williams says, it seems pretty clear that under these circumstances a man should be counted the same if this were done to him, and in the process he were given a new brain (the repairs, let us say, actually required a new part). But, if so, the Physical Criterion of personal identity must, of course, be abandoned. Yet there seems to be nothing that a defender of that criterion, who has followed the route charted above to his position, could convincingly say against Williams's claim. For it is implicit in his position that the reason why (part) brain identity should be preferred to bodily identity as a criterion of personal identity is that it is the brain and not the rest of the body that carries with it psychological identity – identity of memory, personality and character. It is this alone which justifies the privileged status that his criterion of personal identity assigns to that particular bodily organ. But in Williams's case the brain no longer performs this function: psychological identity is secured without identity of brain or part brain, just as in the Brown/ Brownson case it is secured without identity of body. It thus seems quite unmotivated for the defender of the Physical Criterion of personal identity, if he has been led to it by anything like the path sketched above (and what other path could there be?), to resist Williams's conclusion. But to accept it is to abandon his position.

   This argument is an argument against the Physical Criterion of personal identity considered as providing a necessary condition of personal identity. Further development of Williams's story provides an equally powerful argument against the Physical Criterion *qua* sufficient condition of personal identity. For let us suppose that before Brown's brain is transplanted into Robinson's body, it is wiped clean of the information contained in it, and *via* the use of Williams's brain–state transfer device is put into a state information–theoretically identical with that of Robinson's brain. The transplant then takes place, but Brownson now not only has Robinson's body, he also has Robinson's memories, character and personality traits. What he does not have is Robinson's brain, and so by the Physical Criterion of personal identity he is not Robinson but Brown, whose brain he has. But surely this must be wrong, at least if Brownson is Brown in the original version of the story, and the fact that Brownson has Brown's brain must in this case be regarded as being quite irrelevant to the question of his identity with Brown; just as irrelevant as was the fact, in the original version of the story, that he did *not* have Brown's left leg.

   There are further arguments against the Physical Criterion of personal identity. One major difficulty its champion faces is to say something sensible about the situation in which *both* brain hemispheres are transplanted, but into *different* bodies. We shall have much to do with this possibility below. But at this point I wish to note a rather different difficulty for the Physical Criterion.

When philosophers speak of the problem of personal identity they do not use 'person' as a mere synonym of 'human being'. Rather they use it in the sense introduced by Locke (1961): 'a thinking intelligent being with reason and reflection that can consider itself as itself, the same thinking being, in different times and places'. In short, 'person' in the philosophical debate, is a *functional* term, a term that applies to something just in case it has certain capacities (like 'genius' or 'prophet'). The possibility of persons other than human beings is then something that cannot be denied, as Locke himself emphasized by reference to the possibility (which he was in fact rather inclined to accept as an actuality) of a very intelligent rational parrot. (It was in fact Locke's main concern to argue that such a parrot would not be a *man*, but it is implicit in his discussion that it *would* be a person.) But if there can be persons other than human beings there seems to be nothing inconceivable about the idea of persons other than human beings in whom *no* bodily organ occupies the role the brain occupies in the human organism. If so, however, the Physical Criterion of personal identity will be inapplicable to them. Consequently, unless one abandons the demand for a criterion of identity over time for persons *as such*, and settles for the view that there are different criteria of identity for different kinds of person (human persons, parrot persons, extra-terrestrial persons and so on) one must reject the Physical Criterion of personal identity even as an account of the logically necessary and sufficient conditions of identity over time for *human persons*.

I have now outlined, I believe, the main considerations which have been influential in persuading many recent philosophers that personal identity cannot be constituted by the persistence of *any* physical entity.

1.7 The memory criterion

An alternative view, for which many of these arguments seem to provide strong support, is that personal identity is constituted by psychological factors. The essence of this is the thought that, given the importance for our attitudes towards persons of their memories, character and personality traits, continuity in respect of these should be taken to constitute personal identity – whether or not this continuity is caused by the persistence of some bodily organ, such as the brain; and the absence of continuity in these respects involves the absence of personal identity, even if there is identity of body or identity of brain. I shall now explain what this means.

The simplest version of this view is suggested by John Locke's writings. According to this version of the view, what is crucial to personal identity is memory, and it is memory alone that needs to be appealed to in providing a criterion of personal identity. This view is especially tempting because of the fact that memory is crucially involved in our awareness, from the first-person viewpoint, of our own identity over time. But the notion of memory is a very wide one. I can be said to remember my 7 times table, or that Columbus sailed the ocean blue in 1492, or that I am due to take my son to a football match next Saturday. This is factual memory, retention of previously acquired knowledge. I can also be said to remember how to pilot a plane or to do a handstand. This is retention of previously acquired abilities. But there is also the memory of events witnessed or participated in, typically reported in the form: 'I remember X's F-ing' (as opposed to the typical report of factual memory: 'I remember that X F-ed'), and, as a special case of such event-memory, there is the memory of one's own experiences and actions, which one will report in first-person memory claims.

It is such *experience-memory* that Locke's writings suggest should provide the criterion of personal identity over time. However, as numerous writers have noted, this immediately leads into difficulties. I cannot now remember many of the experiences I underwent yesterday, yet it can hardly be denied that I am the same person as the one who underwent those experiences. Again, the account of personal identity in terms of experience-memory appears to conflict with one of the logical properties of identity, namely transitivity. A relation R is transitive just in case, if x is R-related to y and y is R-related to z then x must be R-related to z. Thus if x is taller than y and y is taller than z then x must be taller than z. But it seems that on Locke's account I, as I am now, might be the same person as the 19 year old who went up to Cambridge in 1968, but not the same person as the 11 year old who first went to grammar school in 1961, even though the account certifies that the 19 year old is the same person as

the 11 year old. For I might now have vivid recollections of my first
day in Cambridge, but have forgotten all about my first day at
grammar school, though the 19 year old I was in 1968 still had
recollections of that day. These objections to Locke's account, first
made by his great eighteenth-century opponents Butler and Reid,
are ones we will be looking at much more closely when we come to
examine his views in their own right. But they have led most philosophers basically sympathetic to Locke to a distinction between
psychological connectedness and *psychological continuity*, and to
an explicit restatement of the Lockean account in terms of the latter
notion.

   Let us say that, between *P* today and *P* twenty years ago, there are
direct memory connections if *P* can now remember having some of
the experiences that *P* had twenty years ago. Even if there are no
such direct memory connections between *P* now and *P* twenty years
ago, there may still be continuity of memory. This will be so if
between *P* now and *P* twenty years ago there has been an overlapping chain of direct memories, i.e. if *P* now remembers some of
his experiences of the previous year . . . and nineteen years ago
remembered some of his experiences of the year before. The Lockean account of personal identity can then be revised to read: *P*2 at *t*2
is the same person as *P*1 at *t*1 just in case *P*2 at *t*2 is linked by
continuity of experience-memory to *P*1 at *t*1. Let us refer to this as
the Memory Criterion of personal identity.

1.8 The psychological continuity criterion

But although this reformulation of the Lockean idea avoids the
most obvious objections it still involves the claim that personal
identity is to be accounted for solely in terms of experience-memory.
But many modern philosophers who are otherwise sympathetic to
the Lockean approach think that not only experience-memory, but
other psychological facts, should be taken into account in defining
personal identity. For there is no reason to think that our concept of
ourselves as reidentifiable individuals is so tied up with the notion of
memory as to exclude the relevance of any other types of psychological continuity. Besides direct memories, there are several other
kinds of direct psychological connection. One such connection is
that which holds between an intention and the later act in which this

intention is carried out. Other such direct psychological connections are those which hold when a belief, or a desire, or any other psychological feature, persists. These direct psychological connections are accessible to consciousness, but others need not be. Thus we can count as direct psychological connections the links between childhood experiences and adult character traits, fears and prejudices. In general *any* causal links between past factors and present psychological traits can be subsumed under the notion of psychological connectedness.

We can now define psychological continuity generally in the way we previously defined continuity of experience-memory, namely as the holding of overlapping chains of such direct psychological connections; and then define personal identity over time by saying that $P2$ at $t2$ is the same person as $P1$ at $t1$ if and only if $P2$ at $t2$ is psychologically continuous with $P1$ at $t1$. Let us call this *the Psychological Continuity Criterion* of personal identity.

However, like the other accounts of personal identity already considered, this proposal is not without its difficulties. There are two main lines of objection.

1.9 The circularity objection

The first, originally brought against Locke by Butler, is that the Criterion is viciously circular. Memory cannot occur as an ingredient in a definition of personal identity because memory already presupposes personal identity – as knowledge in general presupposes truth. It is not absolutely clear, when Butler's words are read in context, exactly what point he had in mind. But the argument his words have suggested to the opponents of the Psychological Continuity Criterion is the following. We distinguish between veridical and apparent memory and accept without difficulty that people can seem (to themselves) to remember doing things which they did not do, which were in fact done by other people (the standard example of this given by Flew 1951, is that of George IV, who in his declining years 'remembered' his dashing leadership at the Battle of Waterloo – though he was not even present on that field). But how is this distinction to be made if not by an appeal to personal identity? If so, however, memory not only entails but *presupposes* personal identity: in the sense that the conclusive verification of the proposition that someone genuinely remembers F-ing must involve the conclusive verification of the proposition that he, that same person, did indeed F. To *know* that someone genuinely remembers F-ing one must *know* that he F-ed. Consequently personal identity cannot be defined in terms of memory since one must already be in possession of the concept of personal identity, and be able to determine that it applies, in order to be in a position to operate with the concept of memory at all.

The customary reply to this objection by modern defenders of the Psychological Continuity Criterion, originally given by Sydney Shoemaker, is that while this may be true of the concept of memory one can define a more general concept of *quasi-memory*, of which it is not true, but which is in all other essential respects identical with our ordinary concept of memory. In particular, quasi-memory, like memory, is capable of yielding knowledge of the past which is based neither on evidence nor testimony. Psychological continuity can then be redefined in terms of quasi-memory (and the other types of direct psychological connections mentioned above, generalized where necessary in an analogous fashion) and the Psychological Continuity Criterion of personal identity cleared of the accusation of circularity.

1.10 The reduplication argument

We shall be considering the circularity objection to the Psychological Continuity Criterion of personal identity and the Shoemaker response to it in more detail later. However, whatever is to be said of this matter the second main line of objection to the Psychological Continuity Criterion remains.

This is the famous Reduplication Argument originally proposed by Bernard Williams (1956–7). Williams imagines the case of a man he calls Charles who turns up in the twentieth century claiming to be Guy Fawkes:

> All the events he claims to have witnessed and all the actions he claims to have done point unanimously to the life of some one person in the past . . . Guy Fawkes. Not only do all Charles' memory-claims that can be checked fit the pattern of Fawkes' life as known by historians, but others that cannot be checked

are plausible, provide explanations of unknown facts and so on.
(1956–7:332)

It is tempting in this case to identify Charles, as he now is, with Guy
Fawkes, in other words to regard the case as one of reincarnation.
For what Williams is in effect supposing is that the evidence available in the case is everything for which believers in reincarnation
could possibly wish. But, Williams argues, one is not obliged to do
so, and in fact so to describe the case would be vacuous. For if this
were to happen to Charles it could also happen simultaneously to his
brother Robert. There would then be two equally good candidates
for identity with Guy Fawkes, and since two people cannot be one
person neither *could* be Guy Fawkes. Hence, Williams concludes,
neither should one identify Charles with Guy Fawkes in the original
case where there is no reduplication, for the absence of Robert from
that case has nothing to do with the *intrinsic* relations between
Charles and Guy Fawkes – the relations that obtain between them
independently of what is true of *other* people – but it is absurd to
suppose that whether a later person $P2$ is identical with an earlier
person $P1$ can depend upon facts about people other than $P1$ and
$P2$.

This objection does not apply only to putative cases of reincarnation, where a present-day defender of the Psychological Continuity
Criterion of personal identity might claim that his Criterion is anyway not satisfied (i.e. that the later person merely seems to, but does
not actually have, *genuine* quasi-memories of the earlier person's
experiences). It applies also in cases which the defender of the
Psychological Continuity Criterion of personal identity must regard
as providing undeniable examples of personal identity.

Consider, for example, that variant of the Brown/Brownson
case, suggested earlier as motivating a move from the Brain
Criterion of personal identity to the Physical Criterion, in which
only half of Brown's brain is transplanted into Robinson's body,
with consequent transference of psychological states. The defender
of the Psychological Continuity Criterion ought to regard this as
a paradigm case of personal identity, but consider again the
case – hereafter to be referred to as the *fission case* – in which both
of Brown's brain hemispheres are transplanted, but into different
bodies (and let us suppose for the sake of the example, what is
conceivably but not actually the case, that the two hemispheres are

equipollent in their linguistic abilities, etc.). Williams's Reduplication Argument can now be brought to bear just as in the case of Charles and Guy Fawkes.

Or consider the case in which, *via* Williams's brain-state transfer device, Robinson's brain is put into a state information-theoretically equivalent to Brown's. Again the defender of the Psychological Continuity Criterion must regard the case as a clear example of personal identity. But if this could happen to Robinson it could also happen simultaneously to his friend Smith. Once again, then, the Reduplication Argument can be brought to bear. For its happening simultaneously to Smith would leave the intrinsic relations between Brown and Robinson wholly unaffected.

Consequently the defender of the Psychological Continuity Criterion of personal identity cannot afford just to ignore Williams's Reduplication Argument. He must respond to it.

1.11 The revised psychological continuity criterion

There are two main replies to this argument. One reply, adopted by many defenders of the Psychological Continuity Criterion, is simply to take the bull by the horns and to reject the principle underlying Williams's argument. This is the principle that whether a later individual x is identical with an earlier individual y can depend only on facts about x and y and the relationships between them: no facts about any other individual can be relevant to whether x is y. I shall call this principle *the Only x and y principle*. Applied to the special case of personal identity, it asserts that whether a certain later person $P2$ is identical with a certain earlier person $P1$ can depend only on facts about $P2$ and $P1$ and the intrinsic relationships between them; no facts about individuals other than $P2$ and $P1$ can be relevant to whether $P2$ is the same person as $P1$. If this principle is rejected the Reduplication Argument can be side-stepped very easily by revising the Psychological Continuity Criterion to make psychological continuity a sufficient condition of personal identity only in the absence of a 'rival candidate'. That is, we say: $P2$ at $t2$ is the same person as $P1$ at $t1$ just in case $P2$ at $t2$ is psychologically continuous with $P1$ at $t1$ and there is no 'rival candidate' $P2^*$ also psychologically continuous with $P1$.

But most philosophers who reply to Williams's argument by

rejecting the Only x and y principle also wish to allow that $P2$ can be the same person as $P1$ even if rival candidates exist, so long as $P2$'s claim to identity with $P1$ is *stronger than* those of its rivals. In other words, they prefer a 'best candidate' theory of personal identity to a 'no rival candidate' theory. Such a theory is put forward by Sydney Shoemaker (1970) and by Robert Nozick (1981). Nozick's version of the theory is the most sophisticated in the literature and we shall be examining it in detail later. He refers to it as 'the closest continuer' theory of personal identity. It asserts that $P2$ at $t2$ is the same person as $P1$ at $t1$ just in case $P2$ at $t2$ is (sufficiently) psychologically continuous with $P1$ at $t1$ and there is no other continuer of $P1$ existing at $t2$ who is psychologically continuous with $P1$ to an equal or greater degree. (Actually this statement would need to be further qualified to deal with cases of 'fusion' as well as 'fission', i.e. merging as well as branching of links of psychological continuity, and also to deal with the existence of continuers existing at times between $t1$ and $t2$, but for now we can pass over these details.) We can call this *the Revised Psychological Continuity Criterion*.

Whether this line of reply to the Reduplication Argument can be sustained is a matter of current controversy and we shall be looking at the matter in great detail in what follows. The intuitive objection can be brought out by reflection on the split-brain transplant case. Suppose that I am told that my brain is to be divided into two and the two halves transplanted into different bodies. Then according to the Revised Psychological Continuity Criterion I know that I will not survive and that two new people will be created by the fission. However, if I can persuade someone to destroy the right brain hemisphere before it is transplanted, thus eliminating the plurality of candidates, I will survive and be identical with the recipient of the left-brain hemisphere. Thus according to the Revised Psychological Continuity Criterion in this case my survival is logically dependent upon the non-existence of someone – the person resulting from the right-brain hemisphere transplant – who would not be me even if he were to exist. But how can my survival be thus logically dependent on the non-existence of *someone else*?

1.12 The multiple occupancy thesis

A second way a supporter of the Psychological Continuity Criterion can defend himself against Williams's Reduplication Argument is to question the logic of that argument. According to Williams, in a reduplication situation the rival candidates for identity with the original person must be new existents, identical neither with him nor with one another. But it is possible, or so it has been argued by several recent writers (among them John Perry and David Lewis), to retain the Only *x* and *y* principle while rejecting this description of the reduplication situation. It must, of course, be accepted that the post-fission rivals are distinct people, but it is possible, according to these philosophers, to reject the view that they are new existents; rather they have existed all along, but have only become spatially distinct with the fission. There are various versions of this. Their common element I will refer to, following Robinson (1985), as *the Multiple Occupancy Thesis*. The essence of this thesis is that what makes it the case that two people existing at a certain time *are* two may be facts about what is the case at *other* times, i.e. their distinction at the time in question may obtain only in virtue of facts *extrinsic* to that time, so that at the time, in David Lewis's words (1983, postscript to 'Survival and identity'), they comprise 'two minds with but a single thought', not merely, to quote Robinson, 'as alike as two peas in a pod', but 'as alike as *one* pea in a pod'.

This is another line of argument to be pursued further and to be examined in much more detail. But if it is acceptable it allows us to retain the original version of the Psychological Continuity Criterion and avoid conflict with the Only *x* and *y* principle.

1.13 The simple view

Williams himself appears to take his Reduplication Argument as providing support for some version of the view that personal identity requires some form of physical persistence, indeed for the Bodily Criterion of personal identity. But, as defenders of the Psychological Continuity Criterion were not slow to point out, and as is implicit in the discussion above, there is reason to suppose that if the Reduplication Argument has any cogency at all, then it applies equally to any plausible version of this view. Even if we insist on identity of the whole body as a necessary condition of personal identity, which it is very hard to do when one thinks of cases like the Brown/Brownson case, it does not appear to be impossible to imagine a situation in which we were confronted by two bodies, either of which, but for the existence of the other, we would be happy to identify with a certain body (it seems to be possible to conceive, that is, a situation which we would be tempted to describe as 'a man walking off in two directions'). And if we pass on to versions of the view that personal identity requires physical persistence which allow the identification of Brownson with Brown, it appears to be impossible to find a plausible stopping point before we reach a version which is clearly open to the Reduplication Argument. For if Brownson is Brown in Shoemaker's original case it is surely impossible to deny that he is Brown when he has only half of Brown's brain which nevertheless carries with it full psychological continuity. But any version of the view that personal identity requires physical persistence which licenses the identification in this case is wide open to the Reduplication Argument.

This has led some philosophers to the view that *none* of the proposals so far considered can be a correct account of personal identity. Persistence of body and brain or psychological continuity and connectedness are criteria of personal identity only in the sense of evidence: they are not what personal identity *consists* in. Indeed, there is nothing (else) that personal identity consists in: personal identity is an ultimate unanalysable fact, distinct from everything observable or experienceable that might be evidence for it. Persons are separately existing entities, distinct from their brains, bodies and experiences. On the best known version of this view, a person is a *purely mental* entity: a Cartesian pure ego, or spiritual substance. This is in fact the form in which the view is adopted by its contemporary defenders, amongst whom the most prominent are Chisholm and Swinburne. Following Parfit I shall call this *the Simple View*. The view that there *is* something (else) that personal identity consists in. I shall refer to as *the Complex View*.

Defenders of the Simple View have pointed out that this view is to be found in the writings of Butler (1736) and Reid (1941). Both Butler and Reid insist that personal identity is identity in a stricter sense than the identity of material objects. Butler, for example, maintains that the word 'same' is used in a 'strict and philosophical' sense when applied to persons, but in a 'loose and popular' sense when applied to bodies. In a similar vein, Thomas Reid asserts that 'the identity . . . which we ascribe to bodies, whether natural or artificial, is not perfect identity; it is rather something which for convenience of speech we call identity.' Identity, he says,

has no fixed nature when applied to bodies, and very often
questions about it are questions about words. But identity
when applied to persons has no ambiguity and admits not of
degrees or of more or less. It is the foundation of all rights and
obligations and of all accountableness, and the notion of it is
fixed and precise.

(1941)

The contemporary defenders of the Simple View of personal identity endorse this, and regard it as a great merit of their view that it
does set personal identity apart from the identity of other things.

As I have said, one of the main considerations in persuading its
modern defenders that the Simple View must be accepted has been
the thought that no criterion of personal identity in terms of any
observable or experienceable facts can be sustained in the face of
Williams's Reduplication Argument. That is, as Swinburne expresses
it, no 'empiricist' theory of personal identity is tenable in the light of
this objection. The Simple View is thought to resist this objection
quite easily, for as Swinburne puts it:

The Simple View claims explicitly that personal identity is one
thing, and the extent of similarity in matter and apparent
memory another. There is no contradiction in supposing that
the one should occur without the other. Strong similarity of
matter and apparent memory is powerful evidence of personal
identity. . . . Where there are two later persons P2 and P2'
each of whom has some continuity with the earlier person P1,
the evidence supports to some extent each of two hypotheses –
that P2 is the same person as P1, and that P2' is the same
person as P1. It may give more support to one hypothesis than
to the other, but the less well supported hypothesis might be
the true one, or maybe neither hypothesis is true. Perhaps P1
has ceased to exist, and two different persons have come into
existence. So the Simple View fully accepts that mere logic
cannot determine which experiences will be mine, but it allows
that continuity of memory and apparent memory and brain
provides fallible evidence about this. And, of course, the
duplication objection . . . has no force against the Simple
Theory. For although there can be equally good evidence that
each of two later persons is the same person as the earlier
person, that evidence is fallible, and since clearly only one

person at one time can be strictly the same person as one
person at an earlier time, it follows that in one case the evidence
is misleading – although we may not know in which case.

(Shoemaker and Swinburne 1984:20)

1.14 The determinacy thesis

Another argument in its favour that modern defenders of the Simple
View emphasize is that acceptance of it enables one to endorse what
I shall call *the Determinacy Thesis* concerning personal identity.
Derek Parfit, who rejects it, has formulated this as the thesis that
questions about personal identity must have answers even in cases in
which 'though we know the answer to every other question, we have
no idea how to answer a question of personal identity' (1971). One
initially tempting thing to say about some of the puzzle cases
described in the literature on personal identity is that to ask whether
it is right or wrong to identify the original person in the case with the
candidate for identity with him that the case presents is to ask an
empty question. That is, because of the vagueness inherent in our
concept of personal identity, the statement of identity in question is
neither true nor false and consequently it is neither true nor false
that the original person in the case still exists after the various events
described in it have occurred. (This assumes just one candidate for
identity with the original person. If there is more than one in the case
it is tempting to say that the indeterminacy may be greater still: it
may be indeterminate both whether the original person exists, and,
if so, who he is.)

It is uncontroversial that it is possible to construct puzzle cases
concerning the identity of material objects about which this would
be the correct thing to say. Events can be imagined, indeed events
sometimes really occur, which in Bernard Williams's (1970) nice
phrase 'leave a conceptual shadow' over the identity of a material
object.

One such case is described by Shoemaker (1963). In 1944 the
Germans destroyed the four centuries old bridge of Santa Trinita in
Florence. Six years later it was decided that it (?) should be rebuilt.
On the original site there now stands a bridge of a design exactly like
that of the original, constructed by Renaissance techniques and built
in part with the original stones (each standing in its original place),
in part with new stones taken from the original quarry. These facts

are all clear, but how are we to answer the question 'Is the present bridge of Santa Trinita the very bridge that spanned the Arno 400 years ago?'

It seems clear that in a case like this to persist in arguing about the correct answer to the question would be absurd. Things can be said in favour of the identity and things can be said against it, but there is no right or wrong answer. Rather, what we have is a *borderline case* of identity, as we can have a borderline case of baldness or tallness or fatness. And consequently, if anything practically important turns on whether or not we say that the bridge is the same one, there is room for a decision to be made by the law courts about the matter. Such a decision may be reasonable or unreasonable in the light of the facts and legal precedents, but it cannot be true or false, since it will not be a statement made employing our present concept of sameness of bridge but a recommendation that the concept be made more determinate in a particular direction.

But should we accept in the same way that cases can be imagined in which a conceptual shadow would be cast over the identity of a person? In particular, can I suppose that in certain circumstances it would be indeterminate whether I still existed, and if so, with whom I was then identical? And can I imagine circumstances in which the only sensible thing for me (?) to do if I was concerned about this question would be to seek a decision from the law courts about the matter? The defenders of the Simple View of personal identity argue that these questions must be answered negatively. That is, that precisely because personal identity is something that can be known from the first-person viewpoint, the possibility of borderline cases must be rejected. In this respect, at least, they argue, personal identity must be radically different from the identity of other things. But, they insist, cases are certainly possible in which all the relevant *evidence* leaves the question of personal identity unsettled. And so, they argue, the radical difference between personal identity and the identity of other things which they claim – namely, the impossibility of borderline cases of personal identity – cannot be secured if personal identity is held to consist, as it is according to their empiricist opponents, in the obtaining of any observable or experienceable state of affairs. For any such criterion must be stated in a way that allows borderline cases of personal identity, or, absurdly, it will make the question whether personal identity obtains turn, in some conceivable case, on a question which is of total insignificance in comparison with the importance of the matter of life or death which depends on it. It is Richard Swinburne who has been most vigorous in pressing this argument. He illustrates it (1973–4) by supposing that we are drawn to a theory of personal identity which makes personal survival depend on the survival of exactly half the brain of the original person: one molecule less, according to the theory, and we no longer have personal identity. But, he says, it is absurd that such a small difference can make *all* the difference when the issue is one of life and death. If, on the other hand, this theory of personal identity is revised to allow persistence of *approximately* half of the brain to suffice for personal identity, then, since 'approximately' is a vague term, personal identity becomes something allowing of borderline cases. And it appears that exactly the same dilemma must confront any 'empiricist' theory of personal identity. This, then, is the second important argument used by modern defenders of the Simple View of personal identity. We shall be examining it more closely later on, when we will have to look in detail both at the nature of the indeterminacy which is possible for statements about the identity of things other than persons and at the arguments that for persons, peculiarly, such indeterminacy cannot arise.

1.15 What matters in survival

As well as the question of what personal identity *consists in*, there is also the question of what its significance is, and what the nature is of the special interest we have in our own survival and well-being. This question was introduced into the contemporary debate by Shoemaker (1970), but it is associated particularly with the name of Derek Parfit. Parfit sums up his own view in the slogan 'identity is not what matters in survival'. This slogan might seem baffling. But what Parfit means is that personal identity as such is of *no* significance and our own continued existence and well-being is, as such, of *no* special interest to us.

This needs some explaining.

As I understand it Parfit's thesis is the claim that, contrary to what we are all naturally inclined to believe, we do not have a basic and non-derivative concern for our own future existence and well-being. What *is* of fundamental importance to us is that there be in the future people related by certain links of psychological continuity and connectedness to ourselves as we are now (let us call such future people 'Parfitian survivors'). Now, in the actual world, at the present time, the only way that I can secure that I have a Parfitian survivor tomorrow is to ensure that I myself am around tomorrow – that is, that I still *exist* tomorrow, that one of the people alive tomorrow is *identical* with me. Nevertheless, according to Parfit, my having a Parfitian survivor tomorrow does not *entail* that I exist tomorrow, and in certain conceivable, or possibly actual but merely future, circumstances, in which brain transplants, *Star Trek* technology, etc., are available, it will be possible to ensure a Parfitian survivor for oneself without ensuring one's own future existence (one way to do this, according to Parfit, would be to ensure for oneself a multiplicity of (equally good) Parfitian survivors). Parfit's thesis that identity is not what matters in survival is then the thesis that, given one's fundamental desires and concerns, one would have *no* reason, in such a situation, for preferring a future in which one was present oneself to one in which one merely had Parfitian survivors. Now intuitively this is very implausible. Our interest in personal identity, the kind of importance it has for us, seems totally different from the type of interest we have in the identity of other things. We value the people we care about as tokens rather than as types, as individuals rather than as instantiations of useful or desirable or attractive properties. We do not regard them as replaceable, and we certainly do not regard *ourselves* as replaceable. We can imagine without difficulty a society in which 'teletransportation' of the *Star Trek* variety is in general use as a means of 'transportation' of inanimate objects and food animals – even though it is generally acknowledged in the society that what the process *really* involves is the destruction of one object and the creation elsewhere of a mere replica numerically distinct from the original (of course, in the *Star Trek* series Captain Kirk and his colleagues do not regard teletransportation in this light – they regard it as a genuine form of *transportation*). The willingness of the people in such a society to employ teletransportation in this way would not strike us as in any way odd. But if we try to imagine that the people in this society, *whilst continuing to acknowledge that what the process really involves is the destruction of one object and the creation elsewhere of a numerically distinct replica*, none the less allow themselves and their loved ones to be teletransported, and in fact appear to treat teletransportation as a convenient alternative to travel, we run into immediate difficulties. And at first sight it seems as if we have succeeded only in imagining a society of madmen.

This illustrates the strength of the intuition that Parfit is opposing when he claims that identity is not what matters in survival. For according to Parfit these men are not mad at all. On the contrary, they are acting exactly as it would be rational for *us* to act if we lived in their society and shared their beliefs about the nature of the teletransportation process. It would be quite irrational for us, according to Parfit, if we were in such circumstances, to refuse to step into the teletransporter because we believed that the people who would step out at the other end would not be ourselves but merely numerically distinct replicas. For this could only be relevant if our basic desires and concerns included a desire for *our own* continued existence and well-being. But, Parfit's thesis is, they do not.

Parfit's thesis that identity is not what matters in survival is, then, a quite remarkable one. But he has an argument for it which is well worth considering.

1.16 Parfit's argument

This argument starts, as so much of the recent work on personal identity does, from consideration of the problem of fission. To understand it, however, one needs to make a distinction between two types of opinion we have with regard to such puzzle cases about personal identity. First, we have opinions about how the language of personal identity is to be applied to the case: that is, about what the correct answer to the question of personal identity the case poses actually is (or what the correct *answers* are to the *questions* posed when the case involves more than one later (earlier) candidate for identity with one earlier (later) person). These opinions reflect our mastery of our language, and in particular, our mastery of those parts of our language expressive of the concept of personal identity. In short, they reflect what I will call our 'semantic intuitions', and they are on a par with the opinions we have about the puzzle cases that can be constructed about the identity of things other than persons.

But when we consider puzzle cases about personal identity we often find ourselves with opinions of a second sort. These are opinions about how it is rational for the participants involved in the case – the people whose identity is at issue in it – to behave, given the beliefs they are described as holding. Opinions of this second sort do not merely reflect our semantic intuitions; rather they reflect our fundamental desires and concerns. For we arrive at such opinions by imagining *ourselves* involved in the puzzle case as one of its participants and asking how *we* should then behave.

Now the way Parfit argues for his claim that identity does not matter in survival is as follows. First he describes a fission case, i.e. a case in which each of two later people is related to an earlier person in a way in which, but for the existence of the other 'candidate', we would be very strongly inclined to regard as constituting identity (in fact the fission case he considers is the split-brain transplant case described earlier). Next he argues (a) that the correct description of the case is that given by the Revised Psychological Continuity Criterion of personal identity, namely that the original person ceases to exist, but would not have done so if only one of the fission products had existed, but (b) that it would be quite irrational, if you were the original in the case, for you to be concerned about the impending fission in the same way as you would be about your impending death, or to think that you could gain anything by preventing the fission, e.g. by bribing a nurse to destroy one of the brain hemispheres before the transplant – even though by doing so you would ensure your own future existence (I owe this way of putting Parfit's point to Nozick 1981). Here (a) is an opinion of the first of the two types just distinguished, and (b) an opinion of the second type. Finally, Parfit concludes that these opinions (assuming them to be shared by his readers) can only be reconciled by accepting that our fundamental desires and concerns are not the ones we think we have, and do not include a non-derivative desire for our own continued existence and well-being. In short, he argues that the only explanation of our apparently conflicting intuitions about this case is that we do not in fact regard identity as what matters in survival.

Parfit regards this conclusion as having many corollaries for our views on ethics and the nature of rationality. He also regards it as providing a means of defending the Revised Psychological Continuity Criterion of personal identity against Williams's Reduplication Argument. The principle underlying that argument, it will be remembered, was the Only x and y principle, which, applied to persons, states that whether a later person $P2$ is identical with an earlier person $P1$ can depend only on facts about $P2$ and $P1$

and the intrinsic relations between them: it cannot depend on facts about individuals other than *P2* and *P1*. To accept the Revised Psychological Continuity Criterion of personal identity is to reject this principle. But, Parfit argues, the plausibility of the principle depends on the assumption that personal identity is what matters in survival: for it is only implausible to suppose that my identity or otherwise with a future person can depend on anything other than the intrinsic features of my relationship to him if it is thought to be a matter of great importance whether such identity obtains. If it is a trivial matter then there is no implausibility in supposing it to be something determined extrinsically. Consequently, he argues, once one accepts that identity is not what matters in survival there is no difficulty in accepting also that it has the 'best candidate' structure implied by the Revised Psychological Continuity Criterion of personal identity.

Parfit's arguments present a considerable challenge to those who wish to combine preservation of the common-sense idea that what matters in survival is identity with rejection of the Simple View of personal identity. Consequently they have been the focus of much attention in recent years and have been challenged at several points.

One influential line of argument has been that Parfit is wrong to suppose that the fission case must be described in the way implied by claim (a) above, namely as a case in which the original person ceases to exist when the fission takes place. A version of this criticism is presented in Lewis (1976). According to the theory of personal identity Lewis there states, which entails the Multiple Occupancy Thesis, *no one* ceases to exist when the fission takes place. Rather, two people who have been spatially coincident (and the subjects of the same mental states) now become spatially distinct. But if no one ceases to exist when the fission takes place of course it must be absurd to view it as death.

Another way of responding to Parfit's argument is simply to dig in one's heels and deny his claim (b), that it would be quite irrational to regard one's impending fission as one would regard one's impending death, or to think that one could gain anything by ensuring that only one of the brain hemispheres was transplanted. This line of reply to Parfit has attracted few, but one who does adopt it is Jerome Shaffer, who writes:

Psychological continuity is important where there is identity,
but not otherwise . . . returning to our case of the man who
splits, we would . . . say that since identity is not preserved
even though psychological continuity is preserved, the man
should feel quite differently about it from the way he should
feel about single transplantation.

(1977:157)

However, the difficulty with this is just that Parfit's claim (b) is
so immensely plausible, especially when defended by the argument
from Nozick cited above.

The final possibility is to challenge Parfit's claim that *if* our intuitions about the fission case are as he supposes, namely (a) that the
original person ceases to exist, but (b) that it would none the less be
quite irrational for him to regard the fission as he would regard
death, then the *only* explanation of this can be that identity is not
what matters in survival, i.e. that our own continued existence and
well-being is not something for which we have a basic and non-
derivative concern. It might seem at this point as if this option is a
non-starter; but in fact it is the one I favour, and I shall be elabora-
ting it later.

These arguments against Parfit are ones we will be returning to
later. But Parfit's arguments have also attracted the attention of the
contemporary defenders of the Simple View of personal identity. It
is, of course, part and parcel of the Simple View that identity is what
matters in survival. But, unlike the defenders of the Complex View,
the proponent of the Simple View is not *directly* challenged by
Parfit's argument. As we have seen, since it is essential to his view
that nothing observable or experienceable constitutes personal identity, he can maintain that in the fission case as described by Parfit it
is simply indeterminate whether the original person ceases to exist
and if not, with which of the fission products he is identical. For,
from his point of view, the case is simply underdescribed. Thus the
apparent rationality of the original person's indifference to the fact
of his imminent fission is not, for the defender of the Simple View,
just *tantamount*, as Parfit takes it to be, to the apparent rationality
of his indifference to the fact of his imminent demise. For the Simple
theorist is not committed to saying that the original person in a
fission case does cease to exist when the fission takes place (in this
respect, despite huge differences, his position is akin to that of

David Lewis). Whether it is possible for the proponent of the Simple View of personal identity to develop this into a convincing reply to Parfit is another matter.

I have, I believe, now surveyed the main views and arguments concerning personal identity which have excited the interest of philosophers in recent years. I turn in the next chapter to the history of the problem.

CHAPTER 2

Locke

2.1 Introduction

We shall begin our discussion of the history of the problem of personal identity with John Locke, who gives the problem its first clearly identifiable formulation in the famous chapter 'Of identity and diversity' in his *Essay Concerning Human Understanding* (1961, Book II, Ch. 27). It has been said that all subsequent philosophy consists merely of footnotes to Plato. On this topic, at least, it can be truly said that all subsequent writing has consisted merely of footnotes to Locke. Indeed, many present-day philosophers writing on personal identity would still be happy to describe themselves as 'Lockean' or, at least, 'neo-Lockean' in their approach to the topic, whilst many others would naturally define their positions by their opposition to Locke. Locke's discussion of personal identity is thus far from being of merely historical interest to us.

Nevertheless, it would be a great mistake in reading Locke to neglect the historical context in which he wrote, or the particular concerns which motivated him. For these explain features of his discussion which are both central to it and yet at the same time highly puzzling.

One of the most obvious and important motives for Locke's discussion was to provide an account of personal identity which would make sense of the Christian doctrines of human immortality, the resurrection of the dead and the Last Judgement. And, of course, for Locke these were not mere possibilities or 'puzzle cases', as they might be for many philosophers interested in personal identity in the present day. They were *facts* which any account of personal identity had to accommodate if it was to be considered adequate.

Other philosophers in Locke's time would have agreed, but would have found the solution in the Platonic-Cartesian doctrine of an immaterial, incorporeal, unextended soul, or self, whose identity over time could be taken as unproblematically guaranteeing a personal identity independent of bodily vicissitudes. This was the standard solution – Locke himself refers in an entry in his *Journal* in 1682 to the 'usual . . . proof . . . of the immortality of the soul. . . . Matter cannot think ergo the soul is immateriall, noe thing can naturally destroy an immateriall thing ergo the soul is naturally immortal' (1936:121). But Locke rejects this solution because he rejects the Cartesian claim to demonstrative knowledge that 'that which thinks in us' (as he puts it) is an immaterial substance. It might be the case, Locke thinks, though he says that probably it is not, that that which thinks in us is a wholly material substance to which God has 'superadded' the power of thought (*Essay* IV, iii. 6). This proposal had been made before Locke and typically got a hostile response. Thus Joseph Glanvill (1970), writing before Locke, argues that if 'all things we do are performed by mere matter, and motion, and there is no such thing as an immaterial being then when our bodies are dissolved the man is lost, and our souls are nothing' and consequently the 'dismal conclusion is true and certain' that we are mere mortals. Locke is as much opposed to the 'dismal conclusion' as Glanvill but he does not see that its rejection necessitates acceptance of dualism. 'All the great Ends of Morality and Religion,' he claims,

> are well enough secured, without philosophical proofs of the
> Soul's Immateriality; since it is evident, that he who made us
> first begin to subsist here, sensible intelligent Beings . . . can
> and will restore us to the like state of Sensibility in another
> world and make us capable there to receive the Retribution he
> has designed to men, according to their doings in this life.
> (*Essay* IV, iii. 6)

How this can be so, Locke believes, his account of personal identity explains. Thus he intends this account to be neutral between dualist and materialist accounts of the self, and to make comprehensible the possibility, or rather the fact, of the resurrection of the dead and human immortality, whichever of these two metaphysical systems is correct.

Locke also clearly intends his account of personal identity to make sense of the knowledge we have of our own identities over time. 'Wherever a man finds himself', he says, 'there, another may say, is the same person' (*Essay* II, xxvii. 21). Other accounts of personal identity, and in particular the proposal that personal identity might be grounded in identity of substance (whether material or immaterial), are rejected as incapable of accounting for the certainty we have that we are the same persons as the ones whose actions and experiences we are conscious of having performed and undergone. Although not as close to the surface of Locke's text as his discussion of the possibility of an after-life, this concern with self-knowledge is an equally important theme in Locke's writing on personal identity, and one which reveals that, despite his agnosticism about Cartesian dualism, Locke himself implicitly accepts the Cartesian emphasis on the first-person viewpoint as providing a privileged standpoint from which proposals about the nature of the self can be judged.

Another important aspect of Locke's thought, and one which is mirrored in recent discussions of 'what matters in survival', is indicated by his definition of *self* as 'that conscious thinking thing . . . which is sensible or conscious of pleasure and pain, capable of happiness or misery, and so is concerned for *itself* as far as that consciousness extends' (*Essay* II, xxvii. 17). *Person* he says,

> is the name for this *self*. . . . This personality extends itself
> beyond present existence . . . only by consciousness; whereby
> it becomes concerned and accountable, owns and imputes to
> *itself* past actions, just for the same ground and for the same
> reason that it does the present. All which is founded in a
> concern for happiness, the unavoidable concomitant of
> consciousness: that which is conscious of pleasure and pain
> desiring that that self that is conscious should be happy.
>
> (*Essay* II, xxvii. 26)

One of the merits of his own account of personal identity, Locke thinks, is that it makes comprehensible the way in which our concern about our own pasts and futures is different from the concern we have about those of other people – it explains why personal identity matters. But if the dualist account is accepted this becomes incomprehensible. How can the mere supposition that the same immaterial spirit which inhabits my body now once inhabited that of some person living centuries ago, or will inhabit that of some person living centuries hence, warrant me in being concerned about the activities of such people? How can it provide any more warrant for concern than the supposition that, miraculously, the very same atoms composing me now once composed the person living in the past, and will compose the person living in the future?

> Let anyone reflect upon himself and conclude that he has in himself an immaterial spirit . . . ; let him also suppose it to be the same soul that was in *Nestor* at the siege of *Troy*; but he now having no consciousness of any of the actions . . . of *Nestor* . . . does he or can he conceive himself the same person with [him]? Can he be concerned in [his] actions, attribute them to himself, or think them his own, more than the actions of any other man that ever existed? [N]o more . . . than if some of the particles of matter that were once a part of *Nestor* were now a part of this man: the same immaterial substance, without the same consciousness, no more making the same person . . . than the same particle of matter, without consciousness, makes the same person.
>
> (*Essay* II, xxvii. 14)

Thus, in putting forward his account of personal identity Locke has three main aims. First, to make comprehensible, independently of a commitment to a dualistic metaphysics, the possibility of resurrection and immortality; second, to give an account which is consistent with the fact that we do have knowledge of our own identities over time and is not open to sceptical objection; and third, to make sense of the fact that personal identity is something that *matters* to us, that is, that what we did or suffered and what we will do or will suffer cannot be a matter of indifference to us, in the way in which the activities and sufferings of others can be.

An admirable set of objectives one might think, at least for a philosopher of Locke's time, and yet the resulting theory is an extraordinary one. The core of Locke's view is that, as Locke puts it, 'consciousness makes personal identity'. This idea, by itself, is quite an attractive one, and has been developed by later writers who have defended the Memory and Psychological Continuity Criteria of personal identity. But Locke advocates it in conjunction with a tripartite ontology of *persons, thinking substances* (material or immaterial), and *men*. Persons are not thinking substances, he insists, even though when a person thinks it is a thinking substance that does the thinking for it; and men are not persons, for when man is no longer conscious of a past action he is not the same person as the one who committed the action, though he remains the same man (human courts, in punishing him, treat him *as if* he is the same person, but that is merely because 'the fact is proved against him and want of consciousness cannot be proved for him', *Essay* II, xxvii. 22).

This tripartite ontology is at the same time central to Locke's chapter on identity and the source of the major perplexities about it; understanding it is the key to understanding the chapter as a whole. But in order to do this we must get down to details.

2.2 *The principium individuationis*

The chapter on identity was, in fact, added to the *Essay* only in the second edition, at the urging of Locke's friend William Molyneux, who asked for a fuller discussion of the *principium individuationis*, or principle of individuation. In the first part of the chapter Locke obliges, only moving on to the topic of personal identity in section 9.

Locke begins with an account of our idea of identity: '. . . considering anything as existing at any determined time and place, we compare it with itself existing at another time, and thereon form the ideas of identity and diversity' (*Essay* II, xxvii. 1). Then he quickly moves on to an attempted proof that 'one thing cannot have two beginnings of existence nor two things one beginning'. For

> whatever exists, anywhere at any time, excludes all of the same kind and is there itself alone . . . from whence it follows that (1) one thing cannot have two beginnings of existence, nor (2) two things one beginning: it being impossible for (3) two things of the same kind to be . . . in the same instant in the same place, or (4) one and the same thing in different places. That, therefore, that had one beginning of existence is the same thing; and that which had a different beginning in time and place from that is not the same but diverse.
>
> (*Essay* II, xxvii. 1, my numbering)

Here (1) is inferred from (4) and (2) from (3). The inference of (2) from (3) is valid (though (3) is disputable – recall the Multiple Occupancy Thesis), but (1) does not follow from (4). All that follows from (4) is that if a thing *should* have two beginnings of existence the second beginning will be after the thing's first ceasing to exist. If this is so then the thing will never be in two places at once, which is all that (4) disallows (alternatively, but implausibly, Locke might mean by a beginning of existence, a *first* beginning of existence, in which case (1) does follow from (4), but (1) interpreted in this weak way does not rule out the possibility of a discontinuous existence).

But whatever may be said of the details of his argument, Locke's aim is clearly enough to establish a necessary and sufficient condition of identity: x is identical with y if and only if x and y are of the same kind and have the same beginning of existence. A little later he states explicitly his proposed *principium individuationis*, namely 'existence itself, which determines a being of any sort to a particular time and place, incommunicable to two beings of the same kind' (*Essay* II, xxvii. 3). Here again we are given a sufficient condition of identity: x is identical with y if x and y are of the same kind and at some time occupy the same place; and Locke's previous discussion makes it clear that he would endorse the complementary necessary condition: x is identical with y only if there is no time at which they occupy distinct places.

2.3 Substantial identity

These principles are often said to constitute Locke's general theory of identity, of which the extended discussion of personal identity is meant to provide an illustration. But, in fact, there is little warrant for reading Locke as intending to put forward such a comprehensive theory in the early part of the 'Identity' chapter. And far from illustrating any such general theory, the subsequent discussion of personal identity would have to be regarded as flatly incompatible with it. For it is a consequence of Locke's theory that personal identity is constituted by identity of consciousness, that where identity of consciousness is interrupted, as Locke insists can very well happen, *one person will have two beginnings of existence*. This, in Locke's view, is the correct description of what the resurrection involves, and it is the correct description of such thought-experiments as that presented in section 16, where he asks us to agree that

whatever has the consciousness of present and past actions is the same person to whom they both belong. Had I the same

consciousness that I saw the ark and Noah's flood as that I
saw an overflowing of the Thames last winter, . . . I could no
more doubt that I . . . that saw the Thames overflowed last
winter, and that viewed the flood at the general deluge, was the
same *self*, place that *self* in what substance you please, than I
that write this am the same *myself* now whilst I write . . . that
I was yesterday.

(Essay II, xxvii. 16)

However, we are not forced to regard Locke as putting forward a
general theory of identity in the first section of the 'Identity' chapter, and a more charitable hypothesis, which a modicum of respect
for his logical acumen surely obliges us to accept, is that he is not
here thinking of things *in general* (therefore including persons) at
all, but only of things of the kinds he immediately goes on to list:
(1) God, (2) Finite intelligences and (3) Bodies.

God, he says, is without beginning, eternal unalterable and every-
where, 'and therefore concerning his identity there can be no doubt'
(*Essay* II, xxvii. 2). Finite spirits have their determinate time and
place of beginning to exist, and 'the relation to that time and place
will always determine to each of them its identity as long as it exists',
and the same holds of every particle of matter, 'for, though these
three sorts of substances, as we term them, do not exclude one
another out of the same place, yet . . . they must necessarily . . .
exclude any of the same kind' (*Essay* II, xxvii. 2).

These, Locke says, are the only three kinds of substance of which
we have ideas, 'all other things being but modes or relations termi-
nated in substances' (*Essay* II, xxvii. 2).

What the discussion in the early part of the chapter provides,
then, is not a theory of identity in general but a theory of *substantial*
identity, which need not apply to persons unless persons are substances. But this, as we know, Locke emphatically denies (see, e.g.,
Essay II, xxvii. 7).

But then what does Locke mean by 'substance'? Throughout
most of the *Essay* (as, in fact, in the last passage quoted) substances
are contrasted with modes and relations. Substances are just the
things which possess modes and stand in relations. If Locke were
using the term 'substance' in this way in the 'Identity' chapter, he
ought to find it obvious that persons are substances, for persons are
manifestly things and not modes or relations of things. Indeed,

Locke's own definition of 'a person' tells us this: 'a thinking intelligent being that has reason and reflection and can consider itself as itself, the same thinking thing in different times and places.' But if persons are thinking things and thinking things are substances, then persons are substances, and there can be no possibility that personal identity might not involve identity of substance. Yet this is precisely what Locke asserts. So what is going on?

The same problem arises more generally, for Locke flatly denies in the 'Identity' chapter that animal identity involves identity of substance: 'Animal Identity is preserved in Identity of Life, and not of substance' (*Essay* II, xxvii. 12), but animals, like persons, surely qualify as things and not as modes or relations of things.

This problem, as it applies to persons, was first seen by Butler and Reid and was revived by Shoemaker (1963:454). A fuller discussion of it will be reserved to the next chapter, where Butler's and Reid's views will be explored in more detail. But what the answer to it must be is obvious. In the 'Identity' chapter Locke does *not* use 'substance' as a synonym of 'thing', rather he uses it in a more restricted sense, and persons and animals, though they are things and hence substances in Locke's usual sense, do not qualify as substances in this more restricted sense. This is the solution to the problem given by Alston and Bennett (1988), who go on to identify this special sense of 'substance', namely *thing-like item that is quantified over at a basic level of one's ontology* (*material* substances are then thing-like items quantified over at a basic level in one's ontology of the material world, *thinking* substances are thing-like items quantified over at a basic level in one's ontology of the mental realm, and *immaterial* substances are thing-like, non-material items quantified over at a basic level in one's ontology – presumably of the mental world). Substances, in the special sense in which Locke uses the term in the 'Identity' chapter, are thus the fundamental constituents of reality; those items upon which all the rest depend for their existence and which themselves depend on nothing else. Thus God is a substance, since any account of what there is in the world would have to mention Him, and so are Cartesian immaterial spirits, if they exist, since they cannot be thought of as constructed out of or composed of more fundamental entities. And the same is true of material atoms. On the other hand the whole story about the history of an animal could in principle be told without referring to it, but only to the varying particles of matter which constitute it throughout its history, and, Locke thinks, the same is true of persons: the whole history of a person could in principle be told without ever referring to it, but only to the thinking substances, whether material or immaterial, that constitute it at different times. Thus, though animals and persons are substances in the widest sense – they are things which have properties and relations rather than themselves being properties or relations – they are not substances in the restricted sense, they would not have to be mentioned in an exhaustive inventory of the universe. But if this is correct then when Locke claims that for all he knows personal identity might not involve identity of thinking substance he is involved in no inconsistency, for he is saying merely that for all he knows when a person is present on two occasions, no *basic* substance, no fundamental constituent of reality, might be present, and *that* is a consistent claim, albeit one a Cartesian would find wholly astonishing.

The Alston–Bennett proposal seems to me to be clearly correct and conclusively argued. It makes sense of Locke as no other account can and it fits the text like a glove (apart from the fact that it implies that Locke slips up in classifying masses of matter, or bodies, i.e. aggregates of material atoms, as substances; but on the Alston–Bennett account this is an understandable slip since Locke thinks of the identity of such bodies, in contrast to that of persons and animals, as *determined* by the identity of their atoms, i.e. the basic substances of which they are composed). A firm grip on it is vital to understanding Locke.

But if we now look more closely at Locke's account of what he thinks the identity of a (basic) substance consists in, an interesting – though in the light of the Alston–Bennett proposal unsurprising – result emerges. Namely, that the account is straightforwardly circular. The identity of such a basic substance, Locke tells us, is determined by the time and place of its beginning to exist, and its relation to that time and place will always determine its identity so long as it exists (*Essay* II, xxvii. 2). But what is this 'relation' except its being (identical with) something which came into existence at that time and place? However, if so, no account of identity over time has been given. In the light of this some commentators have attempted to read into Locke the proposal that identity over time for spirits and atoms is a matter of spatio-temporal continuity. This would remove the circularity, but unfortunately Locke's text gives no unambiguous support to the suggestion. It *may* be that Locke is groping towards a spatio-temporal continuity account (e.g., when he writes of 'an Atom, i.e. a continued body under one immutable Superficies, existing in a determined time and place . . . the same with itself, and so must continue, so long as its existence is continued', *Essay* II, xxvii. 3), but the most that can be definitely ascribed to him on the basis of his text, is that spirits and atoms must have a *temporally* continuous existence. But let us now move on from this stony ground to the next part of Locke's discussion.

2.4 Plants, animals and men

Locke moves towards his account of personal identity in carefully controlled stages. Having discussed identity of substance he next moves on to discuss identity of organisms. And here, though his notion of substance in the 'Identity' chapter is, as we have seen, manifestly unaristotelian, something like Aristotle's notion of *Substantial form*, divorced from the notion of substance, has a prominent place in his thought. He is at pains to point out that the identity of organisms

> depends not on a mass of the same particles. . . . For in them
> the variation of great particles of matter alters not the identity:
> an oak, growing from a plant to a great tree. . . is still the same
> oak; and a colt grown up to a horse. . . is all the while the
> same horse, though. . . there may be a manifest change of the
> parts, so that truly they are not either of them the same masses
> of matter, though they be truly one of them the same oak, and
> the other the same horse. The reason whereof is that in these
> two cases of a mass of matter and a living body, *identity* is not
> applied to the same thing.
>
> (*Essay* II, xxvii. 3)

What the identity of an oak does depend on is explained as follows:

> That being then one plant which has such an organization of
> parts in one coherent body, partaking of one common life, it
> continues to be the same plant as long as it partakes of the
> same life. . . . For this organization being at any one instant in
> any one collection of *matter*, is in that particular concrete

distinguished from all other, and is that individual life, which existing constantly from that moment both forwards and backwards in the same continuity of insensibly succeeding parts . . ., it has that identity, which makes the same plant, and all the parts of it parts of the same plant, during all the time that they exist united in that continued organization, which is fit to convey that common life.

(*Essay* II, xxvii. 4)

The case is no different, Locke says, in brutes, for what makes an animal and continues it the same, is 'a participation of the same continued life, by constantly fleeting particles of matter, in succession vitally united to the same organized body' (*Essay* II, xxvii. 6). This quotation is, in fact, from Locke's account of the identity of a *man* through time. '[I]ngenious observation,' he insists,

puts it past doubt that the *idea* . . . of which the sound *man* . . . is the sign, is nothing else but of an animal of such a certain form: . . . whoever should see a creature of his own shape and make, though it had no more reason . . . than a *cat* or a *parrot*, would call him still a *man*; or whoever should hear a *cat* or a *parrot* discourse, reason, and philosophize would call or think it nothing but a *cat* or a *parrot* and say the one was a dull irrational man, and the other a very intelligent rational *parrot*.

(*Essay* II, xxvii. 8)

The identity of *man*, he therefore insists, must be placed in nothing else, but, like that of other animals, 'in one fitly organized body, . . . continued under one organization of life' (*Essay* II, xxvii. 6). Those who disagree, he says

will be led into strange ways of speaking and will find it hard to make an embryo, one of years, mad, and sober, the same man, by any supposition that will not make it possible for Seth, Israel, Socrates, Pilate, St. Austin and Caesar Borgia to be the same man. For if the identity of soul alone makes the same man . . . these men living in different ages . . . may have been the same man . . . which way of speaking must be from a very strange use of the word *man*, applied to an idea out of which body and shape are excluded.

(*Essay* II, xxvii. 6)

Here the opponent Locke is envisaging is, of course, one who believes in the transmigration of souls, and Locke's point is simply that whatever identity of immaterial soul can secure, it cannot, in accordance with ordinary usage, be identity of *man*.

These considerations about the identity of living things are now put forward by Locke as grounds for his conclusion that

> It is not . . . unity of substance that comprehends all sorts of identity . . . but . . . we must consider what idea it is applied to stand for: it being one thing to be the same substance, another the same man, and a third the same person, if *person, man*, and *substance* are three names standing for three different ideas, for such as is the idea belonging to that name, such must be the identity: which if it had been . . . carefully attended to, would possibly have prevented a good deal of . . . confusion . . . especially concerning personal identity.
>
> (*Essay* II, xxvii. 7)

This is the crux for Locke. His account of the identity of organisms shows how one organism may consist at different times of a variety of basic substances united together into a single organization by identity of life. And this provides, he thinks, the analogy which makes the idea that personal identity may be preserved in a variety of thinking substances, material or immaterial, intelligible. But it does so only if Locke can complete the analogy: as sameness of organism is to identity of life, so sameness of person is to identity of – what?

2.5 Personal identity and consciousness

Locke's answer to this question, of course, is: identity of consciousness: 'And as far as this consciousness can be extended backwards to any past action or thought, so far reaches the identity of that *person*' (*Essay* II, xxvii. 9).

Consciousness, in short, is the life of persons. Identity of consciousness determines identity of persons as identity of life determines identity of organism:

different substances by the same consciousness . . . being united into one person, as well as different bodies by the same life are united into one animal, whose *identity* is preserved in that change of substance by the unity of one continued life. For, it being the same consciousness that makes a man be himself to himself, personal identity depends on that only, whether it be annexed only to one individual substance, or can be continued in a succession of several.

(*Essay* II, xvvii. 9)

This analogy is at the heart of Locke's account of personal identity, and he returns to it again and again in his polemic against those who think that it must be identity of (immaterial) substance that makes for personal identity. Thus, for example, he argues at one point against 'those who place thinking in an immaterial substance only', that

before they can come to deal with [their materialist opponents] they must show why personal identity cannot be preserved in the change of immaterial substance . . . as well as animal identity is preserved in the change of material substances . . . unless, they will say, it is one immaterial spirit that makes the same life in brutes, as it is one immaterial spirit that makes the same person in man.

(*Essay* II, xxvii. 9)

Of course, there is a point of disanalogy to be noted. For Locke nowhere suggests that 'sameness of life' may bridge a temporal gap and unite material substances into one animal with a temporally discontinuous existence, and in fact, what he actually says of sameness of life seems inconsistent with this possibility. But the possibility that sameness of consciousness may unite thinking substances into a single temporally discontinuous person is central to Locke's thought. Most importantly, as we have seen, it provides him with his account of the resurrection.

However, quite correctly, Locke does not take this point of disanalogy to undermine the power of his comparison of consciousness to life to make comprehensible the possibility that personal identity might consist in sameness of consciousness and not in sameness of thinking substance.

But *why* is Locke so convinced of the truth of this thesis? When he first introduces it he represents it as a conclusion from his definition of a person. In fact this definition merges insensibly into an argument for the thesis:

> to find wherein *personal identity* consists, we must consider what person stands for; which, I think, is a thinking intelligent being that has reason and reflection and can consider itself as itself, the same thinking thing in different times and places; which it does only by that consciousness which is inseparable from thinking and, as it seems to me, essential to it: it being impossible for anyone to perceive without perceiving that he does perceive. . . .
>
> Thus it is always as to our present sensations and perceptions, and by this everyone is to himself that which he calls *self*: it not being considered in this case whether the same *self* be continued in the same or different substances. For since consciousness always accompanies thinking, and it is that that makes everyone to be what he calls *self*, and thereby distinguishes himself from all other thinking things: in this alone consists *personal identity*. . . . And as far as this consciousness can be extended backwards to any past action or thought, so far reaches the identity of that *person*.
>
> (*Essay* II, xxvii. 9)

But this is not rigorously valid, as Locke probably knows, for an entity could satisfy this definition of a person at a time without its identity over time being constituted by sameness of consciousness. In fact, on Locke's view this will be true of thinking substances, for thinking substances are 'thinking intelligent beings with reason and reflection' and thus answer to Locke's definition of a person at a time, but, of course, their identity over time, Locke thinks, is not a matter of sameness of consciousness.

Locke's real reasons for his conviction that personal identity consists in sameness of consciousness emerge more clearly, however, if we think again of the underlying aims of his discussion. The first of these, I said, was to provide an account of personal identity which made sense of the possibility of resurrection and immortality, but did so in a way that was neutral between dualist and materialist accounts of the self. But, if materialism is true, what *can* be constitutive of personal identity, consistently with the possibility of the resurrection of the dead?

Plainly not identity of (material) substance. For even in this life our *material* substance is in constant flux. Materialists must then conceive personal identity preserved in something other than identity of substance: 'as animal identity is preserved in identity of life, and not of substance' (*Essay* II, xxvii. 12)

But might the materialist not take a hint from this and say that what personal identity consists in *is* identity of life – and that personal identity is just the identity of a special kind of animal? And might he not claim that this is consistent with the possibility of the resurrection?

This might seem a more promising idea. But against it Locke would bring two objections. First, as we have seen, identity of life seems to require spatio-temporal continuity. So on Locke's view the person who is resurrected is *not* united to his earlier self by sameness of life, i.e. he is *not* the same animal.

But second, Locke would say, if personal identity were to be regarded as constituted by identity of life, then there would be no difference between personal identity and human identity. However, Locke thinks that this distinction is one that must be made if the 'forensic' role of 'person' is to be taken seriously.

Thus if Locke is right the materialist who wishes to allow for the possibility of resurrection can regard personal identity as constituted *neither* by identity of substance *nor* by identity of life – he must look elsewhere. But then, since Locke is seeking an account of personal identity which is *neutral* between dualism and materialism, he, too, must look elsewhere. But if neither identity of immaterial soul, nor identity of material particles, nor identity of animal life is acceptable as an account of what makes Socrates 'in this life and after it' the same person, what alternative is there but some form of *psychological* identity? But this is precisely what sameness of consciousness is.

This, then, I suggest, is *one* line of thought lying behind Locke's conviction that personal identity must consist in sameness of consciousness – but it is not, I think, the only one.

Another motive for Locke's conviction, I think, is his belief that an account of personal identity must conform to the facts of self-knowledge. It seems clear that it is part of Locke's thought that since one can know with certainty that one is the person who performed a certain action, and cannot know with certainty that the substance that was the subject of that past action is the subject of one's present actions or thoughts, it cannot be the case that personal identity *consists in* the identity of substance. And this is so, he clearly thinks, even on the assumption that 'that which thinks in us' is an *immaterial* substance. For even if this is the case we cannot be certain that the thinking substance which constitutes us now is the very same as that which constituted us when we performed some remembered action. The fact is that our consciousness is 'interrupted always by forgetfulness', and 'there is no moment wherein we have the whole train of all our past actions before our eyes in one view.' Moreover, 'for the greatest part of our lives, we do not reflect on our past selves', being intent on our present thoughts. Again, 'in sound sleep we have no thoughts at all, or at least none with that consciousness which attends our waking thoughts.' But in all these cases, 'since our consciousness is interrupted and we lose sight of our past selves' we cannot claim to be certain of identity of substance – whether material or immaterial (*Essay* II, xxvii. 10).

Furthermore, even when we have not 'lost sight of our past selves', Locke suggests, sameness of (immaterial) substance is not something of which we can be certain. For we simply do not know whether 'the consciousness of past actions can be transferred from one thinking substance to another', so that 'one intellectual substance may not have represented to it, as done by itself, what it never did, and was perhaps done by some other agent' (*Essay* II, xxvii. 13).

Thus, he argues, even if the dualist thesis that thinking substances are immaterial is right (as he thinks it probably is) personal identity cannot consist in identity of substance, for the fact is that we can be certain that we are the persons who performed our remembered actions but we cannot be certain of identity of substance.

But what *can* I be certain of when I recollect a past action? I cannot be certain of identity of substance, Locke claims, but can I be certain of, for instance, identity of life? Plainly not, as Locke explains it. Clearly, as Locke is viewing the matter, in such a case I can be allowed to be certain only of that which is open to my introspection. But then what *can* I be allowed to be certain of but the fact of my present consciousness of my past action? If so, however, and if it is a requirement on anything's qualifying as a candidate for what constitutes personal identity that it be something that I am certain of when I am certain of my own identity over time, then Locke's conclusion is an obvious consequence: 'self is not determined by identity of substance, which it cannot be sure of, but only by identity of consciousness' (*Essay* II, xxvii. 23).

So far, then, I have suggested that there are two lines of thought in

Locke which lead to his conclusion that personal identity must be a matter of sameness of consciousness. The first we might call metaphysical-theological – since it relates to Locke's concern to provide an account of personal identity which is neutral as to the metaphysical issue between dualists and materalists, but is consistent with Christian doctrine. The second line of thought, just now outlined, is clearly epistemological. But there is also a third line of thought in Locke which leads to the same conclusion. This starts from his conviction that personal identity is of practical concern to us, in a way in which identity of substance is not: '*Self* is that conscious thinking thing . . . which . . . is concerned for *itself* as far as that consciousness extends' (*Essay* II, xxvii. 17).

The dualist might protest that the fact that personal identity matters in the way Locke indicates is no argument against the identification of selves with immaterial substances. But what fuels Locke's thought here is the analogy he sees between material and immaterial substances, and in particular between their identity conditions. The crux is that Locke thinks that in *neither* case has identity of substance anything to do with identity of psychological properties. The same atoms which compose me now might by an amazing coincidence have once composed Nestor or might in the future compose some person not yet born; the fact that I lack any consciousness of Nestor's actions and share none of his (distinctive) psychological properties is perfectly consistent with this hypothesis. Equally, if immaterial substances exist, Locke thinks, it might be the same immaterial spirit which thinks in me now as thought in Nestor thousands of years ago; and again, the fact that I lack any consciousness of Nestor's actions and share none of his (distinctive) psychological properties is consistent with this hypothesis.

But if I became convinced that I was indeed currently composed of some of the material particles which once composed Nestor, still I would not, and could not, 'own and impute' to myself his actions (*Essay* II, xxvii. 17), regarding with remorse those of which I disapprove and with pride those of which I approve. The fact that, as I believe, I am now partly materially identical with the Nestor of long ago would not necessarily make me any more interested in him than I am in any other person of long ago, and in particular it would not, and could not, cause me to adopt towards Nestor's actions any of the backward looking attitudes – of remorse or pride, shame or embarrassment or whatever – that are typical of my relationship to my remembered past. Equally, if I became convinced that someone in the future was going to be composed of the same material particles which compose me in the present, I would not, and could not, in consequence become concerned for that person's well-being as I am concerned for my own. I would not, and could not, come to regard his actions and experiences as appropriate objects of the 'forward looking' attitudes – of fear and dread, or delighted anticipation – which typify my relationship to my own future actions and experiences.

Because these things are so it would be absurd to suggest that personal identity should be regarded as constituted by material identity; it would be absurd because it would be wholly inconsistent with the kind of interest we have in our personal identity. But, Locke argues, for exactly the same reasons it would be absurd to think of personal identity as constituted by sameness of *immaterial* substance. If identity of immaterial substance over time imports no psychological identity then why should it be of any more concern to us than identity of material substance? How can its being immaterial, i.e. as Locke sometimes puts it 'unsolid', substance make all the difference? In fact, Locke thinks, it plainly cannot. The Christian Platonist or Pythagorean who is convinced that '. . . his soul . . . has revolved in several human bodies' (*Essay* II, xxvii. 14), cannot, he argues, thereby become 'concerned in their actions, attribute them to himself, or think them his own, more than the action of any other man that ever existed' (*Essay* II, xxvii. 14). He cannot, that is, adopt towards them any of the 'backward looking' attitudes that typify his relationship to what he thinks of as his own past. And so he must acknowledge that 'he is no more one *self* with them than if the soul or immaterial spirit that now informs him had . . . began to exist, when it began to inform his present body' (*Essay* II, xxvii. 14). But though identity of immaterial substance is not sufficient for personal identity, sameness of consciousness is:

> For as to this point of being the same *self*, it matters not whether this present *self* be made up of the same or other substance, *I being as much concerned and as justly accountable for any action that was done a thousand years since, appropriated to me now by this self-consciousness*, as I am for what I did the last moment.
>
> (*Essay* II, xxvii. 16, last italics mine)

In Locke's view, then, the crucial difference between sameness of substance (whether material or immaterial) and sameness of consciousness, thought of as rival proposals as to what constitutes personal identity, is that the belief that my substance is the same as that of some past person can leave me indifferent to and uninterested in his actions, but once I become *conscious* of that person's actions, though he lived a thousand years hence, I cannot remain indifferent, rather I must then 'own and impute [them] to myself' and regard myself as accountable for them (*Essay* II, xxvii. 26). I must 'extend my personality' to them and regard them as the actions of the same *self* as those of which I am presently conscious. Thus in placing personal identity in sameness of consciousness, Locke thinks, he has an account which not only answers to the metaphysical-theological and epistemological requirements he imposes, but also makes sense of the importance the concept of personal identity has in our lives, and the special concern we have for our own pasts and futures, and in this respect, too, he thinks, his account is superior to the conventional dualist proposal that sameness of person is sameness of soul.

2.6 'Person': a forensic term

The final part of the last section naturally leads on to a consideration of Locke's thesis that 'person' is 'a Forensic term appropriating actions and their merits, and so belongs only to intelligent agents capable of a law, and happiness and misery' (*Essay* II, xxvii. 26).

As Alston and Bennett point out (1988:43ff.) Locke is a conceptual pragmatist. He regards the concepts we have as ones we have chosen, because they best suit our interests and activities, from the superabundant array of possible classifications that nature provides. This conceptual pragmatism is most obvious in Locke's views on how we should regard borderline cases of concepts – monsters and changelings and the like – about which he insists that it is up to us to *decide* how to classify them according to what suits our needs best. However, it is relevant to his views on personal identity, too, where it implies that the reason that we employ the particular concept of a person we do – the particular manner of grouping together collections of thinking substances that our idea of 'same person' signifies – is that it best suits our interests and needs to do so. When Locke says that person is a *forensic* term, then, what he is saying is that the interests which best explain our employment of this particular method of classification are those of morality and law.

Why this is so, Locke thinks, is explained by the facts to which we have just been attending: I can be unconcerned and indifferent to the fate of others, but I cannot be unconcerned or indifferent to my own fate. Thus I cannot but be concerned about the prospect of punishment or reward to be meted out to the agent of those actions which I acknowledge as my own. Hence Locke claims 'In this personal identity is founded all the right justice of reward and punishment; happiness and misery being that for which everyone is concerned for himself, and not mattering what becomes of any substance not joined to or affected with that consciousness' (*Essay* II, xxvii. 18).

The second part of this expresses Locke's conviction that our concern for our own well-being has nothing to do with a concern for the well-being of those persons linked to us by sameness of substance. The first part might seem uncontroversial, until one realizes that Locke is claiming that personal identity is not only a necessary, but also a sufficient condition of warranted accountability.

Of course, this is not what we ordinarily think. For we would ordinarily say, as Flew (1987:136) puts it, 'that there is an abundance of possible extenuations or even of complete excuses' which would justify refraining from punishing (or indeed rewarding) a person for what we would none the less be happy to describe as *his* actions. But Locke thinks of personal identity as the sole condition necessary for proper accountability and seems not to want to have anything to do with the concept of an excuse or extenuating circumstance.

To some extent Locke recognizes the existence of this divergence between his view and our ordinary way of thinking, but he puts it down to the failure of everyday thinking to make his sharp distinction between the concept of a man and that of a person. Ordinarily, for example, we would not think it right to punish a madman for a crime committed when he was sane, or to punish a sane man for a crime committed when he was mad, but we would not deny that we were dealing all along with the same person. Locke acknowledges this but does not take it to be an objection to his view; rather he takes it to be evidence that his distinction between man and person is actually implicit in our ordinary thought:

But if it be possible for the same man to have distinct incommunicable consciousnesses at different times, . . . the

same man would at different times make different persons:
which we see, is the sense of mankind in their solemnest
declaration of their opinions: human laws not punishing the
madman for the sober man's actions, nor the sober man for
what the madman did, thereby making them two persons;
which is somewhat explained by our [saying] such a one is not
himself, or is besides *himself*, in which phrases it is insinuated,
as if those who now, or at least first used them, thought that *self*
was changed, the *self* same person was no longer in that man.

(*Essay* II, xxvii. 20)

But, of course, this cannot be right. The fact is that we do have the
concept of an excuse or an extenuation and so we do not need a
theory of insanity as 'possession' to justify treating the insane man
differently from the sane. And the reason that we do not think it
right to punish a madman for deeds committed before he lost his
reason is that we think that punishment can only be properly meted
out to the sane – who can understand its significance. Locke's proposal that his distinction between man and person is implicit in our
ordinary thought about this case is thus entirely unjustified. But it is
worth noting in addition that it does not even fit the facts, for in the
cases in which human laws do not punish the madman for the sober
man's actions, or the sober man for what the madman did, the
madman and sober man need not have 'distinct incommunicable
consciousnesses', for neither the onset nor the cessation of madness
need create amnesia. Thus whether or not human laws make the
madman or the sober man in such a case two persons, Locke's own
account of personal identity need not do so.

So much, then, for Locke's bizarre insistence that personal identity must be thought of as the sole proper ground for warranted
accountability irrespective of the possibility of excuses or extenuations. I now turn to his seemingly innocuous proposal that it is at
any rate a necessary condition.

I say 'seemingly innocuous' because this proposal, is, of course,
wholly in accord with our ordinary thought. But its content for
Locke is given by his theory of personal identity, and so understood,
it takes on a totally different appearance. For, as Locke notes, so
understood it entails that one can only be held responsible for
having done what one can remember, i.e. is conscious of, having
done. For, of course, on Locke's account one *has* done only what

one is conscious of having done. This consequence of Locke's account has seemed to many readers to be morally repugnant, for it implies that a criminal may escape his just deserts by a convenient attack of amnesia. Locke confronts the problem by considering a case of a criminal act performed during a drunken frenzy with regard to which the man, when sobered up, is wholly amnesic. In Locke's view it cannot be just to punish a man for such an act which he cannot recall, and in fact, such punishment will be on a par with punishing the madman for the sane man's actions, or the sane man for the madman's deeds; it will involve punishing *one* person for the deeds of another. But this, as Locke notes, is not in conformity with how courts ordinarily proceed.

Locke's response to the problem is the following passage:

> But is not a man drunk and sober the same person, why else is he punished for the act he commits when drunk, though he be never afterwards conscious of it? Just as much the same person as a man that walks and does other things in his sleep is the same person. Human laws punish both . . . because . . . they cannot distinguish certainly what is real and what is counterfeit, and so the ignorance in drunkenness or sleep is not admitted as a plea. For, though punishment be annexed to personality, and personality to consciousness, and the drunkard perhaps be not conscious of what he did, yet human judicatures justly punish him, because the fact is proved against him, but want of consciousness cannot be proved for him. But in the Great Day, wherein the secrets of all hearts shall be laid open, . . . no one shall be made to answer for what he knows nothing of, but shall receive his doom, his conscience accusing or excusing him.
>
> (*Essay* II, xxvii. 22)

There is more than one absurdity in this passage. For one thing, as Curley notes (1982:318), in his remarks about sleep-walking Locke seems to be concerned to explain a legal practice which is not a legal practice at all: sleep-walking is and was even in Locke's day, recognized as an excuse in law. Setting this point aside Locke's thesis is apparently that amnesia, and hence, according to his theory, lack of personal identity, *would* be recognized as a reason for withholding punishment by human judicatures if they could be sure of its presence, but not being sure of its presence they assume it not to exist. In other words human judicatures proceed, in this area at least, upon the presumption that the accused is guilty until proven innocent.

But this attempt by Locke to reconcile his theory with ordinary legal practice is wholly implausible. Whether or not God's proceedings on the Day of Judgement, when everyone is known by God to remember all his past, are just, justice is not done by absence of proof of injustice in the meantime. In fact, of course, drunkenness is not widely accepted as an excuse in modern law, and was even less so in Locke's day. But it is fantastic to suppose that this is so because it is, or ever was thought to be, especially easy for a man to counterfeit ignorance of his drunken misdeeds. It is simply because drunkenness unlike madness, is a *voluntarily* contracted state.

As a theory of moral and legal accountability, then, Locke's theory of personal identity is a failure. Partly this is because he insists on regarding it as a *sufficient* condition of proper accountability – in ignorance or defiance of the fact that we ordinarily allow excuses and extenuations even when personal identity is acknowledged. In so far as the faults in the theory derive from this source they do not reflect on Locke's theory of personal identity itself, but only on his over-ambitious employment of it. But, as we have seen, not all the faults in what Locke says about personal identity as the ground of punishment and reward can be traced to this source. In particular, his difficulties with drunken misdeeds cannot. In this case it is the fact that Locke thinks that sameness of consciousness is *necessary* as well as sufficient for personal identity which is the source of the trouble. It seems clear, then, that some modification at least, of Locke's theory is needed. But further discussion of weaknesses in the theory will be reserved to the next chapter.

2.7 Consciousness

I now wish to look more closely at Locke's concept of consciousness, an undersanding of which has been taken for granted in the discussion so far. As we shall see, our appreciation of Locke will benefit.

Locke is often interpreted as putting forward an account of personal identity in terms of memory, but Locke himself never, in fact, uses the word 'memory' or any of its variants in any of the main statements of his view. The expression he constantly uses is 'consciousness'.

As C.S. Lewis details (1967), there were two main meanings of 'consciousness' and its cognates in seventeenth-century English. In its strong, or what Lewis calls its 'consciring' sense, both the meaning of the prefix 'con' (from 'cum'), 'with', and the root 'scio', from the Latin for 'I know', are active. In its weak sense the prefix contributes nothing to the meaning of the word. The *Oxford English Dictionary* cites the following passage from Hobbes's *Leviathan* to illustrate the strong sense: 'where two men, or more men, know of one and the same fact, they are said to be conscious of it to one another'. The modern use of 'conscious' is almost always the weak sense. In the locution 'conscious to himself' (which is common in Locke) 'conscious' is used in the strong sense. When one is 'conscious to oneself' knowledge of something is shared with oneself alone. In this use of the expression one may be thought of as a witness to one's own acts. Consciousness in the sense of 'consciousness to oneself', then, is knowledge of oneself, knowledge of one's own thoughts and actions.

The meaning of the word 'conscience' has also undergone changes since the seventeenth century. Originally it meant 'consciousness' in the *consciring* sense. One's conscience was one's inward knowledge of what one had done. This is significantly different from the modern use of the word, in which it means something like: 'one's judgement as to the moral worth of one's actions'.

To understand Locke's discussion of personal identity it is important to realize that he used 'consciousness' in its strong sense, and uses 'conscience' as a synonym for it. According to Locke consciousness is a reflexive second-order act; the perception of what passes in a man's mind (*Essay* II, xxvii. 9). To be conscious of one's acts is to share, *qua* witness, knowledge of their occurrence with oneself, *qua* agent. And having been a witness in this way to one's own acts one can retain the knowledge of them thus gained. It is such shared knowledge had by a present self of a past self's actions which Locke thinks of as constituting personal identity.

'Conscience' is used similarly by Locke. Thus, when he writes 'But in the Great Day . . . no one shall be made to answer for what he knows nothing of but shall receive his doom, his *conscience* accusing or excusing him' (*Essay* II, xxvii. 22), what he means is '. . . his knowledge of his own acts accusing or excusing him'.

Primarily, then, when Locke says that personal identity consists in sameness of consciousness he means that it consists in shared knowledge – the knowledge shared by the present and past self. Of course, the only knowledge we have of the past which is relevant to Locke's discussion is memory knowledge. Reid gets this absolutely right when he writes: 'Mr Locke attributes to consciousness the conviction we have of our own past actions. . . . It is impossible to understand the meaning of this, unless by consciousness be meant memory' (1941). Nevertheless, the *concept* of consciousness, as Locke uses it, is not that of memory and it is the former concept Locke employs in his account of personal identity. As we shall see in the next chapter this goes some way to explaining why the idea that his account of personal identity might be circular, as Butler argues, simply never occurs to Locke.

2.8 A much disputed passage

I shall end this exposition of Locke's views with a discussion of a passage which hostile commentators have frequently pointed to as a proof of the self-contradictoriness of his position. But we shall see that this charge is unwarranted (whatever other faults can be laid at Locke's door) and in doing so we shall see once more the importance in reading Locke of paying careful attention to his distinction between persons and thinking substances. The tenability of this distinction will then be a main topic of the next chapter.

The passage in question (*Essay* II, xxvii. 13) is one in which Locke first notes that the question whether 'if the same (immaterial) thinking substance be changed it can be the same person?' cannot be resolved 'but by those who know what kind of substance they are that do think; and whether the consciousness of past actions can be transferred from one thinking substance to another'. He goes on:

But . . . why one intellectual substance may not have
represented to it, as done by itself what it never did, and was
perhaps done by some other agent . . . will be difficult to
conclude from the nature of things. And that it never is so will
by us, till we have clearer views of the nature of thinking
substances, be best resolved into the goodness of God, who as
far as the happiness or misery of any of his sensible creatures is

concerned in it will not, by a fatal error of theirs, transfer
from one to another that consciousness which draws reward or
punishment with it.

Many commentators (e.g., Flew 1987:137, Penelhum 1970:76,
Vesey 1974:58-9, Mackie 1976:184) read this passage as deeply confused, involving first a failure on Locke's part to see that his account
of personal identity excludes the possibility of one person being
conscious of another's actions, and secondly an appeal to God's
goodness to close off the gap his theory supposedly leaves open. But
while the passage is strange it is not confused in this way. For the
'sensible creatures' referred to in it are not *persons* but thinking
substances.

Locke's thought is simply that if, as his theory of personal identity
allows, one thinking substance may be conscious of the actions of
another, then the two thinking substances will make one person. But
then in punishing *that* person for his sins on the Day of Judgement
God will punish, or at least hurt, the thinking substance it at that
time 'involves', i.e. which is then doing its thinking for it. However,
that thinking substance may not be the same one which was involved
when the sin for which the person is being punished was committed,
it may simply be one to which a consciousness of that sin has been
transferred; in which case it will be being punished, or at least hurt,
for 'what it never did, and was perhaps done by some other agent
. . .', i.e. some other thinking substance. It is understandable, then,
that Locke speaks of a 'fatal error' involved in the transfer of such a
guilt-bearing consciousness – which can consign its recipient to Hell
– from one thinking substance to another, and the passage involves
no logical incoherence.

What it *does* involve, however, is a momentary piece of back-
sliding on Locke's part. For his 'official' position, of course, is that
personal identity not only is but *ought* to be the sole ground of moral
responsibility: whether punishment falls on a given person on
Judgement Day not only does but *should* depend solely on what sins
that *person* has committed, not upon what sins have been committed by the *thinking substance* it then involves. But if so there is no
'fatal error' involved in condemning a thinking substance to Hell for
a sin *it* never committed – as long as it is the same person as the
thinking substance that did commit the sin then the punishment is
quite appropriate.

Thus the hostile commentators are right in thinking that the passage under discussion reveals a flaw in Locke's position, but what it reveals is not a piece of incoherent thinking, but rather a momentary failure of nerve on Locke's part, in face of the realization of what his theory commits him to.

But the more important point the passage brings out is the seriousness with which Locke treats his description of thinking substances as *thinking* substances – that the only way to consign a sinner to Hell would be to consign thereto a hunk of *non-thinking* substance (whether material or immaterial) would surely have caused him no qualms. When a person thinks, then, it really is the case, in Locke's view, that it does so only because *something else* – some thinking substance which is strictly non-identical with it – does so. As we shall see in the next chapter, this feature of Locke's position is both one of its major strengths and one of its main weaknesses.

CHAPTER 3

Leibniz, Butler and Reid

3.1 Introduction

The heart of Locke's account of personal identity is the claim that identity of substance is irrelevant. What matters for personal identity is sameness of consciousness and this may relate states of different substances, and may fail to relate states of the same substance.

It is precisely their opposition to Locke on this point that unites the writers to be considered in this chapter. Butler's and Reid's views on Locke are well known, and some of their objections to him have become part of the standard anti-Lockean armoury, but Leibniz's views are less often discussed and in some ways more interesting. As we shall see he has a better appreciation of Locke's motives than do Butler and Reid, and in consequence his own account of personal identity, albeit requiring identity of substance as a necessary condition, and in this respect fundamentally opposed to Locke's, is in other respects closer to Locke's than to theirs. The key fact which explains this similarity is that, like Locke, Leibniz regards 'person' as a 'forensic term' and is vividly aware of the need to give an account of personal identity which makes comprehensible *why* it matters. To develop this point we can begin by looking at his treatment of the topic in his *Discourse on Metaphysics* (1953), written at a time before he had encountered Locke's views.

3.2 Discourse on metaphysics

The relevant section of the *Discourse* is section xxxiv, entitled 'Of the difference of Spirits from other substances, souls or substantial forms, and that the immortality which is demanded involves

memory'. The substantial forms of bodies which make *unum per se*,
as man does, and the souls of beasts, Leibniz claims, cannot perish
entirely, any more than atoms or the ultimate parts of matter in the
sentiments of other philosophers. They also express the whole universe, albeit more imperfectly than spirits. But what principally
distinguishes them from spirits is that

> they do not know what they are nor what they do, and that,
> being consequently unable to reflect, they cannot discover
> necessary and universal truths. It is also for lack of reflection
> on themselves that they have no moral quality [orginally: do
> not make a person], whence it comes that passing through a
> thousand transformations, almost like a caterpillar which turns
> into a butterfly, it is all one for morals or practice if they are
> said to perish, as can also be said physically, when we say that
> bodies perish by their corruption.
>
> (1953:57–8)

But

> the intelligent soul, knowing what it is and being able to say
> this *I* which says so much, remains and subsists not merely
> Metaphysically, much more than the others, but it also remains
> the same morally and makes the same person. For it is the
> memory or knowledge of this *I* which makes it capable of
> punishment or reward.

To be the same person, then, according to Leibniz, it is not sufficient to remain the same metaphysically, i.e. to remain the same
substance, it is also necessary to remain the same morally, which
requires the retention of memory or knowledge. This is so because it
is the retention of such memory or knowledge which is the prerequi-
site of moral responsibility. Personal identity, for Leibniz, in the
Discourse, then, just as for Locke, is by definition the ground of
moral responsibility – 'person' is a forensic term appropriating
actions and their merits.

Leibniz goes on to present a remarkable thought-experiment.

> Further, the immortality which is demanded in morals and in
> religion does not consist in this perpetual subsistence alone, for
> without the memory of what one had been it would not be in

any way desirable. Let us suppose that some individual were to become the King of China at one stroke, but on condition of forgetting what he had been, as if he had been born anew, is it not as much in practice, or as regards the effects which one can perceive, as if he were to be annihilated and a King of China to be created in his place at the same instant? Which this individual has no reason to desire.

(1953:58)

The proper response to this thought-experiment has recently become a matter of debate between Simple and Complex theorists of personal identity (see, e.g., Chisholm 1969 and Shoemaker 1969). But what is at present of interest is the similarity between these remarks and some of Locke's. For example:

Let anyone reflect on himself and suppose that he has an immaterial spirit . . . let him suppose it to be the same soul that was in Nestor or Thersites . . . but he now having no consciousness of the actions of Nestor or Thersites . . . can he be concerned in either of their actions, attribute them to himself, or think them his own, more than the actions of any other man that ever existed?

(*Essay* II, xxvii. 14)

Locke's remarks concern the attitude of a present person towards a past one, whereas Leibniz's concern is the attitude of a present person towards a future one: but the thought is clearly exactly the same.

However, Leibniz goes on to argue that even though personal identity, as he defines it, requires more than identity of substance, in fact 'God will always conserve not only our substance but also our person, that is to say the memory and knowledge of what we are'. In other words, the thought-experiment concerning the King of China can be excluded on theological grounds so that in consequence of God's will identity of substance is *de facto* a sufficient condition of personal identity. Here Leibniz departs from Locke, who is happy to allow that it is possible (albeit improbable) that a thinking substance may lose all consciousness of its past life. His reason is:

It must not then be doubted that God has ordered everything in such a way that Spirits not only may live always which is indispensable, but also that they may conserve their moral quality always, in order that his city may not lose a single person, as the world does not lose a single substance. And consequently they will always know what they are, otherwise they would not be susceptible of reward or of punishment.

(1953:61–2)

In sum, then, Leibniz's position in the *Discourse* has one very important point of similarity with Locke's, but two equally important points of difference. The point of similarity is that he makes retention of memory and knowledge a necessary condition of personal identity; the points of dissimilarity are that he thinks that identity of substance is *also* necessary, and that he refuses to envisage as something that God might allow that a substance which at one time qualifies as a person could be stripped of all knowledge and memory of its past life and become another person, in the way Locke supposes to be possible.

3.3 The New Essays

After he had read Locke's *Essay* and reflected on it, Leibniz wrote *The New Essays Concerning Understanding* as a chapter by chapter commentary on Locke's views. Turning to his discussion of Locke's chapter on 'Identity' we find what at first seems to be the same account of personal identity as appears in the *Discourse*. Leibniz writes:

I also hold this opinion, that consciousness or the sense of I proves moral or personal identity. And that is how I distinguish the *incessancy* of a beast's soul from the *immortality* of the soul of a man; both of them preserve real physical identity: but it is consonant with the rules of divine providence that in man's case the soul should also retain a moral identity which is apparent to us ourselves, so as to constitute the same person, which is therefore sensitive to punishments and rewards.

(1981:236)

Nor is Leibniz's next remark incompatible with the *Discourse* account:

You seem to hold, sir, that this apparent identity could be preserved in the absence of any real identity. Perhaps that could happen through God's absolute power; but I should have

thought that, according to the order of things, an identity
which is apparent to the person concerned – one who senses
himself to be the same – presupposes a real identity obtaining
through each immediate temporal transition accompanied by
reflection . . . because an intimate and immediate perception
cannot be mistaken in the natural course of things.

(1981:236)

It would be a misreading of this to take Leibniz to be allowing that
personal identity could be transferred by God's absolute power from
one substance to another; all he says is that *apparent identity* could be
transferred, so that one substance would *mistakenly* think itself the
same person as another one. The *Discourse* requirement that identity
of substance is necessary for personal identity is not abandoned.

However, in the next passage Leibniz does seem to depart from
the *Discourse* account, not, however, by moving closer to Locke,
but by moving further away from him:

I would not wish to deny . . . that 'personal identity' and even
the 'self' persist in us, and that I am that *I* who was in the
cradle, merely on the grounds that I can no longer remember
anything that I did at that time. To discover one's own
moral identity unaided, it is sufficient that between one state
and a neighbouring one . . . there be a mediating bond of
consciousness. . . . Thus, if an illness has interrupted . . . my
. . . consciousness, the testimony of others could fill the gap in
my recollection. I could even be punished on this testimony if I
had done some deliberate wrong . . . which this illness had
made me forget.

(1981:237)

Memory, then, Leibniz is saying, in apparent disagreement with
the *Discourse* account and certainly in disagreement with Locke, is
not necessary for moral, and hence, personal identity. The next
statement is a still more extreme expression of the point:

if I forgot my whole past, and needed to have myself taught all
over again, even my own name and how to read and write, I
could still learn from others about my life during my preceding
state; and, similarly, I would have retained my rights without
having to be divided into two persons and made to inherit

from myself. All this is enough to maintain the moral identity which makes the same person.

(1981:237)

This should remind us of Leibniz's remarks about the individual who becomes King of China, who according to the *Discourse* account would *not* retain his moral identity in the absence of any memory or knowledge of his past life.

In fact, however, Leibniz's position in the *New Essays* is less of a radical departure from that in the *Discourse* than this makes it appear, as becomes evident later when he takes up explicitly Locke's question whether

the same individual substance remaining, there may be two distinct persons; which question seems to me to be built on this, whether, the same immaterial being may be stripped of all sense of its past existence, and lose it beyond the power of ever retrieving again; and so as it were beginning a new account from a new period.

(1981:238)

His reply is instructive:

An immaterial . . . spirit cannot 'be stripped of all' perception of its past existence. It retains impressions of everything which has previously happened to it, and it even has presentiments of everything which will happen to it; but these states of mind are mostly too minute to be distinguishable and for one to be aware of them, although they may perhaps grow some day. It is this continuity and interconnection of perceptions which makes someone really the same individual: but our awareness – i.e. when we are aware of past states of mind – proves a moral identity as well . . . it is unreasonable to suppose that memory should be lost beyond any possibility of recovery, since insensible perceptions . . . serve a purpose here too, preserving the seeds of memory.

(1981:239)

Thus Leibniz is in agreement with Locke that personal identity implies some kind of psychological connectedness. But he does not regard this as in conflict with the requirement of substantial identity, since it is itself the basis of substantial identity. In virtue of the interconnectedness and continuity of its insensible perceptions, which make a spirit the same substance, it retains its moral identity because it can and will ultimately recall its past actions, whatever transformations it undergoes in the meanwhile. Thus, just as in the *Discourse*, identity of substance is not only necessary for identity of person, but also sufficient – but what is meant by a substance here is not a bare substratum of mental life, as Locke thinks of it, but an active monad whose identity over time does not have to be taken as an unanalysable datum but is grounded in the connectedness between its states. And so Leibniz sums up:

> I have shown you the basis of true physical identity and have shown that it does not clash with moral identity or with memory either. And I have also shown that although they cannot always indicate a person's physical identity either to the person in question or to his acquaintances, they never run counter to physical identify and are never totally divorced from it. Finally, I have shown that there are always created spirits who know or can know the truth of the matter, and that there is reason to think that things which make no difference from the point of view of the persons themselves will do so only temporarily.
>
> (1981:247)

It remains only to note, before leaving the *New Essays*, Leibniz's remarkable anticipation of Bernard Williams's Reduplication Argument to Locke's theory:

> suppose in another region of the universe or at some other time there may be a sphere in no way sensibly different from this sphere of earth on which we live, and inhabited by men each of whom differs sensibly in no way from his counterpart among us. Thus at one time there will be more than a hundred million pairs of similar persons, i.e. pairs of persons with the same appearances and states of consciousness. God could transfer the minds, by themselves or with their bodies, from one sphere to the other without their being aware of it; but whether they are transferred or left where they are, what would your authorities say about their persons or 'selves'? Given that the states of consciousness and the inner and outer appearance of the men on these two spheres cannot yield a distinction between them, are they two persons or are they one and the same? . . .

they could be told apart by God. . . . But since according to
your theories consciousness alone distinguishes persons, with
no need for us to be concerned about the real identity or
diversity of substance or even about what would appear to
other people, what is to prevent us saying that these two
persons . . . are one person? Yet that would be a manifest
absurdity.

(1981:245)

In view of the impact Williams's Reduplication Argument had on
the personal identity debate when it was published in 1956 one can
only speculate how the discussion on personal identity would have
gone if this argument had come to the attention of philosophers
sooner.

3.4 Butler and Reid

Unlike Leibniz, Butler and Reid show no sympathy for Locke's
treatment of personal identity, and many of their arguments against
it seem to be based on perverse misunderstandings. Nevertheless
their replies to Locke are important for two reasons. First, because
in the course of criticizing Locke they present their own view of
personal identity as (as Butler puts in) 'strict and philosophical'
identity, or (as Reid puts it) 'perfect identity', and despite the fact
that their arguments for this view are virtually non-existent, it is, as
we saw in Chapter 1, a view with considerable attractions, which has
become increasingly popular in recent years. The second reason for
the importance of Butler and Reid is simply that amongst the many
bad arguments they bring against Locke there are several good ones,
and some which raise issues of considerable importance for how
Locke is to be understood.

As we have seen, one of the thoughts at the heart of Locke's
position is that there is an analogy between personal identity and
animal or vegetable identity: as sameness of life makes for identity
in the case of animals and vegetables, so sameness of consciousness
makes for identity in the case of persons. Butler and Reid reject this
analogy outright. Butler writes:

The inquiry, what makes vegetables the same in the common
acceptance of the word, does not appear to have any relation

to that of personal identity; because the word *same*, when
applied to them and to persons, is not only applied to different
subjects, but it is also used in different senses.

(1735)

He goes on to introduce his distinction between 'strict and
philosophical' and 'loose and popular' senses of identity, explaining
that

> when a man swears to the same tree . . . he means only the
> same as to all the purposes of property and uses of common
> life, and not that the tree has been all that time the same in the
> strict and philosophical sense of the word.

He makes it very clear what this strict and philosophical sense of
sameness implies – that there can be no change in the parts of the
entity to which it is applied. He then tells us, giving no reason, that
'sameness is used in this latter sense, whenever applied to persons.
The identity of these, therefore, cannot subsist with diversity of
substance', as, that is, Locke had claimed.

Reid is similarly dogmatic:

> The identity, therefore, which we ascribe to bodies, whether
> natural or artificial is not perfect identity: it is rather something
> which for conveniency of speech we call identity. It admits of a
> great change of the subject . . . ; sometimes even of a total
> change. . . . It has no fixed nature when applied to bodies, and
> questions about the identity of a body are very often questions
> about words. But identity, when applied to a person, has no
> ambiguity, and admits not of degrees, or of more and less. It
> is the foundation of all rights and obligations and of all
> accountableness; and the notion of it is fixed and precise.

(1941:206)

Why this is so, Reid thinks, is because the 'identity of a person is a
perfect identity . . . and it is impossible that a person should be in
part the same, and in part different; because a person is a *monad*,
and is not divisible into parts' (1941:204).

Reid has a peculiar argument for this assertion, which goes as
follows:

A part of a person is a manifest absurdity. When a man loses
his estate, his health, his strength, he is still the same person
and has lost nothing of his personality. If he has a leg or an
arm cut off, he is the same person as he was before. The
amputated member is no part of his person, otherwise it would
have a right to a part of his estate, and be liable to a part of his
engagements. It would be entitled to a share of his merit and
demerit, which is manifestly absurd. A person is something
indivisible, and is what Leibniz calls a *monad*.

(1941:202)

The crux of this argument is the claim that to qualify as a part of a
person a thing must have a right to a part of his estate and be liable to
a part of his engagements. Everything that is *in fact* (as we would
ordinarily say) part of a person (his arms, legs, kidneys, etc.), of
course, has no right to part of that person's estate, but Reid regards
the fact that something is not entitled to part of a person's estate as a
reason for saying it is not part of a person. However, if none of the
things that are in fact parts of persons are to be called 'parts of
persons' then indeed presumably nothing else should be called parts
of persons.

But Reid's reason for denying that arms, legs, etc., are parts of
persons is no reason at all. Whether something is a part of a person
is not a moral question, as Reid implies, but a physical one. The
considerations Reid adduces are thus irrelevant. All he establishes
(or rather reminds us of) is simply that for *moral* purposes a person
(as opposed to families, organizations, etc.) is the smallest unit. But
this is irrelevant to the question he is considering.

We shall look more closely at Butler and Reid's Simple View of
personal identity in a later chapter, but now let us move on to their
explicit arguments against Locke.

One objection Butler makes is perfectly straightforward: 'to say
that [consciousness] . . . is necessary to our being the same persons,
is to say, that a person has not existed a single moment, nor done one
action, but what he can remember: indeed none but what he reflects
upon' (1736). Clearly this is absurd, whatever Locke claims, and
even self-contradictory, given the logical properties of identity, as
Reid hammers home with his famous Paradox of the Gallant Officer:

Suppose a brave officer to have been flogged when a boy at
school for robbing an orchard, to have taken a standard from

the enemy in his first campaign, and to have been made a
general in advanced life; suppose also . . . that, when he took
the standard, he was conscious of his having been flogged at
school, and that, when made a general, he was conscious of his
taking the standard, but had absolutely lost the consciousness
of his flogging. . . . it follows, from Mr. Locke's doctrine,
that he who was flogged at school is the same person who took
the standard, and that he who took the standard is the same
person who was made a general. Whence it follows, if there be
any truth in logic, that the general is the same person with him
who was flogged at school. But the general's consciousness
does not reach as far back as his flogging; therefore according
to Mr. Locke's doctrine he is not the same person who was
flogged. Therefore, the general is, and at the same time is not,
the same person with him who was flogged at school.

(1941:213)

Obviously, these objections hit their target, but they do not go
deep. For Locke's account can easily be revised to render them
ineffective. We saw this in the last chapter. What is needed is just the
distinction between *connectedness* of consciousness and *continuity*
of consciousness, where continuity is defined in terms of connectedness by saying that a later person $P2$ at $t2$ has a consciousness which
is continuous with that of an earlier person $P1$ at $t1$ just in case he is
the last link in a chain of connecting persons beginning with $P1$ at $t1$,
each of whom is conscious of the experiences and actions of the preceding link in the chain. With continuity of consciousness defined in
this way a revision of Locke's account which makes personal identity consist in continuity of consciousness is immune to these objections of Butler and Reid.

The only question that might be raised is whether this revision,
which would also get Locke out of his difficulties with drunks and
madmen, is consonant with Locke's motives in giving his account of
personal identity. But it seems clear that it is. Like Locke's original
account the revised account is neutral between dualist and materialist accounts of the self, but leaves open the possibility of the resurrection. Again like Locke's original account it does not make
incomprehensible, as the bare substratum theory does, the practical
importance of personal identity. And finally, since it still allows
that sameness of consciousness is a *sufficient* condition of personal

identity, it accords with Locke's desire to provide an account of personal identity which is in accord with its first-person knowability.

The next objection we should consider is the famous vicious circularity objection, which Butler gives in the very next sentence following the passage last quoted. As we shall see, this raises more interesting questions.

3.5 The circularity objection

Butler writes: 'And one should really think it self-evident that consciousness of personal identity presupposes, and therefore cannot constitute, personal identity, and more than knowledge, in any other case, can constitute truth, which it presupposes.' This is often taken to be an objection to defining personal identity in terms of memory, on the ground that the analysis of the notion of memory requires appeal to the notion of personal identity if we are to distinguish veridical from non-veridical memory. That is, the point is often read as a point about the concept of memory itself and its involvement with the concept of personal identity, irrespective of the *content* of the memory in question. This had led philosophers sympathetic to Locke to see whether or not memory could be defined without such an appeal, or whether some analogous notion of *quasi-memory* might be developed that differs from memory only by lacking the identity-presupposing element in the latter. This line of enquiry has been very fruitful, as we shall see in Chapter 8. However, it seems clear that to read Butler as making so sophisticated an objection, is mistaken. His thought is simply that, in general, one cannot define *what it is for it to be the case that P* in terms of *what it is for it to be known that P*, and that, as a special case of this, one cannot define *what it is for personal identity to obtain* in terms of *what it is for it to be known – or to be an object of consciousness – that personal identity obtains*. On this understanding his objection is the same as the one Reid puts more bluntly: 'to say that my remembering that I did such a thing, or . . . my being conscious that I did it, makes me to have done it, appears to me as great an absurdity as it would be to say, that my belief that the world was created made it to be created', it is 'to attribute to memory or consciousness a strange magical power of producing its object, though that object must have existed before the memory or consciousness which produced it' (1941:204 and 214).

If this is the objection, however, Locke can answer it. The notion of consciousness he employs in his account of personal identity is indeed a notion of knowledge, but its content is not personal identity, and its possessors are not persons but *thinking substances*. The last point is the crucial one: it is because Locke so carefully keeps the notions of a person and a thinking substance distinct that he is not vulnerable to the circularity objection. For the relation in terms of which Locke defines personal identity, that is, sameness of consciousness, is not a relation between persons, but a relation between thinking substances.

To see this point it is useful to think of Locke's account of personal identity in the light of a more recent paradigm of what an account of a criterion of identity should be, namely Frege's specification (1950) of the criterion of identity for directions as the relation of parallelism between lines. According to Frege's familiar proposal we can introduce the functor: 'the direction of' by the stipulation that:

the direction of a = the direction of b if a is parallel to b.

We thereby fix the criterion of identity for directions as the relation of parallelism between lines.

With this fixed we can go on to explain 'x is a direction' as meaning 'there is some line of which x is the direction', and we can go on to explain the predicates of directions in terms of those satisfiable by lines, subject to the constraint that the truth-conditions of each statement of the form 'the direction of a is F' be given by a statement of the form 'line a is F^*', where 'F^*' denotes a property of lines for which parallelism is a congruence relation (i.e. a property shared by all parallel lines). Thus, starting from the criterion of identity for directions, we can go on to explain the whole 'language game' (to lapse into Wittgensteinian terminology) in which we speak of directions.

This approach is susceptible to generalization. For *any* kind of object K we can ask (although we cannot always receive an answer): (i) what entities play the role for K's that straight lines play for directions, and (ii) what relation plays the role for K's that parallelism plays for directions?

We can apply this Fregean approach to problems of identity over time also. The entities which stand to K's as straight lines stand to directions might be ordered pairs of persisting things (of a distinct kind K^*) and times, and the relation which serves as the criterion of identity over time for K's might be a relation between pairs of such ordered pairs.

Where a and b are K^*'s the criterion for K-identity over time could then be given in the form:

> the K of which K^*a is a manifestation at t = the K of which K^*b is a manifestation at t' if $\langle a,t \rangle R \langle b,t' \rangle$.

Being a K could then be explained as being the K of which some $\langle a,t \rangle$ is the manifestation, and the satisfaction conditions of predicates satisfiable by K's could be explained in terms of the properties possessed by K^*'s at times (equivalently, relations between K^*'s and times, or properties of ordered pairs of K^*'s and times).

With this Fregean perspective in mind we can then think of what Locke is doing in his discussion of personal identity as follows. He begins with the notion of a thinking substance – these are his K^*'s. He notes a relation which can hold between a thinking substance at one time and a thinking substance at another, namely being conscious of the same actions or experiences – this is his relation R. He then specifies the criterion of personal identity over time by stipulating that:

> the person in which thinking substance a thinks at time t = the person in which thinking substance b thinks at time t' if thinking substance a is conscious of the same actions and experiences as thinking substance b.

This is not then a circular procedure. But it still seems odd. What makes it seem so is that Locke not only ascribes consciousness to thinking substances, he also ascribes it to persons. And in general it appears that whatever psychological characteristics thinking substances have are also possessed by persons, and conversely. This makes it difficult to see how Locke can hold apart the two notions of a thinking substance and a person, as he needs to, both to answer the circularity objection and, more generally, to maintain the possibility of a divergence between personal identity and identity of thinking substance. This leads us on very naturally to Butler and Reid's next objection to Locke, which is precisely that Locke *cannot* hold these two notions apart.

3.6 The Butler–Reid–Shoemaker objection

Butler states this objection as follows:

> The thing here considered is proposed by Mr. Locke in these words, *whether it*, i.e. the same self of person, *be the same identical substance*? And he has suggested what is a much better answer to the question than that which he gives it in form. For he defines person, a thinking intelligent being, etc., and personal identity *the sameness of a rational being*. The question then is, whether the same rational being is the same substance; which needs no answer, because being and substance, in this place, stand for the same idea.
>
> (1736)

Reid restates the objection:

> [Locke] defines a person to be an intelligent being . . . from this definition of a person it must necessarily follow, that, while the intelligent being continues to exist and to be intelligent, it must be the same person. To say that the intelligent being is the person, and yet that the person ceases to exist while the intelligent being continues, or that the person continues while the intelligent being ceases to exist, is . . . a manifest contradiction. . . .
>
> (1941:212)

Shoemaker also notes the difficulty (hence the title of this section):

> Locke defines 'person' as meaning 'a thinking, intelligent being . . . .' If persons are thinking things and thinking things are substances then persons are substances. And if it follows from the definition of a 'person' that a person is a substance, it is surely self-contradictory to say that the identity of a person does not involve the identity of a substance.
>
> (1963:45–6)

This objection has not been much discussed in the literature on Locke, but very recently Alston and Bennett (1988) have addressed it. As they point out, the inference from '*x* is a person' to '*x* is a thinking substance' is not obligatory, given the sense 'substance' has in Locke's 'Identity' chapter, i.e. '*basic* thing-like item'. That this *was* Locke's notion of substance in this chapter we saw in Chapter 2, and we also saw how crucial it was for understanding Locke that this point be appreciated. What we are now concerned with reinforces this. Thus the Alston–Bennett line enables us to give an effective answer to the objection in so far as it depends on the false assumption that, as Butler puts it, 'being and substance, in this place, stand for the same idea'.

However, this is only half of the problem. For just as, if persons are thinking substances, the same person must be the same thinking substance, so, by parallel reasoning, if thinking substances are persons, then the same thinking substance must be the same person. The inference from '*x* is a person' to '*x* is a thinking substance' can be resisted, since to be a possessor of the psychological attributes in Locke's definition of a person is not necessarily to be a *basic* constituent of reality. But the inference from '*x* is a thinking substance' to '*x* is a person' cannot similarly be blocked, since it surely cannot be said to be a necessary condition of a thing's being a person that it *not* be a basic constituent of reality. In fact it seems clear that thinking substances, or at least those which 'think in' persons (to use Locke's locution) are bound to possess all the psychological properties in Locke's definition of a person, for persons 'borrow', as it were, their psychological attributes from the thinking substances that think in them.

To get a clearer sense of the difficulty facing Locke here, and perhaps to get a clue as to why Butler and Reid are so confident in their rejection of his position, it will be useful at this point to follow through some reasoning of R.M. Chisholm's, who is the most careful recent defender of the significance of Butler's distinction between 'strict and philosophical' and 'loose and ordinary' senses of identity.

Chisholm argues (e.g. 1976:89ff.) that entities which are capable of surviving change of parts (hereafter 'mereologically variable objects'), and thus qualify as identical over time, according to Butler, only in a loose and popular sense, have to be regarded as ontologically parasitic on, or logical constructions out of, objects which possess identity in a strict and philosophical sense – mereologically constant objects. If a mereologically variable material object, such as a table, possesses a property at a time it must be in virtue of the properties of the mereologically constant objects (roughly, the hunks of matter) constituting it at the various times in its history. Thus, in making any claims about the ontologically parasitic table we could always retreat to the philosophically stricter, and more austere, way of talking, which involves references to the mereologically constant objects alone. In descriptions of the universe, references to the table can be systematically eliminated in favour of references to its constituents.

In particular, and crucially, according to Chisholm, of the properties that a mereologically variable object has at a time there is a subset which it has only because the mereologically constant object constituting it at the time has them – these properties are what Chisholm describes as 'rooted only in the times at which they are had', roughly, properties which a thing has at a time only in virtue of its intrinsic character at the time, and independently of its past and future history. Thus, if a mereologically variable object has such a property at a time it 'borrows' it from the mereologically constant object constituting it at that time.

Appealing to this framework, Chisholm is able to argue that *if* persons are mereologically variable objects, that is, are objects with only Butlerian loose and popular identity over time, then the properties they possess which are rooted only in the times at which they are had, must be borrowed from mereologically constant objects which constitute them. Given that such psychological properties as 'hoping for rain' (1976:104) are rooted only in the times at which they are had, it follows that if persons are mereologically variable objects, they can only possess such psychological properties because they have 'borrowed' them from other, numerically distinct, mereologically constant, objects. In other words, if I am a mereologically variable object then I can hope for rain now only because *something else*, something numerically distinct from me, hopes for rain now, just as the table I am writing on now can only weigh 50 pounds now because the hunk of matter now constituting it weighs 50 pounds.

Now one might not have thought that one was letting oneself in for such a consequence merely in virtue of accepting the common-sense view that people, like tables, have parts and are capable of undergoing a change of parts. And indeed it is surely possible to resist Chisholm's conclusion – either by denying that such properties as 'hoping for rain' *are* rooted only in the times at which they are

had, or by denying that such a property can be possessed by a mereologically variable object at a time only if it 'borrows' it from some
mereologically constant object, which then composes it. But at
present the point of interest is just that Chisholm's conception of
what persons must be like if they are mereologically variable objects
corresponds exactly to the picture of personal identity that Locke has.
Persons, which are mereologically variable objects, are for Locke
ontological parasites on, or logical constructions out of, thinking
substances, which are mereologically constant objects. They possess
their (psychological) properties only because the substances composing them, or 'thinking in them', possess those properties, and so
whenever a person hopes for rain then indeed something else, some
thinking substance strictly non-identical with him, hopes for rain.

Thus Locke is set up perfectly for Chisholm's intended *reductio
ad absurdum* of the suggestion that persons might be mereologically
variable entities ('*entia per alio*'):

> Consider the simplest of Cartesian facts – say, that I now hope
> for rain. Hoping for rain is one of those properties that are
> rooted only in the times at which they are had. And so if I am
> an *ens per alio*, an *ens successivum*, like our simple table . . .
> then I may be said to hope for rain only in virtue of the fact
> that my present stand-in hopes for rain. I borrow the property,
> so to speak, from the thing that constitues me now. But surely
> *that* hypothesis is not to be taken seriously. There is no reason
> whatever for supposing that *I* hope for rain only in virtue of
> the fact that some *other* thing hopes for rain – some stand-in
> that, strictly and philosophically, is not identical with me, but
> happens to be doing duty for me at this particular time. If
> there are thus two things that now hope for rain, the one doing
> it on its own and the other such that its hoping for rain is done
> for it by the thing that now happens to constitute it, then I am
> the former thing and not the latter thing.
>
>   (1976:104)

This, I submit, is an impressive argument and it may well be that
their perception of its vulnerability to it lay behind Butler's and
Reid's conviction of the wrong-headedness of Locke's position. But
it is not the *reductio ad absurdum* that Chisholm thinks it is (what is,
in philosophy?). For Locke's position has not been shown to be

inconsistent, and so he can simply stand his ground and accept the consequences Chisholm points out. It is not simply a *given*, he can say, that when he hopes for rain it is not in virtue of some other object's doing so, so if the best philosophical theory of the mind dictates that that is so, as it does, then so be it: there are no undeniably hard data concerning the number of thinking things which theory is constrained to accommodate. And indeed, if Locke says this he will not be without present-day company. For as we shall see later (Chapter 5), it is an acknowledged consequence of the much admired theory of personal identity put forward by David Lewis (1976) that when I hope for rain I do so only in virtue of the fact that something else – my present person-stage – does so. And the same is true, on Lewis's theory, of all my present temporally intrinsic psychological properties.

However, this is not the end of the matter. For the difficulty still remains that on Locke's picture thinking substances and persons no longer seem to be distinguishable in the way they have to be in order to have different identity conditions. The only grip we have on the idea of a person, it seems, is that which is given to us by Locke's definition: 'a thinking intelligent being that has reason and reflection', but this idea, so defined, now seems to be applicable both to persons and to thinking substances. But if so, what can Locke mean by claiming that persons and thinking substances (i.e. persons) have different identity conditions, and what sense can the question, 'In what does personal identity consist?' actually possess? Locke insists that identity is 'suited to the idea', that there is no point in asking for an account of identity *simpliciter*, but only for an account of what it is to be the same thing *of a certain kind*. But if the idea to which identity is relativized applies equally well to things of *distinct* kinds, with distinct identity conditions, how can the relativization yield a sensible question?

What these questions bring out, I believe, is that Locke cannot consistently maintain his position against the Butler–Reid–Shoemaker objection if he says that the content of his idea of a person is exhausted by the list of psychological properties he gives in his definition. But he does not need to say this, for he has another resource. As we have seen, Locke uses the term 'person' inter-changeably with the term 'self'. What he is interested in, is, in fact, *the identity of the object of first-person reference*, or as Leibniz puts it 'this I which means so much'. In order to render his position consistent in the face of the Butler–Reid–Shoemaker objection what Locke must do is to insist on the distinctness of the idea of the I from the idea of that which possesses the psychological properties he lists in his official definition of a person. In other words he must insist that when a thinking substance thinks an 'I'-thought its referent is not that thinking substance *itself* but the person it then constitutes. (David Lewis must similarly deny that a person-stage's 'I'-thoughts are about thoughts itself, i.e. thoughts which are verified or falsified by *its* possession or lack of properties.) Once again, R.M. Chisholm brings the matter into clear focus. If, as on the Lockean theory, I am placed in a thinking substance but not identical with that thinking substance, he asks, 'If I want my dinner, does it follow that two of us want my dinner? Or does the thinking substance want its dinner and not mine?' (1976:108). The answer the Lockean must give, to be consistent, is that the thinking substance wants *me* to have *my* dinner, but the only way it can think that thought is by thinking 'I want my dinner'. Once again, lest it be too hastily concluded that this is a *reductio ad absurdum* of the Lockean theory, let it be remembered that David Lewis's much admired theory of personal identity has the same consequence, modulo the substitution of 'person-stages' for 'thinking substances.'

I conclude, then, that the Butler–Reid–Shoemaker objection does not refute Locke's position. But it is, I submit, certainly the most interesting of the objections we have considered in this chapter, and I have been more concerned to see what Locke *must* say in response to it than to assess the plausibility or otherwise of the reply. I would not regard it as an unreasonable response to this discussion to say that Locke's theory *has* been refuted – along, of course, with any modern theory of personal identity with comparable features.

3.7 Conclusion

In this chapter we have looked at three philosophers who maintain, in defiance of Locke's arguments, that personal identity is identity of substance, and maintain, in consequence, that personal identity is somehow more real or genuine than the identity of other things. In the next chapter we will be examining the views of a philosopher who agrees with Locke that personal identity is not identity of substance, but who maintains in consequence that it is not really identity at all. This philosopher is David Hume.

CHAPTER 4

Hume

4.1 Introduction

Hume discusses personal identity in two places: in the main body of the *Treatise of Human Nature* (1978), in Section VI of Part IV of Book I, entitled 'Of personal identity', and in an Appendix published a year later with Book III, in which he declares himself wholly dissatisfied with his treatment of the topic in that section, but confesses that he now finds the whole matter a 'labyrinth' and that he knows neither how to correct his former opinions nor how to render them consistent: there is no discussion of the topic in the *Enquiry Concerning Human Understanding*.

Unfortunately Hume fails to make clear in his recantation what he finds objectionable in his earlier account, and though commentators have produced a variety of suggestions, no consensus as to what Hume's worry is has emerged. But we shall return briefly to this matter later. First we need to get clear about what the problem is that Hume is concerned with in the section 'Of personal identity', and what solution he there offers to that problem.

In Chapter 1 I began be saying that the problem of personal identity over time was the problem of giving an account of what (if anything) *constitutes* personal identity over time. This is a fair statement of the problem as it is debated by the philosophers discussed so far, but it is not Hume's problem. For, according to Hume, personal identity is a fiction; the ascription of identity over time to persons is a mistake. It is an explicable mistake, and one we all necessarily make, but none the less, it is a mistake. For persons just do not endure self-identically over time. Consequently since there is no such thing as personal identity over time, nor is there any problem of the metaphysical-cum-semantical variety presented by the question:

in what does personal identity over time consist? The only problem that exists is the *genetic* one of specifying the psychological causes of the universal but mistaken belief in the existence of enduring persons, and this is the problem to which Hume addresses himself in his discussion of personal identity.

It is not, however, in Hume's view, if I may so put it, a peculiarity of persons that they do not endure self-identically over time; nor does anything else which we ordinarily think of as doing so. For the idea of identity, Hume thinks, is incompatible with the idea of change: it is the idea of an object which 'remains invariable and uninterrupted thro' a suppos'd variation of time' (1978:253). Most, if not all, objects of ordinary discourse, plants, animals, artefacts and the rest, are like persons in failing to satisfy this definition, and so when we ascribe identity to them, Hume says, it is only in an 'improper sense'. Thus for Hume the genetic problem of accounting for our false belief in the existence of enduring persons is just a part of the wider genetic problem of accounting for our false belief in the identity over time of changing things generally. In fact, he thinks, the *same* mechanism which accounts for our ascriptions of identity over time to plants, animals and so on can equally well account for our ascriptions of identity over time to persons. This is so because:

> The identity which we ascribe to the mind of man, is only a fictitious one and *of a like kind* with that which we ascribe to vegetable and animal bodies. It cannot, therefore, have a different origin, but must proceed from a like operation of the imagination upon like objects.
>
> (1978:253, my italics)

The mechanism, then, which generates the belief in the fiction of personal identity (the identity we ascribe to 'the mind of man') is an operation of the imagination. In fact it is an operation by which the imagination is led to ascribe an identity to *distinct perceptions*, however interrupted or variable. Then:

> In order to justify to ourselves this absurdity, we often feign some new and unintelligible principle, that connects the objects together, and prevents their interruption or variation. Thus we feign the continued existence of the perceptions of our senses, to remove the interruption; and run into the notion of a *soul*,

and self, and *substance*, to disguise the variation. But we may
further observe, that when we do not give rise to such a fiction,
our propensity to confound identity with relation is so great,
that we are apt to imagine something unknown and mysterious,
connecting the parts, beside their relation, and this I take to be
the case with regard to the identity we ascribe to plants and
vegetables. And even when this does not take place, we still feel
a propensity to confound these ideas, though we are not able
fully to satisfy ourselves in that particular, nor find anything
invariable and uninterrupted to justify our notion of identity.

(1978:254–5)

Hume indicates here how general is the application of the mechanism by which the fiction of personal identity is generated: it not only
accounts for our belief in personal identity, and the identity over time
of such changeable things as plants and animals, it is also the source of
our belief that there is an external world at all, and the explanation
of our regarding things (ourselves included) as substances possessing
properties rather than as mere collections of qualities. These applica-
tions of the genetic account are given in earlier sections of the
Treatise, as we shall see later. But for now the important point to note
is just that it is an essential part of this story, as Hume tells it, that the
propensity we have to identify distinct perceptions is a propensity to
regard them as answering to the idea of identity which he himself
defines: 'an object which is invariable and uninterrupted through a
supposed variation in time'. If this was not our idea of identity then
the psychological mechanism could not operate as he suggests. If, for
instance, our idea of identity was consistent with the idea of interruption (that is, if we thought it possible that one thing might have two
beginnings of existence) then our propensity to identify (resembling
but) temporally separated perceptions would not lead us to 'feign the
continued existence of the perceptions of our senses', and thus would
not lead us to our belief in an external world. Again, if we thought of
identity over time as consistent with change we would not be disposed
to 'run into the notion of a *soul*, and *self* and *substance*' or 'apt to
imagine something unknown and mysterious' to *disguise* the variation. Thus it is essential to Hume's account that our idea of identity
is, in fact, the one he describes, and it is because this is so that he says:

the controversy concerning identity is not merely a dispute of
words. For when we attribute identity . . . to variable or

interrupted objects, our mistake is not confined to the expression, but is commonly attended with a fiction, either of something invariable and uninterrupted, or of something mysterious and inexplicable, or at least with a propensity to such fictions.

(1978:255)

In denying that there is identity over time in those cases in which everyone would assert it, Hume thinks, he is not merely quibbling, for the fact is that such assertions are mistaken not just by some strict and philosophical standard with which no one but philosophers operate but by our everyday standards for identity, and thus our everyday assertions of identity over time and through change are not merely indicative of a looseness in speech, but of actual errors in thought.

Thus, according in Hume, given that our idea of identity is as he describes, we must be in error in ascribing identity over time to 'variable or interrupted' things – ourselves included, but given that this is *in fact* our idea of identity, plus the rest of the genetic story he tells, this error is an explicable one.

But why does Hume think our idea of identity is as he supposes, and what does he think is its source?

4.2 Our idea of identity

Hume addresses this question in the earlier section, 'Of scepticism with regard to the senses'. Here he gives the first employment of the psychological mechanism discussed above, in an attempt to explain the genesis of our belief in an external world existing independently of being perceived.

He begins his account of identity by posing a dilemma:

the view of any one object is not sufficient to convey the idea of identity. For in that proposition *an object is the same with itself*, if the idea expressed by the word, *object*, were no ways distinguished from that one meant by *itself*, we really should mean nothing. . . . One single object conveys the idea of unity, not that of identity. On the other hand, a multiplicity of objects can never convey this idea, however resembling they may be supposed.

(1978:200)

Hume then professes himself baffled: 'Since then both number and unity are incompatible with the relation of identity, it must lie in neither of them. But to tell the truth, at first sight this seems utterly impossible. Betwixt unity and number there can be no medium' (1978:200).

To solve this problem Hume has recourse to the idea of time or duration. Earlier in the *Treatise* he has argued that time implies succession, i.e. change, and that the idea of time or duration, is not applicable in a proper sense to unchanging objects:

> the idea of duration is always derived from a succession of
> changeable objects, and can never be conveyed to the mind by
> any thing steadfast and unchangeable . . . it inevitably follows
> . . . that since the idea of duration cannot be derived from such
> an object, it can never in any propriety . . . be apply'd to it,
> nor can anything unchangeable be ever said to have duration.
>
> (1978:37)

When we think of an unchanging object as having duration, then, this is only by a 'fiction of the imagination', by which 'the unchangeable [*sic*] object is suppos'd to participate of the changes of the co-existing objects and in particular that of our perceptions'. The unchanging object does *not* endure, strictly speaking, but this 'fiction of the imagination almost universally takes place'; and it is by means of it, Hume thinks, that we get the idea of identity. The way this is supposed to work will be easier to comprehend if we think in terms of an example. Suppose we are gazing at the wall, on which hangs a picture of David Hume and a clock with a second hand. The picture is an unchanging object which reveals no interruption or variation and, therefore, considered in isolation, will yield the idea of unity but not that of time or duration. If the picture were *all* we were surveying and if nothing else was going on in our minds then it would be as if no time had passed. But the picture is not all we are surveying: we can also see the clock. In consequence, as well as the unchanging sequence of perceptions of the picture there is the changing sequence of perceptions of the clock. This second sequence, which answers to our idea of number, gives us the idea of time, which genuinely applies to it. And now, Hume suggests, when we survey these two sequences together we suppose the unchanging sequence to participate in the changes of the changing sequence and thus imagine *it* to have genuine duration. Thus we arrive at the idea of identity, viz. 'the invariableness and uninterruptedness of any object, thro' a suppos'd variation in time'. Here, then, Hume triumphantly concludes, 'is an idea which is a medium betwixt unity and number; or more properly speaking, is either of them, according to the view in which we take it: And this idea we call that of identity' (1978:201).

Although this is hardly clear, or even coherent, one point at least emerges fairly evidently. Namely, that it cannot just be to *variable* or *interrupted* objects, in Hume's view, that the idea of identity must be inapplicable; the same must be true of invariable and uninterrupted objects. The idea of identity, to be distinct from the idea of unity, must imply duration, but duration implies change. Even the paradigm from which we get the idea of identity, then, must be a case to which it does not apply. For the notion of an object existing through a period of time without change is a contradiction in terms.

If this is right, the reasons for persons' lacking genuine identity, which Hume puts forward in his section on personal identity, are misleading or at least superfluous: given his analysis of the notion of identity *nothing*, not even a soul or self or substance, *could* possess it. However, the radical scepticism to which this line of thought would lead is not addressed by Hume; he is content to insist that identity is, at least, incompatible with change or interruption and with this conclusion in hand he proceeds to explain first our belief in an external world and then our belief in enduring selves.

4.3 The reification of perceptions

Hume's insistence that our notion of identity is the one he analyses is then one source of his belief that personal identity is a fiction. But it is not the only one. Another is his conception of what the nature of the self or mental subject would have to be, if it existed, and, correlatively, his view of the status of the items he calls 'perceptions' – which is his general term for all the contents of the mind (in what follows I am greatly indebted to Shoemaker 1986 and Cook 1968).

One of the best-known passages in Hume's chapter on personal identity – indeed, one of the most famous passages in any philosophical text – is Hume's denial that he is introspectively aware of any self or mental substance:

> For my part, when I enter most intimately into what I call *myself*, I always stumble on some particular perception or other, of heat or cold, light or shade, love or hatred, pain or pleasure. I never can catch myself at any time without a perception, and never can observe anything but the perception.
>
> (1978:252)

Many philosophers who have read this denial have found themselves in agreement. But the passage is a puzzling one. Humes writes as if it is just a matter of fact that on looking into himself he fails to find anything but perceptions, but, as many commentators have noted, this sits ill with his emphatic denial that he has any idea of a self distinct from perceptions. I can be confident that I am not observing a tea-kettle now because I know what it would be like to be doing so. But if Hume has no idea of a self he presumably has no conception of what it would be like to observe one. In that case, however, how does he know that he is not doing so? Maybe he is, but just fails to recognize the fact.

Another difficulty is that, as Chisholm puts it (1976:39), it looks very much as though the self that Hume professes to be unable to find is the one that he finds to be stumbling – stumbling onto different perceptions. For Hume reports the results of his introspection in the first person: '*I* never catch myself without a perception', '*I* never observe anything but the perception'. Nor can he avoid doing so, if the basis of his denial is merely empirical. For suppose instead of '*I* never observe anything but perceptions' he had written 'Nothing but perceptions is ever observed'. Then his assertion would have committed him to denying that *anyone* ever observes anything but perceptions, and so would have gone far beyond the evidence available to him. For how could he know that? As he himself writes a little later:

> If anyone upon serious and unprejudic'd reflection, thinks he has a different notion of *himself*, I must confess I can reason no longer with him. All I can allow him is, that he may be in the right as well as I, and that we are essentially different in that particular. He may, perhaps, perceive something simple

and continu'd which he calls *himself*, tho' I am certain that
there is no such principle in me.

(1978:252)

Of course, this is irony, for Hume immediately goes on: 'But
setting aside some metaphysicians of this kind, I may venture to
affirm of the rest of mankind, that they are nothing but a bundle or
collection of different perceptions' (1978:252). But Hume is not
entitled to the irony, or to any claim about the rest of mankind if, as
he represents it, the basis of his report of his negative finding is
empirical. For to be so entitled he needs to be able to assent not
merely to the (apparently self-defeating) claim that *he* never finds
anything but perceptions, but also to the subjectless claim that nothing but perceptions is ever *found*.

Hume's denial is not therefore the straightforward empirical assertion it might at first appear to be. But then what *is* his basis for it?

Earlier in the *Treatise* he writes: 'To hate, to love, to think, to feel,
to see; all this is nothing but to perceive' (1978:67). This gives us our
clue. Hume starts from a conception of mental states according to
which to be in a mental state is for a certain relational statement to
be true of one: for one to be in any mental state is for one to be
perceiving a certain sort of *perception*. But if this is correct it is very
natural that he should deny the introspective observability of the
self. For if to be in any mental state is to possess a relational property
of the type: perceiving a perception of type *x*, then *no* mental state
can be an *intrinsic* property of its subject. Given that the only states
of which one can be introspectively aware are mental, then, introspective awareness of a self would require awareness of it without
any awareness of its intrinsic properties. But surely it makes no
sense to speak of observing something introspectively if the thing
has no intrinsic properties whatsoever which one can observe by
introspection. As Shoemaker (1986) puts it, this makes no more
sense than it does to speak of seeing or feeling a point in empty
space.

The introspective inaccessibility of the self is thus an obvious
consequence of the conception of all mental states as relational
which, if we take it literally, is implied by the remark quoted from
Hume at the beginning of the last paragraph. And the same line of
thought can be pressed further. For Hume was undoubtedly enough
of a dualist to take it for granted that a mental subject would have no

intrinsic properties that were *not* mental, i.e. that the physical properties of a person's body were not intrinsic properties of a self. But,
if so, it follows from the Humean conception of the mental that a
self can have no intrinsic properties at all – it must be a 'bare particular' whose only properties are relational. However, it is not hard
to see how someone thinking this could conclude that no such thing
could exist.

These simple reflections suffice, I think, to explain Hume's confi-
dence in his denial of the introspective accessibility of the self. But
they can be taken further if we now turn from what the Humean
conception of the mental implies about the *subject* of mental
states – namely that its only properties are relational ones of the
type 'perceiving a perception of type x' – to what it implies about
their *objects*, Hume's perceptions. What the conception implies, of
course, is that these perceptions are *things* to which the subject of
mental states is related in somewhat the way in which, as we ordinarily think, we are related to trees or tables. However, this seems to
have the absurd implication that just as trees and tables might exist
unperceived, so a pain or a dizzy spell or thought might occur without occurring to anyone. Hume accepts the implication. In fact he
gives an argument for it. Here is what he says:

> we may observe that what we call a *mind*, is nothing but a heap
> or collection of different perceptions, united together by certain
> relations. . . . Now as every perception is distinguishable from
> another, and may be consider'd as separately existent; it
> evidently follows, that there is no absurdity in separating any
> particular perception from the mind; that is, in breaking off all
> its relations, with the connected mass of perceptions, which
> constitute a thinking being.

> (1978:207)

This argument occurs in Hume's section 'Of scepticism with
regard to the senses' and is used at this point to show that 'the
vulgar', the non-philosophers, are not inconsistent, but just mistaken, in supposing that their perceptions continue to exist when not
perceived. The argument, of course, presupposes the account of
personal identity Hume has yet to defend, and as several commentators have observed, even in its own terms it is inadequate. For
suppose a perception P might have existed outside of the bundle of
perceptions with which it is in fact combined; it does not follow that

P might have existed outside of *any* more comprehensive bundle of perceptions – outside of *any* mind. But actually the difficulties with the argument as quoted are unimportant, for it is clear that Hume here takes himself to be merely repeating a familiar line of reasoning which he uses elsewhere, and expounds most fully in the section 'Of the immortality of the soul', which immediately precedes the section on personal identity. Here Hume attempts to establish that the definition of a 'substance' as *something which may exist by itself* 'agrees to everything that can possibly be conceived; and never will serve to distinguish substance from accident, or the soul from its perceptions'. He argues thus:

> whatever is clearly conceiv'd, after any manner, may exist after
> the same manner. This is one principle. . . . Again, everything
> which is different is distinguishable, and everything which is
> distinguishable, is separable by the imagination. This is another
> principle. . . . since all our perceptions are different from each
> other, and from everything else in the universe, they are also
> distinct and separable, and have no need of anything else to
> support their existence. They are, therefore substances, as far
> as this definition explains a substance.

(1978:233)

Here Hume's argument does not presuppose the account of personal identity he goes on to give in the next section, i.e. the conception of the mind as a bundle of perceptions, and so it is possible to see how he might have thought this conception could have been non-question-beggingly supported by the conclusion for which he argues here. Of course, the conclusion of the argument is an astonishing one. For what it says is that the ache I now have in my big toe, or my present thought that David Hume was a genius, or my promise to myself that I will get a cup of coffee when I have finished this section, *might have been the only thing in the universe*. In fact, since the argument is supposed to be quite general, applying to everything which can possibly be conceived, then, as John Cook points out, we must take Hume to be arguing not only that a pain or a dizzy spell or a thought might occur 'loose and separate' without belonging to anyone, but also:

> that there could be a scratch or a dent without there being
> anything scratched or dented. Indeed if we take Hume at his

word, we must take him to be saying that he would see no
absurdity in Alice's remark: 'Well!, I've often seen a cat
without a grin, but a grin without a cat! It's the most curious
thing I ever saw in all my life!'

(1968)

Fortunately, Cook is able to expose the flaw in Hume's reasoning:
the fact that x is distinct from y does not entail that it is distinguishable from y, not, at least, if this is to entail that 'x exists' is to be
compatible with 'y does not exist'. For the fact that x is distinct from
y does not entail that x can be identified independently of y. Thus,
the dent in my fender is distinct from the fender: 'the dent in my
fender' does not stand for the same object as 'my fender'. But the dent
is not distinguishable from the fender – I could not get someone to
understand which dent I was referring to without identifying the
fender in which it was a dent. Hence we can deny that Hume's argument establishes that dents are substances and by parity of reasoning
we can deny that it establishes that perceptions are substances.

But the important point for our purposes is not what Hume's
argument *does* prove, but what he *thinks* it proves. For if perceptions are thought of as substances, i.e. as ontologically independent entities, then the self, thought of as that which *has* perceptions,
must now appear to have a very problematic status indeed. It is
implicit in this conception of the self, whether or not it is thought of
as introspectively observable, that it *is* thought of as having a special
ontological status *vis-à-vis* its perceptions and not merely as being
ontologically on a par with them. And, of course, this is quite right.
But it is quite right just because being in a mental state is *not* to be
understood as bearing a special relation of 'perception' to something which has a (logically) independent existence, anymore than
smiling or walking is to be understood as bearing a certain special
relation (of 'wearing' or 'taking') to an entity (a smile or a walk)
logically capable of an independent existence. The grammar of the
noun 'perception' (and that of 'idea' and 'impression') is like that of
'smile' or 'walk'. The concept of *someone's having* a perception is
logically prior to the concept of *a perception*.

To put the same point in different terms, the relation between the
self and its perceptions is analogous to that between the sea and its
waves. The waves are modifications of the sea and perceptions are
modifications of the self. But Hume, in claiming that perceptions

are ontologically independent, denies this, and thus denies the only possible basis for regarding the self, *qua* perceiver, as ontologically prior to its perceptions. That he should claim that the self is in reality nothing but a bundle of its perceptions in the section following is thus entirely intelligible. Once perceptions are reified as substances no other conception of the self makes any sense at all.

Once again, John Cook's remarks are perceptive. He points out that if the argument Hume gives were a good one then it would establish not only that perceptions are capable of an independent existence, but also that the same is true of qualities generally (and indeed Hume applies the argument to yield this conclusion himself (1978:222)). Then Descartes's famous analogy in the *Second Meditation*, in which he compares the relation between a piece of wax and its qualities to the relation between a man and his clothes, would be an appropriate one. But one consequence of this analogy is that the wax is represented as hidden beneath its garments and so as in itself unobservable. This is because the analogy implies that the assertion that the wax has any quality is in reality an assertion of a relation between it and something else. And a second consequence of the analogy is that the qualities of the wax are represented as being themselves substantial, as though they can 'stand by themselves', as a suit of armour can when no man is wearing it. But these consequences of the analogy, which is an *appropriate* one if the Humean argument is a good one, make it obvious that if the wax is so conceived its existence, as anything other than that of a collection of qualities, must be regarded as highly problematic. Exactly the same is true of the self if Hume's argument is correct.

4.4 Of soul and self

With this background in mind we can now turn to the details of Hume's section on personal identity. In fact this section is continuous with the preceding one, which though entitled 'Of the immateriality of the soul', contains a largely even-handed critique of both materialist and immaterialist doctrines of a substantial self, together with the striking criticism of the 'doctrine of the immateriality, simplicity and indivisibility of a thinking substance' that 'it is a true atheism, and will serve to justify all those sentiments, for which Spinoza is so universally infamous' (1978:240). The basis of this last criticism is again Hume's conception of perceptions as ontologically independent entities.

> there are two different systems of beings presented, to which I suppose myself under a necessity of assigning some substance, or ground of inhesion. I observe first the universe of objects or of bodies: the sun, moon, stars, the earth . . . Here Spinoza tells me that these are only modifications; and that the subject in which they inhere is simple, uncompounded, and indivisible. After this I consider the other system of beings, viz the universe of thought, or my impressions and ideas. There I observe *another* sun, moon and stars. . . . Upon my enquiring concerning these Theologians . . . tell me, that these also are modifications . . . of one single substance. Immediately . . . I am deafen'd with the noise of a hundred voices, that treat the first hypothesis with detestation and scorn . . . and the second with veneration and reverence . . . I turn my attention to these hypotheses, and find that they have the same fault of being unintelligible . . . and [are] so much alike, that . . . any absurdity in one . . . is common to both.
>
> (1978:234, my italics)

Nor are matters improved for the Theologians, according to Hume,

> if instead of calling thought a modification of the soul, we should give it the more ancient, and yet more modish name of an *action*. By an action we mean . . . something which, properly speaking, is neither distinguishable, nor separable from its substance. But nothing is gained by this change of the term modification, for that of action. . . . First . . . the word *action*, according to this explanation of it, can never be justly apply'd to any perception. Our perceptions are all really different, and separable, and distinguishable from each other, and from anything else. . . . [In] the second place, may not the Atheists likewise take possession of [the word *action*], and affirm that plants, animals, men, etc., are nothing but particular actions of one simple substance? This . . . I own 'tis unintelligible but . . . assert . . . that 'tis impossible to discover any absurdity in the supposition . . . which will not be applicable to a like supposition concerning impressions and ideas.
>
> (1978:245-6)

There could not, I think, be a clearer illustration than this of the lengths to which Hume is prepared to go in following through the consequences of his reification of perceptions – if a tree cannot be a modification of Spinoza's God my idea of a tree cannot be a modification of me!

Turning now to the section 'Of personal identity' Hume proceeds very rapidly, and confidently, for reasons that I hope will now be perfectly understandable, to his conclusion that the self is nothing more than a bundle of perceptions. The whole business takes less than two pages.

Some philosophers have thought that 'we are every moment instinctively conscious of what we call our *SELF*.' But: 'Unluckily all these positive assertions are contrary to that very experience which is pleaded for them, nor have we any idea of self, as it is here explained, for from what impression could this idea be derived?' Since the self is supposed to be an unchanging object any impression of self must be constantly the same throughout the whole course of our lives. But, Hume finds, looking within himself, 'There is no impression constant and invariable. Pain and pleasure, grief and joy . . . succeed each other. It cannot therefore, be from any of these perceptions, or from any other that the idea of self is deriv'd; and consequently there is no such idea' (1978:251–2)

Hume goes on to raise explicitly the difficulty that his conception of perceptions as ontologically independent creates for the notion of a substantial self:

> But farther, what must become of all our particular perceptions upon this hypothesis? All these are different, and distinguishable, and separable from each other, and may be separately consider'd, and may exist separately, and have no need of any thing to support their existence. After what manner therefore do they belong to self; and how are they connected with it?
>
> (1978:262)

It is immediately after this that he issues his denial of the observability of a self distinct from perceptions, and concludes that the self can be nothing but a bundle of perceptions.

The same structure is exhibited in the Appendix, in which Hume summarizes his arguments *for* the bundle theory before making his famous confession of bafflement. After arguing that we have no impression of self or substance as something simple or individual from which these ideas might be derived he goes on to spend no less than three paragraphs insisting on the ontological independence of perceptions, finally concluding that since ' 'tis intelligible and consistent to say that objects exist distinct and independent, without any common *simple* substance or subject of inhesion' (i.e. it is intelligible and consistent to deny Spinoza's doctrine), 'This proposition can never, therefore, be absurd with regard to perceptions' (1978:263–4).

In the immediately following paragraph he denies the observability of the self and derives the bundle theory.

So much, then, for Hume's arguments for the bundle theory of the self. Taken together with his analysis of identity, they entitle him, he believes, to the conclusion that personal identity is a fiction, that 'the mind is a kind of theatre, where several perceptions successively make their appearance. . . . There is properly no *simplicity* in it at one time, nor *identity* at different' (1978:253). For the idea of identity is that of an object, that 'remains invariable and uninterrupted thro' a suppos'd variation of time'. But if the bundle theory is correct a person is nothing but a sequence of different (ontologically independent) objects existing in succession, and connected by a close relation – something like a thunderstorm. But 'as such a succession answers perfectly to our notion of diversity, it can only be by a mistake that we ascribe to it an identity' (1978:255).

The only question that remains then, Hume thinks, is to explain the psychological mechanism that accounts for this mistake.

4.5 The source of the mistake

Hume summarizes his account of this as follows. In contemplating an identical, i.e. an invariable and unchanging object, we are doing something very different from contemplating a succession of objects related by links of resemblance, causation and contiguity but:

> That action of the imagination, by which we consider the uninterrupted and invariable object, and that by which we reflect on the succession of related objects, are almost the same to the feeling, nor is there much more effort of thought requir'd in the latter case than in the former. The relation facilitates the transmission of the mind from one object to another, and

renders its passage as smooth as if it contemplated one
continu'd object. This resemblance is the cause of the confusion
and mistake, and makes us substitute the notion of identity,
instead of that of related objects. However at one instant we
may consider the related succession as variable or interrupted,
we are sure the next to ascribe to it a perfect identity, and
regard it as invariable and uninterrupted.

(1978:254)

Hume's discussion of personal identity is merely the last of several discussions in which he appeals to this mechanism. The first, in which he explains it most carefully, occurs in the section 'Of scepticism with regard to the senses', where Hume undertakes to explain 'what causes induce us to believe in the existence of body'. Stripped to its bare essentials the explanation goes as follows: I often have impressions which seem to remain invariable and uninterrupted over a stretch of time – as when I gaze for ten minutes at a picture of David Hume. This may be depicted thus:

(1) A A A A A A A A A

I take this to be the contemplation of an identical, i.e. invariable and uninterrupted object.

But if I close my eyes or look away for a few seconds I will have instead an interrupted sequence of perceptions:

(2) A A A A A B A A A A A

However, in contemplating situation (2) there is 'the same uninterrupted passage of the imagination' (1978:203) as in situation (1). Situation (2) places the mind in the same 'disposition and is considered with the same smooth and uninterrupted progress of the imagination, as attends the view of' situation (1). But 'whatever ideas place the mind in the same disposition or in similar ones are apt to be confounded' (1978:203). Thus I confound situation (2) with situation (1). But since I take situation (1) to be a view of an identical object I do the same with situation (2) and 'confound the succession with the identity' (1978:202).

However, I cannot fail to notice the apparent interruption in situation (2), but consistently with maintaining that (2) *is* a view of an identical object I cannot allow that there really is an interruption.

Consequently I unite the 'broken appearance' by means of 'the fiction of a continued and distinct existence' (1978:205). That is, I come to believe that the identical *perception A* which I earlier perceived has continued in existence whilst I was not perceiving it and is now again being perceived by me. This is, in Hume's view, the form that the 'belief in body' takes in the minds of the vulgar, i.e. the non-philosophers. They believe that their *perceptions* exist unperceived and have a 'continued and distinct existence'. Philosophers know better. Not, however, because the unperceived existence of perceptions is a contradiction. It isn't, as we have seen. But because, as a matter of empirically discoverable fact, Hume thinks, perceptions are 'dependent and perishing existences'. But the mechanism by which we are led to confound situation (2) with situation (1) is too powerful even for philosophers to resist. They cannot help, anymore than the vulgar, regarding situation (2) as a view of an identical object. However, they know that perceptions do not continue unperceived. To resolve their conflict all they can do is to distinguish between *objects* and *perceptions*, ascribing the continuity and distinctness to the former, and the interruptedness to the latter. But such a system of 'double existence', Hume thinks, is only a 'palliative remedy' and 'contains all the difficulties of the vulgar system, with others, that are peculiar to itself' (1978:211). Thus the psychological mechanism which leads us to confound situation (2) with situation (1) necessarily involves us, whether we are philosophers or the vulgar, in intellectual error.

The same is true of the next operation of the mechanism Hume examines, namely that which produces our, or rather the 'antient philosophers' ', belief in *substance*.

'Tis evident, that as the ideas of the several distinct *successive* qualities of objects are united together by a very close relation, the mind, in looking along the succession, must be carry'd from one part of it to another by an easy transition and will no more perceive the changes than if it contemplated the same unchangeable object. . . . The smooth and uninterrupted progress of the thought, being alike in both cases, readily deceives the mind, and makes us ascribe an identity to the changeable succession of connected qualities. But when we alter our method of considering the succession, and instead of tracing it gradually thro' the successive points of time, survey

> at once any two distinct periods of its duration . . . the
> variations do now appear of consequence, and seem entirely
> to destroy the identity. . . . In order to reconcile which
> contradiction the imagination is apt to feign something
> unknown and invisible which it supposes to continue the same
> under all variations . . . a *substance* or *original* and *first matter*.
>
> (1978:220)

Once again the story is one of conflation and error produced by the faculty of 'fancy' or 'imagination'.

It is exactly the same, Hume thinks, in the case of personal identity. The same mechanism of the imagination is at work and it produces conflation and error in just the same way. The succession of my perceptions is merely a succession of distinct related objects. But because the objects in the succession are closely related the action of the imagination in surveying the succession is 'almost the same to the feeling' as the action of the imagination in considering an uninterrupted and invariable object. As in the other cases, the similarity between the two acts of mind leads me to confound the two situations and thus to regard the succession of related perceptions as really united by identity. And so I am led to believe in the unity of the self, which is as much a fiction as in the other cases of the operation of the mechanism, and, 'proceed[s] entirely from the smooth and uninterrupted progress of the thought along a train of connected ideas according to the principles above explain'd' (1978:260).

All that remains to be said, Hume thinks, is what relations do link my successive perceptions so as to bring about this uninterrupted progress of the thought.

His answer is: resemblance and causation.

Our perceptions at successive times resemble each other for a variety of reasons, of course, but the one Hume stresses is that people can remember their past experience:

> For what is the memory, but a faculty by which we raise up the
> images of past perceptions? And as an image necessarily
> resembles its object must not the frequent placing of these
> resembling perceptions in the chain of thought, convey the
> imagination more easily from one link to another, and make the
> whole like the continuance of one object?
>
> (1978:260-1)

Given this copy theory of memory, then, Hume is able to regard memory not merely as providing us with access to our past selves, but also as contributing to the bundles of perceptions which we can survey elements which represent, and thus resemble, earlier elements; and so, since resemblance is a relation which enables the mind to slide smoothly along a succession of perceptions, as strengthening our propensity to believe in the fiction of a continuing self. In this particular case, then, Hume is able to say, with a nod of agreement to Locke, 'memory not only discovers but produces personal identity' (1978:166)

But we do not remember all, or even most of, our past actions or experiences. Yet we do not affirm, because we have entirely forgotten the incidents of certain past days, that the present self is not the same person as the self of that time. Consequently there must be something else which enables us to think of our identity as extending beyond our memory.

Here it would have been entirely appropriate for Hume to point out that memory is not the only source of the resemblances among our perceptions and thus that we can imagine such resemblances extended beyond the range of our memory and by this means can comprehend ourselves as existing at times we have now forgotten. But he does not do so. Instead he appeals to causality, which has been previously introduced in his account of

> the true idea of the human mind . . . a system of different
> perceptions or different existences, which are linked together
> by the relation of cause and effect. . . . Our impressions give
> rise to their correspondent ideas: and these ideas in their turn
> produce other impressions. One thought chases another, and
> draws after it a third, by which it is expelled in its turn. In this
> respect I cannot compare the soul more properly to anything
> than to a republic or commonwealth, in which the several
> members are united by the reciprocal ties of government and
> subordination, and give rise to other persons, who propagate
> the same republic in the incessant change of its parts.
>
> (1978:266)

When we think of ourselves as existing at times we cannot remember we do so, Hume says, by imagining the chain of causes and effects we remember extending beyond our memory of them. So the causal links between our perceptions, as well as their resemblances, are crucial to our belief in a continuing self which exists at times it no longer recalls. Consequently, Hume is able to say, this time in agreement with Locke's opponents: 'In this view memory not so much *produces* as *discovers* personal identity, by shewing us the relation of cause and effect among our perceptions' (1978:262).

4.6 Objections to Hume

Two objections must be noted at the outset. First, Hume is just wrong to reify perceptions or to think of them as capable of an independent existence. The comparison of the mind to a republic and of its perceptions to the citizens of the republic is thus fundamentally flawed. Second, Hume is again just wrong to think that identity is incompatible with change. Whether this is so depends on the kind of thing to which identity is being ascribed. Some things are perhaps by definition unchanging things. But in the case of most things this is not so. They cannot survive just *any* change, but what kind of changes they can survive depends on the kind of thing they are. To know what such changes are is part of knowing the definition of the kind. And persons, in particular, are entities which can survive many changes without ceasing to exist (Penelhum 1955 is the classic source of this second criticism).

These are radical objections. If correct they show that the whole Humean enterprise is misconceived from the start. I think that they do show this. But there are other objections even if these are set aside.

One of the most obvious is the following. We not only regard ourselves as unified selves, we also have particular beliefs about which perceptions are ours. But it is not the case that all the perceptions we ascribe to ourselves are related either by resemblance or by causality. In particular, this is not true of what Hume calls 'impressions of sensation'. At present I have an impression of a desk top partly covered with sheets of writing paper. If I turn my head to the left I have an impression of a book case filled with books. The impression of the desk top neither resembles nor is a cause of the impression of the book case (nor is the desk top itself a cause of the book case); yet I regard both impressions as mine. Why, on Hume's story, should this be so? According to the story we are led to ascribe perceptions to a single self only when we have a propensity to identify them; and such a propensity is produced only if the action of the mind in surveying them resembles that in surveying a constant and uninterrupted object. But in the present case this will not be so. On Hume's account, therefore, I ought to have no inclination to regard both these perceptions as mine. But I do.

This criticism of Hume can be deepened by recalling his views on causality. According to these causality is not a relation we perceive between objects; rather we regard a pair of objects as related as cause and effect when we have observed a constant conjunction of similar pairs of contiguous objects and as a consequence of this observed constant conjunction are led to expect the second member of the pair on perceiving the first. For two of my perceptions to be related as cause and effect, then, is for them to be an instance of an observed constant conjunction between similar pairs of perceptions which has produced in me a disposition to expect the second member of such a pair whenever I perceive the first. And this is to say that for my perceptions to be causally linked in the way Hume suggests (1978:261) they would have to exhibit a multitude of long-standing constant conjunctions. But they do not do so.

Once one puts Hume's views on causality together with his account of the genesis of our belief in personal identity, therefore, it becomes evident that the latter requires the possession by the human mind of a good deal more regularity and less novelty than it actually has.

The converse objection to the one just stated is worth considering. Not only do perceptions which we self-ascribe *fail* to be related by resemblance or causality in the way Hume requires; these relations *do* obtain between perceptions which we do not self-ascribe. Many of one's perceptions are bound to resemble those of others, given that we all inhabit the same world. Presumably, also, one's perceptions, one's mental states, sometimes stand in causal connections with those of others, for instance when one talks with them. Why, then, am I not disposed to regard (some of) your perceptions as mine? Why, on the contrary, do I think of you and I as having separate minds?

Of course, Hume has an easy answer to this question. *Your* perceptions are not available to me as input to the mechanism which generates my belief in the unity of my mind; for I cannot 'look into your breast' as Hume puts it, and observe them. Hence the fact that they stand in relations of resemblance and causality to my perceptions and thus *would* be self-ascribed by me if I *could* observe them is neither here nor there.

But this defence of Hume merely gets us to the crux of the matter. The Humean story requires that perceptions be *pre-bundled*, as it were, before the belief-producing mechanism he describes can operate. So Hume cannot after all reject the metaphysical-ontological question of what *in fact* distinguishes one mind from another and what *in fact* unifies the elements within a single mind. For the genetic-psychological question he explicitly addresses *presupposes* that this other question is answerable.

This is not to say that the metaphysical-ontological question is *not* answerable in Humean terms. Obviously any simple appeal to relations of resemblance and causality is bound to fail, given what we have already seen. But maybe some ingenious construction out of these relations might individuate minds in a way that fits our pre-philosophical ideas. However, Hume never addresses this question and says nothing that makes it seem at all likely that it might be so. We shall see in a moment that there is, given certain of Hume's assumptions, strong reason for supposing that it could not be so.

The same point – that the Humean story requires that minds be 'pre-bundled' antecedently to the operation of the belief-producing mechanism Hume describes – emerges again if we look at another obvious criticism of Hume's account.

This is the criticism that Hume's account of how we mistakenly come to believe in the existence of a unitary self itself *presupposes* the existence of unitary selves. For the story Hume tells can be true only if the mind (or the 'imagination'), as a result of surveying a certain succession of perceptions, is *mistakenly* led to believe in the existence of a unitary self. But if that belief is mistaken *what* is it that surveys the sequence of perceptions and is led into this error? Does it not seem that it must be a unitary entity of precisely the type Hume repudiates?

In short, on the face of it, the explanatory story Hume tells seems internally inconsistent. What he says is that the mind, as a result of surveying a certain sort of sequence of perceptions, is caused to have a mistaken belief in the existence of a unitary self. But since 'mind' and 'self' are in this context interchangeable this seems to mean, quite absurdly: the mind, as a result of surveying a certain sequence of perceptions, is caused to have a mistaken belief in *its own* existence.

And, it might be added by a proponent of this criticism, perhaps Hume himself half-recognizes the difficulty he faces. For it is a notable fact about the section on personal identity that, despite the fact that the primary object of Hume's account must be to explain the belief each of us has in *his own* identity, the perspective from which he presents the problem is determinedly *third-personal*; in fact, this comes out even in his manner of posing the central question of the section 'whether in pronouncing concerning the identity of a person we observe some real bond among his perceptions, or only feel one among the ideas we form of them' (1978:259).

This is the most obvious objection to Hume's discussion of personal identity. But, as Pike (1967) demonstrates, it is far from clear that it is a good one. According to Hume each mind is nothing but a bundle of perceptions. And so for a mind to perform a mental act is simply for a perception to occur in it. The mind's 'activity' consists in nothing more than perceptions occurring in it. Of course, it seems odd to say 'a bundle of perceptions confuses certain sequences of perceptions with others' (say), but that is merely because it is out of line with our ordinary manner of speaking. But that manner of speaking, according to Hume, embodies a falsehood.

What goes for the mind's activities also goes for its propensities or dispositions. They must be regarded as dispositions of certain bundles of perceptions to develop in certain ways over time. For example, the cash value of the claim that we are all disposed to confuse constant but interrupted series of perceptions with similar uninterrupted series is just that whenever an uninterrupted series of perceptions occurs in the particular bundle which is someone's mind, and then a similar but interrupted series occurs there, that mind or bundle will also come to contain the lively idea, or belief, that the second series is like the first.

Thus, it seems, Hume's enterprise is not self-defeating in the way in which the objection under discussion envisages. For he can reinterpret talk of the mind's activities or dispositions in a way that is consistent with his belief that all that really exist are bundles of ontologically independent perceptions.

But, of course, not all bundles of perceptions will display the patterns of development which correspond, in Hume's view, to the dispositions and propensities he ascribes to minds. These patterns of development will be displayed only by certain bundles of perceptions – what we might call 'personal' bundles. But now, which are they?

We have come back to the point that Hume needs an answer not only to the genetic-psychological question: 'What causes induce us to believe in unitary selves?', but also to the metaphysical-ontological question: 'What in fact unites the perceptions within a single mind and distinguishes one mind from another?' For the picture with which he operates, and with which he cannot dispense, is of perceptions *objectively* tied together in well-individuated bundles, prior to the operation of the belief-forming mechanism which generates, in each bundle which qualifies as a mind, a belief in its own unity.

As I said previously, Hume tells us nothing that suggests that he might be able to provide a good answer to this question. But matters are worse than that. For as Don Garrett has recently ingeniously argued (1981), given Hume's views about causation, the relations of causation and resemblance, or any however ingenious construction therefrom, are *necessarily* insufficient to provide an answer to the metaphysical-ontological question, *necessarily* insufficient to provide an 'idea of the human mind' that corresponds to our actual idea, even after that has been purged of its vague association with metaphysical substance.

He argues the point thus: When we regard a pair of objects as related as cause and effect, according to Hume, all that is objectively present in the situation is precedence and contiguity in time or place. In addition there will have been an observed constant conjunction of similar pairs of objects in like relations of precedency and contiguity, as a result of which we are led, mistakenly, to regard the objects as necessarily connected.

Two *exactly resembling* perceptions in distinct minds can differ in their causal relations, therefore, only by differing in their relations of precedence or contiguity to other perceptions. But *simultaneous* exactly resembling perceptions occurring in distinct minds can differ in their causal relations only by differing in their spatial locations. However, Hume is emphatic that many, in fact most, of our perceptions do not have spatial locations. This indeed is one of his main theses in the section immediately preceding his discussion of personal identity, and one of the principal components of his argument against a materialist conception of the self. He asserts:

> *an object may exist and yet be nowhere*, and I assert, this is not only possible, but that the greatest part of beings do and must exist after this manner. . . . This is evidently the case

with all our perceptions, except those of sight and feeling. A moral reflection cannot be placed on the right or on the left hand of a passion, nor can a smell or sound be either of a circular or a square figure. These objects and perceptions, so far from requiring any particular place, are absolutely incompatible with it, and even the imagination cannot attribute it to them.

(1978:235–6)

But, of course, if there are two exactly resembling and simultaneous perceptions, *a* and *b*, in distinct minds, neither of which is spatially located – two moral reflections or two passions, say – they cannot fail to stand to all other perceptions in exactly the same relations of resemblance and causality. If there is a bundle of perceptions containing *a* which qualifies as a mind in virtue of all its members being interrelated by some relation constructed out of resemblance and causality, there will be an exactly similar bundle of perceptions consisting of all the rest of the perceptions in the first bundle together with *b* instead of *a*. And the Humean account will be quite incapable of saying why this bundle also should not qualify as a mind.

However complicated an account, in terms of resemblance and causality, Hume might give in attempting to answer the metaphysical-ontological question concerning the principle of individuation for minds, then, it must necessarily be inadequate. For any two qualitatively identical perceptions which are neither of sight nor touch and occur simultaneously will be incapable of being distinguished either by their similarity relations or by their causal relations. To be able to embrace such a 'Humean' principle of individuation for bundles one must, therefore, *either* abandon Hume's own most emphatically expressed view of the possibility of spatially unlocated perceptions, *or* reject the common-sense view that qualitatively identical perceptions may occur in two minds at the same time; in which case one can hardly claim to be giving an account of the unity of the mind in any sense that at all approximates to the one we actually have.

In presenting these criticisms of Hume's theory I have not suggested that they were the source of his subsequent dissatisfaction with his account. Whether they were, or whether it was some quite different difficulty that was worrying Hume, it is quite impossible to say. Hume is far too inexplicit. All he says is

all my hopes vanish, when I come to explain the principles,
that unite our successive perceptions in our thought or
consciousness. I cannot discover any theory, which gives me
satisfaction on this head. . . . In short, there are two principles,
which I cannot render consistent; nor is it in my power to
renounce either of them, viz. *that all our distinct perceptions
are distinct existences*, and *that the mind never perceives any
real connexion amongst distinct existences*.

(1978:636)

Clearly Hume no longer believes that the belief-generating
mechanism he has described is sufficient to generate the belief in a
unitary self. But since, as all commentators have noted, the two
principles he claims that he cannot render consistent clearly are
consistent, he gives no clue as to why this is so. Hume scholars will
doubtless continue to speculate.

4.7 Conclusion

That completes my discussion of Hume's views of personal identity.
I have argued that his account is radically defective in so far as it
rests on the mistaken views that identity is incompatible with change
and that perceptions are ontologically independent entities. But I
have also argued that even on its own terms it is a failure, since it
cannot explain the pattern of self-ascriptions of mental states which
actually exists, and is in principle incapable of providing an adequate principle of individuation of minds.

Most subsequent philosophers have not followed Hume in regarding the unity of the self as a fiction, but in two other ways his discussion has been immensely influential.

First, his writings are the primary source of the idea, now
accepted by all proponents of psychological continuity criteria of
personal identity, that memory alone cannot constitute personal
identity, but must figure merely as one of the great variety of *causal*
links between the earlier and later psychological states of a person
which constitute his identity (or at least, what matters in his
identity).

Second, Hume, and in particular his analogy between self and
state, is the primary source of the reductionist tradition in discus-

sions of personal identity, which dominated the logical empiricists' writings on this topic and is still alive and well today in the writings of Derek Parfit. Indeed Parfit may not unreasonably be thought to have attempted the most systematic contemporary extension of Hume's theory.

A further examination of this reductionism is one of the topics of the next chapter.

CHAPTER 5
Identity and Personal Identity

5.1 Introduction

Discussions of personal identity typically take it for granted that the problem is easy to characterize and clearly intelligible, and concentrate on explaining its various possible solutions. So far this discussion has been no exception. In this chapter, however, I want to get clearer about what the problem is, and about its relation to problems about identity over time more generally. I shall also devote part of the discussion to an examination of the distinction between the Simple and the Complex Views of personal identity – which will turn out to be, not one distinction at all, but a conflation of (at least) three different distinctions.

First of all, then, what is the problem of personal identity? In Chapter 1 I described it as the problem of specifying the criterion of diachronic identity for persons, where what is in question is not an evidential or heuristic principle, but a metaphysical-cum-semantic one. The provision of a criterion of diachronic identity for persons would not merely be a statement of what would count as *evidence* for the identity over time of persons, but a statement of what the identity over time, and hence the persistence of a person, would *consist in*. But what precisely are we asking when we enquire, about persons, or things of any other kind, what their identity over time consists in?

At first sight there seems to be no difficulty. For any kind of persisting thing K, in addition to the identification problem for K's, i.e. the problem of specifying logically necessary and sufficient conditions for being a K, there is also the problem of specifying the logically necessary and sufficient conditions for the identity of a K existing at one time and a K existing at another. Thus the problem of personal identity over time is the problem of saying, 'What are the logically necessary and sufficient conditions for a person $P2$ at a time $t2$ to be the same person as a person $P1$ at an earlier time $t1$?' (Swinburne 1976:223). The (less interesting) problem of ship identity over time is precisely analogous: 'What are the logically necessary and sufficient conditions for a ship $S2$ at a time $t2$ to be the same ship as a ship $S1$ at an earlier time $t1$?' And *mutatis mutandis* for the rest of the problems of identity over time discussed by philosophers.

In addition to these problems of diachronic identity, there are also problems of synchronic identity, which can be stated similarly. Thus there is the problem of synchronic identity for persons: 'What are the necessary and sufficient conditions for two persons [i.e. persons identified by distinct descriptions] at a given time to be the same person?' (Swinburne 1976:228). There is the less interesting problem of synchronic identity for ships and so on.

5.2 A puzzle

That these problems make sense seems evident. For what else are we discussing when we debate such puzzle cases as Locke's Prince and Cobbler, Shoemaker's Brown and Brownson, the ship of Theseus, or the (non-fictional) cases of 'split-brain' patients? Either these debates are a lot of nonsense, it seems, or these problems about identity are genuine ones. And so most philosophers are content to hold that they are indeed genuine ones (cf. Kripke's unpublished lectures on identity over time for similar remarks).

But when one looks more closely at the formulations of these apparently genuine problems it is easy to become puzzled. They *seem* to be requests for the specification of the satisfaction conditions of certain relations – personal identity over time, or ship identity over time, for example. But how can this be? There are not different *kinds* of identity, to be differently analysed. There is just the *one* relation of identity, and there is nothing in any way puzzling about it. As David Lewis puts the point:

> Identity is an utterly unproblematic notion. Everything is identical to itself. Nothing is identical to anything else. There is never any problem about what makes something identical to itself; nothing can fail to be. And there is never any problem

about what makes two things identical: two things never can be identical.

(1986:192–3)

How, then, can it make sense to ask, for example, what makes a person existing at one time identical with a person existing at another? If the person existing at the earlier time *is* identical with the person existing at the later time, the question is a request for an account of what makes a thing identical with itself. While if the earlier person is distinct from the later one, the question is a request for an account of what makes *two* things identical. In either case it is unanswerable. The same problem confronts a request for an account of what makes two persons (persons specified by distinct descriptions) at one time identical. Either they are, or they aren't. If they aren't nothing makes them identical. If they are, then their identity is the identity of a thing with itself, and so again nothing makes 'them' identical. Of course, statements of identity can be informative, and so the possibility is still left open of evidential or heuristic principles stating what evidence would count in favour of claims of personal identity or ship identity, or whatever. But the 'semantic-cum-metaphysical' problem of what *constitutes* identity (whether diachronic or synchronic) for things of a kind now begins to look like nonsense (for this line of thought see also, apart from Lewis, Brody 1980).

5.3 A solution

The basic thought underlying this argument has two components. The first is that there is just the one relation of identity, the relation everything has to itself and to nothing else. Identity is not, in the Lockean phrase, 'suited to the idea', not at least if this is interpreted (controversially) to mean that there is a multiplicity of distinct sortal-relative identity relations. The second component of the thought is now just that there is no possibility of analysing this one notion of identity in any more fundamental terms (note, for example, that the gloss I just gave: 'the relation everything has to itself and to *nothing else*', itself uses the notion of identity, for 'nothing else' means 'nothing not identical with it'). How, then, can there be *both* a problem about personal identity *and* a distinct problem about ship identity? How can there be *both* a problem about diachronic personal identity *and* a distinct problem about synchronic personal identity? And, more fundamentally, how can *any* of these problems make sense?

One response to this difficulty would be to side with Locke, interpreted as above, and to deny the uniqueness of the identity relation. To pursue this line of response would be to endorse the views of the Relative Identity Theorists (see, e.g., Geach 1962, and 1967). But there is a better way, which is to deny that the *genuine* problems which philosophers are concerned with when they debate topics under the title of 'problems of (synchronic and diachronic) identity' are problems about *identity* at all. Rather, they are problems about kind-membership.

This suggestion is, of course, a wholly unoriginal one, the clearest expression of which is in Quine (e.g. 1976).

According to Quine 'any collection of particle stages, however spatio-temporally gerrymandered or disperse' counts as a physical object. The world's water is a physical object. There is a physical object part of which is a momentary stage of a silver dollar sometime in 1976 and the rest of which is the temporal segment of the Eiffel Tower through its third decade. Any two momentary objects, taken at different moments, are time slices of one physical object – time slices indeed of many such.

However, most such physical objects are irrelevant to our concerns, and go unnamed in our language. But some do not; though ontologically on a par with the rest, these occupy a favoured place in our language and conceptual scheme. For any such favoured kind of K of physical object there is the problem of specifying the conditions a physical object has to satisfy to be a K. Thus there is the problem of specifying the conditions a physical object has to satisfy to be a ship, or a person, a river, or a body of water.

Now according to Quine the temporal parts of a physical object need be related in no way that is of interest to us. But when we consider, say, what conditions a physical object has to satisfy to be a river, the situation is different. It is not enough for a physical object to be a river that its momentary stages have a certain character: in addition they must be interrelated in a certain way – they must be *river-kindred*. In Quine's view it is the specification of this relation which philosophers are concerned with when they debate the 'criterion of diachronic identity' for rivers. But in specifying the conditions of river-kinship we are not stating conditions for *identity*, but merely conditions for *being a river*.

It is, in Quine's view, the same with the problem of synchronic identity for rivers. In so far as it makes sense it is not a problem about identity at all. Though it is not sufficient for a physical object to be a river that its momentary stages have a certain character, still, it is necessary. A momentary stage of a river differs in intrinsic character from, say, a momentary stage of a cow. Thus there is the problem of saying what this character is. But nothing can count as a river-at-a-moment unless its parts at that moment stand to one another in certain relations. It is these relations that are discussed under the misleading title 'the criterion of synchronic identity for rivers'.

The Quinean conception of problems of synchronic and diachronic identity as reducible to problems about kind membership seems to me very plausible, indeed wholly compelling. But it is bound up in Quine, as in the exposition above, with an idea that many philosophers find a good deal less compelling, namely, the idea that everyday things like ships and people are 'four-dimensional worms', with temporal as well as spatial parts.

But I want to suggest that we can take on board the more attractive of these Quinean ideas without committing ourselves to the less attractive one. However, in order to make good the claim that the so-called problem of identity over time for a particular kind of thing *K* is not a problem about identity at all, but solely a problem about kind-membership, we need a formulation of the problem in which the notion of identity does not occur. In the absence of such a formulation the claim is a fraud.

So what might such a formulation be if we do not presuppose the four-dimensional ontology?

We can approach an answer to this question if we begin by asking what information a solution to the problem of *K*-identity over time would provide. The answer is that it would provide an account of the distinction between those changes a *K* can survive, and those it cannot. In other words, it would provide an account of the sort of history that is a possible one for a *K*, an account of the variations and constancies that such a history *must* display, and those it *may* display.

Thus, a solution to the problem of personal identity over time would provide an account of the sort of history that is a possible one for a person. It would provide answers (or, conceivably, tell us that no answers are to be had) to such questions as, 'Can a person have different bodies at different times?, 'Can a person be a saint at one time and a psychopath at another (Dr Jekyll and Mr Hyde)?'

These questions *can* be rephrased to speak of personal identity (e.g., 'Can the *same* person have different bodies at different times?'), but as they stand they do not do so. As they stand they are simply questions of the form 'Can a person be *F*?' (which is equivalent to: 'Is it necessarily true that all persons are non-*F*?'), i.e. questions about the necessary conditions for *being a person*.

Similarly for other cases. An account of the identity of a ship over time would enable us to answer (or state to be unanswerable because of the vagueness of the concept) such questions as, 'Can a ship have all its parts replaced one at a time by new ones?', 'Can a ship be disassembled, transported from one country to another and then reassembled?' Such questions *can* likewise be rephrased to speak of ship identity – 'Can the *same* ship . . .?' – but as they stand they do not do so. As they stand they are simply questions about the necessary conditions for *being a ship*, on a par with such questions as, 'Can a ship travel underwater?'

In general, then, in asking what *K*-identity over time consists in, what one is asking for, in part, is a specification of certain necessary conditions of being a *K*, namely those identifiable by specification of the relations *R* satisfying the following schema:

(1) Necessarily, for any (thing of kind) Kx, for any times t, t', if x exists at t and t' then $Rxtt'$.

The hope is that such conditions can be informatively specified, i.e. can be specified without the use of the very concept *K* which is being analysed (whether the concept of *identity* needs to be employed is neither here nor there).

But, of course, in asking what constitutes *K*-identity over time one is asking for more than the specification of certain *necessary* conditions of *K*-hood.

The four-dimensional theorist can explain this 'more' very simply: what one is asking for, he can say, is a specification of a relation *R* such that it is a sufficient condition of a physical object being a *K* that all its temporal parts are pairwise related by *R* (sometimes, as in Perry 1972, such a relation is called the 'unity relation' for K's). But if we do not presuppose the four-dimensional ontology, we must express the request differently, namely, as the request for a specification of a relation R such that for any x, it suffices for x's being a K that R relates all ordered triples $\langle x,t,t' \rangle$ where t and t' lie within the period of x's existence. That is, the request is for a specification of a relation R satisfying the condition:

(2) Necessarily, for any x, if for every t and t' if x exists at t and x exists at t' then $Rxtt'$ then x is a K.

However, the specification of such a relation may be wholly uninformative (naturally the same is true of the specification of a four-dimensional unity relation). To ensure that this is not so (to ensure, in other words, that the specification contributes to the *analysis* of the concept of a K) we need to appeal once more to schema (1) and require (at least) that the relation satisfying (2) can be specified as the relation whose satisfaction by any ordered triple $\langle x,t,t' \rangle$ is entailed by (and entails) the joint satisfaction by that triple of some set of relations R', each of which satisfies schema (1), but is specified without the use of the concept of a K. (In other words, the specification of the relation satisfying (2) must be of the form 'the relation R such that necessarily, an ordered triple $\langle x,t,t' \rangle$ satisfies R iff it satisfies all of $R1 \ldots Rn$', where $R1 \ldots Rn$ are relations satisfying schema (1) and specified in the description given without the use of the concept of a K.)

This, then, I suggest, is what the request for 'a criterion of diachronic identity for K's', or an account of what constitutes K-identity over time, comes down to when properly expressed. It would perhaps be better described as a request for 'the diachronic criterion of K-hood'.

The problem of personal identity over time is thus the problem of specifying a set of relations $R1 \ldots Rn$, and a relation R, such that (a) necessarily an ordered triple $\langle x,t,t' \rangle$ satisfies R iff it satisfies all of $R1 \ldots Rn$, (b) $R1 \ldots Rn$ can be specified without the use of the concept of a person, and (c) $R1 \ldots Rn$ and R satisfy, respectively, the schemas

($P1$) Necessarily, for any person x, for any times t and t', if x exists at t and t' then $Rxtt'$

and

(*P2*) Necessarily, for any *x*, if for every *t* and *t'*, if *x* exists at *t* and *x* exists at *t'* then *Rxtt'* then *x* is a person.

The specification of such a set of relations would be an account of the diachronic criterion of personhood.

But it is usually assumed in the literature on problems of identity that in addition to problems of diachronic, there are also problems of *synchronic* identity.

What, then, of the request for a criterion of synchronic identity for *K*'s, and its customarily assumed distinctness from the request for a criterion of diachronic identity? Familiar examples (e.g., in Perry 1972) make it evident that it is at least logically possible to be in a state in which one's grasp of the concept of a *K* is partial in such a way as to make it tempting to say that whilst one grasps the criterion of synchronic identity for *K*'s one does not grasp their criterion of diachronic identity. But how is the demand for a criterion of synchronic identity to be expressed if the notion of identity is not to be used?

Once again, if the four-dimensional ontology is presupposed the answer is simple, as we have seen. But what if it is not? Then, I suggest, the only intelligible question to be asked is: What are the necessary conditions for a *K*'s existence at a time? That is, what conditions *C* satisfy the following schema:

(3) Necessarily, for any *K x*, for any time *t*, if *x* exists at *t*, then *Cx* at *t*.

Anything sensible that can be said in answer to the request for a criterion of synchronic identity for *K*'s must, therefore, be comprised in the answer to this question.

Of course, one such necessary condition is that *x be a K*. So there is no hope, unless we presuppose the four-dimensional ontology, of treating the request for a criterion of synchronic identity for *K*'s as wholly distinct from the request for a criterion of diachronic identity. But it may none the less be possible, by suitable choice of '*C*' in (3) to give an informative specification of *some* necessary conditions of *K*-hood without thereby specifying or presupposing the diachronic criterion of *K*-hood. Many such necessary conditions will have nothing in common with what philosophers typically have in mind when they talk of the criterion for the synchronic identity of

K's, but this need not be true of all of them. A subset of such necessary conditions, in the case of spatially extended objects, for example, will concern the interrelations of their (spatial) parts, and when we ask for a criterion of synchronic identity for, say, ships or tables, it is largely information about this that we are seeking (see once again Perry 1972). In the case of persons our interest in a criterion of synchronic identity is rather an interest in the relationship which must obtain between simultaneously occurring, co-personal, mental states. But this can similarly be understood as an interest in the truth-yielding specifications of (3), with 'K' read as 'person'.

But what now of what might be called the *exclusion* principle for K's, the principle that two K's cannot occupy the same place at the same time, i.e. that K's occupying the same place at the same time must be identical? For some specifications of 'K' ('person' being one) such principles are much debated by philosophers. But such a principle cannot be regarded as specifying a necessary condition of K-hood in the manner of an instance of schema (3), yet it seems, at first sight, a perfectly intelligible thesis about K-identity at a time. How, then, can this be reconciled with the Quinean thesis that all questions about criteria of identity, whether diachronic or synchronic, for things of a particular kind, must reduce to questions about the criteria for membership in that kind?

The easiest way to understand the role of such exclusion principles, I think, is to revert yet again to the point of view of the four-dimensional theorist. From this point of view there is, of course, no difficulty whatsoever in the idea of two *physical objects* being in the same place at the same time. So what, from this point of view, can we be doing when we say (using the concept of a familiar kind of physical object): two K's cannot occupy the same place at the same time? The answer is that even though we are not specifying a necessary condition of K-hood (what Frege in Geach and Black 1952 calls a 'mark' of the concept) we *are* specifying a constraint on the concept of a K: a condition any concept must satisfy if it is to qualify as the concept of a K (or equivalently, a condition the unity relation for K's must satisfy). And, of course, the role of the principle remains the same even if the four-dimensional point of view is rejected.

But, if this is the way in which exclusion principles are to be understood, we can reaffirm the Quinean thesis of the reducibility of questions about identity criteria to questions about kind-membership. For, if this is the case, for any kind K, whether the exclusion principle for K's is true will be determined once the necessary and sufficient conditions for membership in the kind (the marks of the concept) have been fixed: if true its status will thus be that of a merely derivative truth which does not have to be mentioned in a full account of the concept (cf. the way in which the specification of the necessary and sufficient conditions of K-hood, together with the facts, will determine, without the aid, or the possibility, of any further delimitation of the concept, the truth-value of the proposition 'K's exist').

Whether, once this is accepted, one continues to speak of the exclusion principle for K's (for those kinds for which the exclusion principles are true) as an aspect of the conditions of K-identity at a time is, of course, a matter of no importance. But it is important, if we choose to do so, to note the difference between *this* aspect of the conditions of K-identity at a time and those which can be subsumed under a specification of the conditions C satisfying schema (3); and to be aware also that it will be impossible to specify the conditions on the concept of a K which determine the truth of the exclusion principle without specifying the *diachronic* criterion of K-hood.

5.4 An alternative solution

I have now explained my favoured framework for the discussion of so-called problems of diachronic and synchronic identity, for persons or any other things. But I must now outline another line of solution to the puzzle I set forth in section 5.2, a solution which has also had an influence on the discussion of problems of identity over time. We can call this, for brevity, the Fregean solution (though Frege himself never applied it to problems of identity over time).

According to Frege's familiar proposal (Frege 1950) we can introduce the functor 'the direction of' by the stipulation that:

the direction of a = the direction of b iff a is parallel to b.

We thereby fix the criterion of identity for directions as the relation of parallelism between lines.

With this fixed we can go on to explain 'x is a direction' as meaning 'for some line a, x is the direction of a', and we can go on to explain the predicates of directions in terms of those satisfiable by lines, subject to the constraint that the truth-conditions of each statement of the form 'the direction of *a* is *F*' be given by a statement of the form 'line *a* is *F**', where '*F**' denotes a property of lines for which parallelism is a congruence relation (i.e., which is possessed both by a line *a* and by a line *b* if *a* is parallel to *b*). Thus, starting from a specification of the criterion of identity for directions we can go on to explain the whole 'language game' in which we speak of directions. (In fact Frege himself proceeded somewhat differently, explicitly defining directions as classes of parallel lines (or rather, as the extensions of certain concepts), but this difference need not trouble us.)

This approach is susceptible to generalization. For *any* kind of object *K* we can ask (although we cannot always receive an answer): (i) what entities play the role for *K*'s that straight lines play for directions, and (ii) what relation plays the role for *K*'s that parallelism plays for directions?

We can apply this Fregean approach to problems of diachronic identity and we can do so without presupposing the Quinean four-dimensional scheme. The entities which stand to *K*'s as straight lines stand to directions might be ordered pairs of persisting things (of a distinct kind *K**) and times, and the relation which serves as the criterion of diachronic identity for *K*'s might be a relation between pairs of such ordered pairs.

Where *a* and *b* are *K**'s the criterion of diachronic identity for *K*'s could then be given the form:

the *K* of which *K*a* is a manifestation at *t* = the *K* of which *K*b* is a manifestation at *t'* if $\langle a,t \rangle R \langle b,t' \rangle$.

Being a *K* could then be explained as being the *K* of which some $\langle a,t \rangle$ is the manifestation, and the satisfaction conditions of predicates satisfiable by *K*'s could be explained in terms of the properties possessed by *K**'s at times.

Thus (if one is prepared to discount the possibility of disembodied existence) one might take the problem of diachronic personal identity to be the problem of specifying the relation which body *a* existing at time *t* must bear to body *b* existing at time *t'*, if the person occupying *a* at *t* is to be identical with the person occupying *b* at *t'*. Here the *K**'s are bodies.

Or, if one finds the idea of Lockean thinking substance intelligible, one might take it to be the problem of specifying the relation which thinking substance *a*, existing at time *t*, must bear to thinking substance *b*, existing at time *t'*, if the person in which *a* thinks at *t* is to be identical with the person in which *b* thinks at *t'*. Here the *K**'s are thinking substances (cf. Chapter 3).

But although the Fregean approach *can* be applied to problems of diachronic identity without presupposing the four-dimensional scheme, it is not, of course, incompatible with it; so one might also take the problem to be that of specifying the relation which must hold between person-stage *a*, existing at *t*, and person-stage *b*, existing at *t'* if the person of which *a* is a stage at *t* is to be identical with the person of which *b* is a stage at *t'*. Here the *K**'s are person-stages, and if they are momentary the reference to times is redundant.

The Fregean approach, then, provides a second way of making unproblematic sense of requests for criteria of diachronic identity.

But what, then, is the relation of this approach to problems of diachronic identity to the approach outlined in the previous section? The answer, I think, is that the Fregean approach is just another way of developing the Quinean insight that questions about identity criteria reduce to questions about kind-membership: in specifying the Fregean criterion of identity for directions one is specifying exactly what it is to *be* a direction, namely something for which questions of identity and distinctness are reducible to questions of parallelism between lines. That is *all* there is to being a direction. Similarly, a Fregean criterion of identity for persons would be at one and the same time an answer to questions about personal identity and a specification of what it means to be a person.

Thus the Fregean approach to problems of diachronic identity explained in this section is not in competition with the approach described in section 5.3. However, there remains a substantial difference between them. For in order to provide a Fregean criterion of diachronic identity for *K*'s one must identity *another* kind of thing *K** and a relation *R* between ordered pairs of *K**'s and times in terms of which *K*-identity over time can be explained. (In the terminology to be introduced shortly, in order to provide a Fregean criterion of diachronic identity for *K*'s one must show that facts about *K*-identity are *reducible* to facts about relations between *K**'s.) But no such restriction applies to the provision of a diachronic criterion of

K-hood as explained in section 5.3. Thus even if a Fregean criterion of diachronic identity for *K*'s cannot be given, it may well be that a diachronic criterion of *K*-hood is still capable of being specified. As a basis for discussion of problems of diachronic identity, including the problem of diachronic identity for persons, the approach outlined in section 5.3 thus remains preferable. (And, it should be added, a Fregean approach to problems of *synchronic* identity would be wholly implausible.)

5.5 The simple and complex views

With this clarification of the nature of the problem of personal identity we are now in a position to look more closely at the fundamental division between the Simple and Complex Views of personal identity.

I gave a rough summary of the distinction between these two views in Chapter 1. The proponent of the Simple View of personal identity will say that personal identity is an ultimate unanalysable fact, which resists definition in any other terms. By contrast a proponent of the Complex View will maintain that an informative account of what personal identity consists in *is* possible, since personal identity is nothing over and above those observable and introspectable facts of physical and psychological continuity which provide the only evidence for it. Again a proponent of the Simple View will say that persons are 'separately existing' entities, distinct from their brains, bodies and experiences, whilst a proponent of the Complex View will say that persons are nothing 'over and above' their brains, bodies and experiences.

But what exactly does this disagreement amount to? I shall argue that there are, in fact, at least three distinctions customarily conflated in the current debate about the Simple and Complex Views. I shall explain one of these in this section and the two others in the two following sections.

The first distinction is between those who maintain and those who deny the possibility of an informative diachronic criterion of personhood, i.e. between those who maintain and those who deny the possibility of a specification of a set of relations $R1 \ldots Rn$ and a relation R, satisfied respectively by schema ($P1$) and by schema ($P2$) and satisfying the other conditions explained in section 5.3. It is obvious that anyone who puts forward any version of the Complex View of personal identity, i.e. any of the Bodily, Brain, Physical, Memory or Psychological Continuity Criteria, must maintain the possibility of such a diachronic criterion of personhood. It is equally obvious that anyone who supports the Simple View must deny it.

In fact, supporters of the Simple View must, and do, go further. Not only must they deny that any informative criterion of diachronic identity for persons can be given, they must also deny that any informative list of *necessary conditions* of personhood can be given by a specification of relations satisfying schema ($P1$).

That this *is* denied by supporters of the Simple View is evident from their writings. Nothing more can be required for personal identity over time, they insist, than the persistence of the self or 'I', and they resist any attempts by their opponents to suggest that a person's history must satisfy any independently specifiable constraint. There is nothing unintelligible, nothing self-contradictory, they insist, in the idea of a person having different bodies at different times, there is nothing self-contradictory in the idea of his having different *sorts* of bodies at different times; there is nothing self-contradictory, indeed, in the idea of a person having a body at one time and not having a body *at all* at other times. Equally there is nothing self-contradictory in the idea of a person having a discontinuous set of memories and radically different character and personality traits at different times. Nor is there anything self-contradictory in the combination of these ideas: the idea of a person *simultaneously* acquiring a new (sort of) body, or becoming disembodied, and *at the same time* losing all his memories of his previous life, and his old psychology, and acquiring a new set of memories and a new set of character and personality traits. In short, there is nothing self-contradictory in the idea of a person's history exhibiting *no* sort of physical or psychological continuity whatsoever. As R.M. Chisholm succinctly expresses the point: 'my future experiences need not be linked by any of our present criteria of personal identity to my present self' (Chisholm 1969:138; see also Swinburne, in Shoemaker and Swinburne 1984:25).

Thus the first distinction to be made between proponents of the Simple View and proponents of the Complex View is that the former deny the possibility of any informative specification of constraints on the possible history of a person (by way of specifications of relations R satisfying schema ($P1$)), whilst the latter not only affirm this possibility but also maintain the possibility of specifying an informative diachronic criterion of personhood in the sense introduced in section 5.3. But it is apparent, then, that there is a possible position which proponents of *neither* view endorse, namely that there *are* relations satisfying (P1) whose specification informatively constrains the class of possible personal histories, but there is no *set* of such relations, related to a relation satisfying (P2) in the way required to provide an informative diachronic criterion of personhood (or as we might put it, for easier intelligibility: there are informatively specifiable *necessary* conditions of personal identity over time, but no informatively specifiable *sufficient* conditions). For concepts other than that of a person this would seem to be quite a plausible position, but it has no place in the debate over personal identity. In order to preserve the convenient terminological convention that an opponent of the Simple View is a proponent of the Complex View, and conversely, I therefore hereby stipulate that I shall use the expression 'a proponent of the Simple View' to mean just: 'one who denies the possibility of specifying informative constraints on the class of personal histories', and the expression 'a proponent of the Complex View' to mean just: 'one who affirms the possibility of specifying such constraints'. By this pair of stipulations a defender of the unoccupied position just characterized is classified as a Complex theorist. (The opposing pair of stipulations whereby he was classified as a Simple theorist would, of course, be equally acceptable.)

5.6 Reductionism and non-reductionism

So much, then, for the first distinction which a philosopher may have in mind when thinking of the contrast between the Simple and Complex Views, a distinction with which, for terminological convenience, I have in fact now identified that contrast. A second distinction, often conflated with this one, is that between *non-reductionist* and *reductionist* accounts of personal identity. It is perhaps in Parfit (1984) that this second distinction has figured most prominently in recent years, and in insisting on its non-identity with the first distinction I am heavily indebted to Shoemaker's 'Critical Notice' of Parfit's book (Shoemaker 1985).

The general notion of reductionism is clearly explained by

Dummett (1982). A reductionist thesis always concerns the relationship between two classes of statements: the 'given' class and the 'reductive' class. Reductionism, properly so-called, is the thesis that there exists a translation of statements of the given class into the reductive class. This translation is proposed not merely as preserving truth-values, but as part of an account of the meanings of statements of the given class: it is integral to the reductionist thesis that it is by an implicit grasp of the scheme of translation that we understand these statements. Often, however, what goes on under the name of reductionism is a weaker form of thesis, which Dummett calls a *reductive* thesis. A reductive thesis, like a fully-fledged reductionist thesis, is concerned with the relation between two classes of statements, the given class and the reductive class. But it claims only that no statement of the given class can be true unless some suitable statements of the reductive class are true, and conversely, that the truth of these statements of the reductive class guarantees the truth of the corresponding statement of the given class. It is, once again, essential that the reductive thesis be advanced not as a mere observation concerning the connection between the truth conditions of statements of the two classes, but as part of an account of the meanings of statements of the given class: the proponent of the thesis holds that an understanding of these statements involves an implicit grasp of their relation to statements of the reductive class, that is, an implicit acceptance of the reductive thesis.

A famous example of a reductive thesis is the thesis of the Logical Positivists that facts about nations are logical contructions out of facts about people, i.e. that if any statement about nations is true it will be true in virtue of the truth of certain other statements referring to people and not to nations. According to this claim there are no facts about nations 'over and above' facts about people, and it is part of understanding talk of nations that one implicitly accepts that this is so.

However, even if this is so, there need not be any *translation* of statements about nations into statements about people and their behaviour: for it might be that any particular statement about nations is such that there is an infinite number of statements about people which would make it true; or that it entails an infinite number of statements about people: or both these things might be so. Under any of these suppositions there could be no finite translation of a statement about nations into a statement referring only to people, but it would still be the case, in the sense required by the Logical Positivists' reductive thesis, that nations were not entities 'over and above' people.

As well as providing a good example of the distinction between full-blooded reductionism and a reductive thesis, the Logical Positivist thesis also illustrates another feature of many reductionist or reductive theses.

This is that the 'given' class of statements can be characterized as a class in which there is a reference to or quantification over entities of a certain kind A, whilst the 'reductive' class contains no statement of this type, nor any statement involving reference to or quantification over entities which are ontologically or conceptually dependent on A's, that is, which could exist only if A's existed or could be referred to only by language users also capable of referring to A's.

Thus, it is undeniable that people are neither ontologically nor conceptually dependent on nations and equally undeniable that nations are both ontologically and conceptually dependent on people. (This is, of course, why the Logical Positivists were so fond of illustrating their notion of a 'logical construction' by referring to this thesis.)

In explaining his Reductionist View of personal identity Parfit repeatedly compares it to the Logical Positivists' thesis concerning the relationship between nations and their citizens (see Parfit 1984) thereby continuing, of course, a tradition begun by Hume. The Reductionist View, as Parfit characterizes it, is, in fact, in the terms just introduced, a reductive, though not a reductionist, thesis. The core idea is that people stand to their experiences as nations stand to their citizens. Facts about people and their identity over time are nothing 'over and above' facts about experiences and their relations. As statements about people constitute a 'reductive' class relative to statements about nations, so statements about experiences constitute a 'reductive' class relative to statements about people. And just as people are neither ontologically nor conceptually dependent on nations, so experiences are neither ontologically nor conceptually dependent on people (thus at one point (1984:211) Parfit proposes to use the word 'event' rather than 'state' to refer to experiences precisely because a state must be a state *of* some entity, whereas this is not true of events – see also Parfit 1984:209–13).

This view is, of course, very reminiscent of Hume's (except that

Parfit never suggests that there is anything 'fictional' about personal identity). All there are in reality are bundles of experiences (or 'perceptions') linked together by certain relations of psychological continuity and connectedness (and causally related to happenings in brains and bodies). The whole truth about reality could be given by an 'impersonal' description, in which neither persons nor any entities which are either ontologically or conceptually dependent on persons are referred to or quantified over.

Evidently, on the face of it (as Parfit indeed insists), this Reductionist View of personal identity is utterly implausible. For, on the face of it, it is just wrong to think of experiences, or mental states in general, as Hume thought of his 'perceptions'. Rather they should be thought of precisely *as* states in the sense to which Parfit objects, that is as entities which are ontologically and conceptually dependent on persons. That is, for an experience to occur just as for a person to be in a certain state, just as for a dent to exist is just for a surface to be dented. In short, experiences are 'adjectives of' their subjects and not independent entities in their own right (see Shoemaker 1985, Cook 1968).

The Reductionist View of personal identity thus seems to be merely a philosopher's dream. But my present purpose is not to argue that this is so (actually, of course, the onus of proof is surely on the Reductionist), but simply to insist on the difference between the Reductionist View, as now characterized, and the Complex View. And this difference should I hope by now be perfectly apparent. There is no conceivable reason why a defender of the thesis that there are relations satisfying (P1) whose specification informatively constrains the class of possible personal histories should have to maintain that experiences are anything other than they appear to be, that is states (in the sense Parfit objects to) of persons. Nor does acceptance of the thesis that a diachronic criterion of personhood can be informatively specified (a thesis accepted by all actual Complex theorists) involve a commitment to Parfitian Reductionism. Of course, a defender of this thesis *is* committed to reductionism about persons as this notion is characterized by Dummett, since he is committed to holding that the truth-conditions of statements in which the term 'person' occurs can be given by statements in which the word 'person' does not occur. But to be committed to reductionism in this sense is not to be committed to Reductionism in Parfit's sense, which is a far more specific thesis, particularly in respect of the nature of the reductive class to which statements about persons are to be reduced.

5.7 *Persons as endurers or persons as perdurers?*

I have now explained two distinctions between views on personal identity which have often been conflated in recent writings on the topic. I turn now to a third such distinction, namely, that between regarding persons as *perdurers* and regarding persons as *endurers*, I take this terminology from Lewis (1984). It is an uncontroversial thesis that persons persist, i.e. exist at more than one time – that is the neutral word. But *how* they do so is controversial. According to one view persons persist by having *temporal parts* which exist at different times and are to be distinguished by the times at which they exist – this is the view that persons *perdure*. Other philosophers deny that this is so: according to them when a person is present at two times he is *wholly* present at those times, for he has no temporal parts but only spatial ones. This is the view that persons *endure*. I referred to this controversy earlier in section 5.3 when I introduced the Quinean thesis that intelligible problems about identity conditions reduce to problems about kind-membership. I now want to elaborate it just far enough to make clear the difference between this latest distinction and the ones characterized in the previous sections.

Some philosophers, Quine perhaps being the most eminent, maintain as a general thesis that the only way an entity can persist is by perduring, i.e. by having temporal parts. I shall refer to such philosophers as 'four-dimensional theorists'. What distinguishes the position of the four-dimensional theorist from that of his opponent is, as Quine puts it, that he rejects the point of view inherent in the tenses of our natural language. From that point of view people, and other persisting things, endure and change through time but do not *extend* in time; they extend only in space and their only parts are spatial parts, which likewise endure and change through time but do not extend in time. Thus people and other persisting things are to be sharply distinguished from events or processes, precisely in the respect that unlike the latter, they lack temporal parts. One way of describing the position of the four-dimensional theorist, then, is to say that he denies the existence of a distinct ontological category of persisting *things*, or substances. Thus Quine writes: 'physical objects conceived thus four-dimensionally in space and time are not to be distingushed from events, or in the concrete sense of the term, processes. Each comprises simply the content, however hetero-genous, of some portion of space-time, however disconnected or gerrymandered' (1960:171).

A point that was mentioned in passing before, but now needs more emphasis, is implicit in this passage: one of the features of the four-dimensional scheme is that it entails that the familiar persisting things of our everyday acquaintance are a mere subset of the totality of physical objects, ontologically on a par with the rest, and assigned a favoured position in our language and conceptual scheme only because of interest-relative considerations. Thus not only are there people, there are also temporal parts of people, but not only are there temporal parts of people, there are physical objects of which people are temporal parts: for example, that spatio-temporally discontinuous object of which George Washington is the first spatio-temporal stage and Ronald Reagan the second, or that spatio-temporal discontinuous object of which George Washington is the first spatio-temporal stage and the Post Office Tower the second. In addition there are such objects as that which consists of the first three decades of Washington and the last four decades of Reagan, or this table until midnight yesterday and this pen from midnight today. According to the four-dimensional scheme all these entities are perfectly real, albeit of no interest to anyone but a phi-losopher making a point. But this ontological pluralism is certainly one reason why some philosophers are reluctant to accept the four-dimensional scheme.

The four-dimensional analysis of tensed discourse (see Quine 1960: Section 36) has singular terms standing for times and temporal intervals. Times and temporal intervals are added to ordinary past, present and future objects in one large domain of quantification. This also contains objects' temporal parts (and all arbitrary sums thereof). The temporal parts of an object a are referred to by completing a functor 'a-at- . . .', associated with the entire object a, with a temporal term 't' referring to the corresponding time or temporal interval; equivalently, 'a-at-t' can be thought of as the result of the completion of a functor '. . . -at-t' by the term 'a'. In either case what is denoted is the overlap of a and t. Quine suggests that ascription of a property G to an object a at a time t should be analysed as an ascription of G to the temporal part a-at-t (thus

'Tabby is eating mice at t' becomes 'Tabby at t is eating mice'). Temporal sentences are analysed using a term for the present time, a *later than* predicate and quantification into the argument place for times. Thus 'a is now G' becomes '$G(a$-at-t-now)'; 'a was G' becomes '(for some u) (later(now,u) & $G(a$-at-u)'. Assertions of temporal existence and non-existence are analysed without any special first-level predicate of existence using Russell's theory of descriptions. Thus 'a no longer exists', for example, becomes 'a-at-now does not exist', i.e. there is nothing which is (uniquely) a present temporal part of a.

Arguments for this analysis of tensed discourse are not our present concern, but one, which has been emphasized recently by Lewis (1986:198), is worth noting for the light it throws on the disagreement between the four-dimensional theorist and his opponent. If the four-dimensional analysis is rejected the ascription of dated or tensed properties to objects must be regarded as assertions of *irreducible* relations between objects and times. If Tabby is fat on Monday that is a relation between Tabby and Monday, and if the four-dimensional scheme is rejected it is an irreducible relation between Tabby and Monday. On the four-dimensional scheme it is still, of course, a relation between Tabby and Monday, but it is not an irreducible one: it holds between Tabby and Monday only because the temporal part of Tabby, Tabby-on-Monday, is intrinsically fat. If the four-dimensional scheme is rejected, however, no such intrinsic possessor of the property of fatness can be recognized: Tabby's fatness on Monday must be regarded as an irreducibly relational state of affairs.

So much, for the time being, for what is involved in the dispute between the four-dimensional theorist and his opponent. A philosopher who maintains that persons persist by perduring may then do so either because he thinks that *in general* to persist is to perdure, i.e. because he is a four-dimensional theorist, or because he thinks that there are special reasons for thinking that persons, as opposed to, say, typewriters, must have temporal parts (for the view that some but not all of the entities we ordinarily think of as persisting *things* – as opposed to processes – have temporal parts see Butterfield 1985). On the other hand a philosopher who holds that persons persist by enduring may do so because he is opposed to the four-dimensional scheme in general, or it may be that he thinks that other persisting things can be allowed to have temporal parts, but that there are special reasons for denying that this is true of persons.

The four-dimensional scheme will be examined further in the next chapter, but I have now elaborated it sufficiently for my present purpose, which is to make clear the difference between the third distinction – between the view that persons perdure and the view that persons endure – and the two others already drawn.

That this distinction is not identical with that between the Complex View and the Simple View, as explained above, should be evident. It may be that there are arguments that a Complex theorist should maintain that persons perdure. But if so this is not obvious: the thesis that persons perdure is not a mere *rephrasal* of the Complex View – as is made evident by the number of philosophers who accept the Complex View but reject as self-evidently absurd the thesis that persons perdure (someone who adopts just this position is Shoemaker 1984). On the other hand the opponent of the Complex View, the Simple theorist, does not *need* to deny that persons perdure, for he may hold that the relation between two thing-stages which make them temporal parts of one person is primitive, unanalysable, etc.

It is less obvious, but none the less quite true, that the position one takes on Parfitian Reductionism is, at least in one way, independent of one's view of whether persons perdure or endure. Of course, it is hard to see how a Parfitian Reductionist could deny that persons have temporal parts, for according to his view a person is something like a thunderstorm, a complex series of interrelated events. But such an entity is a paradigm of what has temporal parts. The interesting question, however, is whether someone who rejects Parfitian Reductionism can accept that persons have temporal parts.

The answer to this question is affirmative. In fact, that this is so is implicit in the four-dimensional analysis of tensed discourse given above. According to that analysis the temporal part of *a* at *t*, *a*-at-*t*, possesses a property *G* just in case *a* is *G* at *t*. But then temporal parts of persons are not bundles or collections of mental events, thought of as akin to Humean perceptions, but, like the persons of which they are parts, the *subjects* of mental states. Any brief examination of the literature on personal identity will reveal that this is how the proponents of the view that persons perdure typically think of person-stages. But the point is made most explicitly and vividly by David Lewis, who explains what he means by a person-stage as follows:

A person-stage is a physical object, just as a person is.

(If persons had a ghostly part as well, so would person-stages.) It does many of the same things that a person does: it talks and walks and thinks, it has beliefs and desires, it has a size and shape and location. It even has a temporal duration. But only a brief one, for it does not last long. (We can pass over the question how long it can last before it is a segment rather than a stage, for that question raises no objection of principle.) It begins to exist abruptly, and it abruptly ceases to exist soon after. Hence a stage cannot do everything that a person can do, for it cannot do these things that a person does over a longish interval.

(1983:76)

In fact, on this account, it looks as if it might be hard to deny that person-stages *are* persons. For they walk and talk and think, and have beliefs and desires. What more could one ask? But whatever may be right or wrong about this proposal, it is clear (and something to which Lewis himself draws attention) that such a person-stage existing on its own, and not as a proper part of a larger aggregate of person-stages, will be a person. So person-stages cannot be thought of as more basic entities than persons, out of which persons can be 'logically constructed' in the way in which nations can be 'logically constructed' out of people, as required by Parfitian Reductionism. For the existence of person-stages *logically entails* the existence of persons. Lewis again could not be clearer on the point:

When I say that persons are maximal R-interrelated aggregates of person-stages I do *not* claim to be reducing 'constructs' to 'more basic' entities. . . . Similarly, I think it is an informative necessary truth that trains are maximal aggregates of cars interrelated by the ancestral of the relation of being coupled together (count the locomotive as a special kind of car). But I do not think of this as a reduction to the basic. Whatever 'more basic' is supposed to mean I don't think it means 'smaller'.

(1983:177)

(To prevent misunderstanding the following should be noted at this point. Even though, if one accepts that persons have temporal parts one is not committed to *Parfitian* Reductionism, one is, of course, committed to reductionism or at least, reductivism, with a small 'r', as that was characterized above. For if persons perdure facts about persons will obtain in virtue of facts about person-stages and their interrelations. On the account given above of the notions of reductionism and reductivism, then, in this case statements about person-stages will constitute a 'reductive' class relative to the class of statements about persons (*qua* the given class). But that this is so does not entail that person-stages are a class of entities conceptually or ontologically independent of persons, which is what Lewis is denying that he is committed to. So what is illustrated here is merely, once again, the point made above: that even though many reductionist theses do take the form of offering translation of discourse about *A*'s into discourse in which neither *A*'s nor any entities conceptually or ontologically dependent on *A*'s are referred to or quantified over, the general notion of reductionism does not require such a restriction on the 'given' class of statements.)

5.8 Conclusion

To sum up, then, the latter part of this discussion: we have seen that acceptance of the Complex View of personal identity is consistent with several substantially distinct positions: (1) One may be a Complex theorist whilst rejecting *both* Parfitian Reductionism *and* the thesis that persons perdure – this is Shoemaker's position; (2) One may be a Complex theorist and accept that persons perdure but still reject Parfitian Reductionism – this is Lewis's position; and finally, (3), like Parfit himself one can accept all three theses.

In what follows it will be important to keep this variety of views in mind.

CHAPTER 6
Identity and Determinacy

6.1 Introduction

In this chapter I wish to look more closely at the Determinacy Thesis concerning personal identity introduced in Chapter 1. Recently discussions of personal identity have come to be focused more and more on this thesis, with proponents of the Simple View stoutly defending it, and proponents of the Complex View denying it.

I shall also devote part of this chapter to a further look at the thesis that persons perdure. At first sight it might seem as if this is a topic that has little connection with the debate over the Determinacy Thesis. But we shall see that this appearance is illusory.

6.2 The determinacy thesis

When one thinks of some of the puzzle cases described in the literature on personal identity it is tempting to say that to ask whether it is right or wrong to identify the original person with the later candidate for identity with him that the case presents is to ask an empty question. That is, the statement of identity in question is neither true nor false because of the vagueness inherent in our concept of personal identity, and consequently it is neither true nor false that the original person in the case still exists after the various events in it have occurred. According to the Determinacy Thesis such cases, in which statements of personal identity over time would be indeterminate in truth-value, are impossible. Whatever happens, either I will exist tomorrow or I will not; whatever happens, of each of the people in existence tomorrow it will be definitely true that he is identical with me, or definitely true that he is not. Thus, according to the Determinacy Thesis, if it is true (a) that there is just one person in place *p* at time *t* and true (b) that there is just one person in place *p'* at time *t'* then either it will be definitely true that the person in *p* at *t* is identical with the person in *p'* at *t'*, or this will be definitely false. The statement of identity in question will not be indeterminate in truth-value, even if no one is able to say what its truth-value is.

The opponent of the Determinacy Thesis, on the other hand, holds that such 'borderline cases' of personal identity can occur, i.e. are conceivable, whether or not they actually do occur. And at first sight this seems an entirely reasonable thing to say. As it is often said, the concepts we have serve our practical needs in the situations in which we find ourselves, but there is no reason to suppose that they must have a determinate application in every bizarre situation that philosophic ingenuity can conceive. With regard to such situations the only sensible policy is Wittgenstein's: 'say what you like so long as you are clear about the facts'.

It is uncontroversial that it is possible to construct puzzle cases about the identity of entities other than persons about which this would be the correct thing to say. Events can be imagined, indeed events sometimes occur, which in Bernard Williams's nice phrase 'cast a conceptual shadow' over the identity of a material object. One such case is Shoemaker's case, of the four centuries old bridge of Santa Trinita in Florence (see Chapter 1). A similar case described by Parfit (1984:213) shows how a conceptual shadow might easily come to be cast over the identity of a club. Suppose that a certain club exists for, say, five years, holding regular meetings. The meetings then cease. A year later, some of the members of this club form a club with the same name and the same rules, which then continues to exist for a further twenty-five years. We ask: 'Have these people reconvened the very same club? Or have they merely started up another club, which is exactly similar?' There might be an answer to this question. The original club might have had a rule explaining how, after such a period of non-existence, it could be reconvened. Or it might have had a rule preventing this. But suppose that there is no such rule, and no legal facts supporting either answer to our question. And suppose that the people involved would be unwilling to give it an answer, and yet we still ask: 'Is this club the same as the earlier one?'

It seems clear that in cases like these to persist in arguing about the correct answers to such questions would be absurd. Things can be said in favour of the identity claims and things can be said against them, but there are no right or wrong answers. Rather we have borderline cases of identity over time, just as we can have a border-line case of baldness or tallness or fatness. That is, it is definitely true (a) that there is just one bridge (club) in a certain location p at a time t, definitely true (b) that there is just one bridge (club) in a certain location p' at a time t', but neither true nor false that the bridge (club) in p at t is the bridge (club) in p' at t'.

But can we also accept that cases are conceivable in which a conceptual shadow would be cast over the identity of a person? In particular, can I suppose that in certain circumstances, e.g. after an only partially successful brain transplant of the Brown/Brownson variety, it would be indeterminate whether I still existed and if so with whom I was then identical? And is it imaginable that there might be circumstances in which the only sensible thing for me (?) to do if I was concerned with this question would be to seek a decision from the law courts about the matter? The proponents of the Determinacy Thesis claim that this makes no sense. Just because personal identity over time is something which can be known from a first-person viewpoint, the possibility of borderline cases must be rejected. In this respect, at least, they argue, personal identity must be radically different from the identity of other things.

6.3 Types of indeterminacy

In fact, in thinking about the Determinacy Thesis there are two types of case to consider.

One is the type illustrated by the only partially successful brain transplant. In this type of case the people whose identity is in question are linked by *some* of the relations of physical and psychological continuity which typically link successive stages of a single person's life, but, in consequence of some event, a discontinuity has been introduced which is not present in ordinary cases. This is the type of case to which Shoemaker's example of the bridge and Parfit's example of the club provide non-personal analogues.

But there is another type of case which must also be taken into account, illustrated by the example of Methuselah (Lewis 1976).

In this case, between successive stages of a life there are all the normal psychological and physical connections, but because the life is so long there are no psychological connections between its early and late stages. Methuselah, aged 900, shares none of the ambitions or interests of Methuselah aged 24, has no memories at all of his activities and none of his character traits. Of course, one may not wish to accept that this is a case in which personal identity is anywhere indeterminate, for one may wish to say that, in virtue of the physical and psychological *continuity* which links these two stages of his life, Methusalah aged 900 *is* (determinately) the same person as Methuselah aged 24.

But one may also be tempted to say, as Lewis does, that 'for Methuselah . . . the fading out of personal identity looms large as a fact of life. It is incumbent on us [i.e. as philosophical analysts] to make it literally true that he will be a different person after one and one half centuries or so' (1976:66).

If Lewis is right about this case there will be no one identifiable statement of identity of which it will be correct to say that *it* is neither true nor false. But there will be a *series* of statements about identity: (1) 'Methuselah aged 1 = Methuselah aged 2' (2) 'Methuselah aged 2 = Methuselah aged 3' . . . (899) 'Methuselah aged 899 = Methuselah aged 900' – not all of which can be true, given the transitivity of identity, but no one of which can be definitely false. Thus, though no one of these statements can be identified as neither true nor false, one or more of them *must* be.

A non-personal analogue of the Methuselah case (on Lewis's interpretation of it), is provided then neither by Shoemaker's example of the bridge nor by Parfit's example of the club.

But consider a case of the following sort. An artefact of one type, say a table, is very gradually transformed into an artefact of a different type, say a chair. Each small change in the transformation is *so* small as to make it seem utterly implausible to regard it as destroying identity. Yet after the whole process is over it is very plausible to say that there is no single artefact which has survived throughout the whole series of changes. (For otherwise what kind of (gradual) Protean change *could* we disallow?) Hence, at some point in the transformation, identity must have failed to have been preserved, even though there is no one of the small changes which can be regarded as *destroying* identity. Consequently, if we refer to the artefact present before any change as '*A*', the artefact present after the first change as '*B*' and so on, then, just as in the Methuselah case, there will be a series of identity statements (1) '*A* = B', (2)

'*B* = *C*' . . . no one of which is definitely false, but not all of which
are definitely true. One at least of these statements must thus be
indeterminate in truth-value.

This, then, is one non-personal analogue of the Methuselah case,
construed as Lewis wishes to construe it. Another is perhaps provided by the history of a nation which undergoes no major dis-
ruptions or discontinuities, but gradually evolves and changes over a
thousand years or so, so that language, culture, customs, etc.,
though changing only gradually, are radically different at the end of
the period.

6.4 Indeterminacy as semantic indecision

Let us now try to get clearer about the nature of the indeterminacy
which (uncontroversially) is possible for statements of identity
about entities other than persons.

Consider the following case given by Shoemaker (in Shoemaker
and Swinburne 1984:146). A structure consists of two halls, Alpha
Hall and Beta Hall, linked by a rather flimsy walkway. Smith is
lecturing in Alpha Hall, Jones is lecturing in Beta Hall. The nature
of the structure is such that the identity statement 'The building
Smith is lecturing in is the building Jones is lecturing in' is neither
true nor false, because it is indeterminate whether Alpha Hall and
Beta Hall count as two distinct buildings or merely as two parts of
one and the same building.

In this case, I think, it is absolutely clear what is going on. The
term 'building' is vague in a way that makes it indeterminate
whether it applies to the whole structure or just to the two halls.
Consequently, it is indeterminate what 'the building in which Smith
is lecturing' denotes: Alpha Hall or the entire structure. The same is
true *mutatis mutandis* of 'the building in which Jones is lecturing'.
For each of these definite descriptions there are two candidates for
what it denotes, each of which *would* be denoted by it on a possible
sharpening of the meaning of the term 'building'. Since both sharpenings are possible, however, neither candidate is *presently*
determinately denoted by the description and so the identity statement in question is neither true nor false.

Thus the source of the indeterminacy is *semantic indecision*: perhaps for good reason or perhaps for no good reason we have simply

not made the term 'building' precise enough to give it a determinate application in a case such as this, and the vagueness of the general term, by infecting definite descriptions containing it, has the consequence that statements of identity employing them may be indeterminate in truth-value (cf. Quine 1985).

6.5 Indeterminacy and identity over time

So much is obvious. But when one turns to the possibility of indeterminacy in statements of identity *over time*, matters stand differently, and in fact there has been a great deal of recent controversy about how such indeterminacy is best explained.

To see what the issues are here, let us look more closely at Parfit's example of the club, in which the facts render the identity statement 'the club existing earlier is the club existing later' indeterminate in truth-value.

Now applying the thesis that such indeterminacy must be due to semantic indecision we get the following account of the case. The source of the indeterminacy is that the terms 'the earlier club' and 'the later club' do not have determinate denotations. Let us fix on the former term. Because our notion of a 'club' is imprecise there are two candidates for the denotation of this term, each of which would count as a club on some, but not all, acceptable sharpenings of the imprecise expression 'club'. One of these candidates is an entity which lasts a mere five years, and ceases to exist when the members of the earlier club cease to hold regular meetings. Another is an entity which exists throughout those five years, and also exists throughout the twenty-five year period after the members of the original group get together again at the end of the period of inactivity. This latter entity is also a candidate for being the denotation of the description 'the later club', but there is another entity which is a candidate for this, too, which comes into existence only after the period of inactivity and exists only for twenty-five years. Since these descriptions are thus indeterminate in denotation it is not puzzling that the identity statement 'the earlier club is the later club', in which they occur, is indeterminate in truth-value.

This is the explanation of the indeterminacy involved in Parfit's example of the club which is parallel to the obviously correct explanation of the indeterminacy involved in Shoemaker's example of

Alpha Hall and Beta Hall. But in this application, it has seemed to many philosophers, the explanation is not obviously correct. For it is not obviously correct that there *are* the two candidates for the denotation of 'the earlier club' that the explanation implies. It was undeniable that both Alpha Hall and the entire structure consisting of Alpha Hall, Beta Hall and the walkway existed, because one could specify quite straightforwardly what their relation was: Alpha Hall was simply a *part* of the entire structure, of which Beta Hall and the walkway were two other parts. But unless one thinks of persisting entities like clubs as having temporal parts one cannot specify in the same way the relationship between the two possible candidates for the denotation of the description 'the earlier club' whose existence the explanation just given implies. Of course, to a four-dimensional theorist the existence of these two candidates is a total triviality. But many philosophers reject the four-dimensional framework and for them the difficulty involved in believing in the existence of the relevant rival candidates must, I suggest, be a real one, and a reason for resisting the view that where there is indeterminacy in statements of identity over time, this must be seen as arising from semantic indecision. Even though this is the obviously correct way to explain indeterminacy in statements of synchronic identity, when diachronic identity is at issue matters are less clear.

6.6 Fuzzy objects

In fact there is an alternative account which some philosophers have recently defended. According to this account (most clearly defended by John Broome 1984) the source of the indeterminacy in such a case as this is not semantic indecision. Each of the descriptions 'the earlier club' and 'the later club' has a determinate denotation, but the objects determinately denoted by these descriptions are *vague* objects with *fuzzy boundaries*. The reason why the identity statement 'the earlier club is the later club' is neither true nor false is because the relationship which obtains between the earlier club and the later club is neither identity nor non-identity, but the intermediate relation of *indefinite identity*, which can obtain between one vague object and another.

Now, as I have said, this alternative account of the indeterminacy in Parfit's example of the club ought to be at least tempting to a philosopher who is reluctant to accept the four-dimensional theorist's very extensive ontological commitments (and perhaps it ought to be even more tempting to him as an account of the indeterminacy involved in Shoemaker's analogous case of the reconstructed bridge), but nevertheless, I think, it must be rejected.

The principal objections to it are two.

First, there is an argument against it put forward, independently, by Gareth Evans (1978) and Nathan Salmon (1981: 244ff.).

Informally presented, the basic argument is a *reductio ad absurdum*. Let '*a*' and '*b*' be two terms, such that the identity statement '*a* = b' is indeterminate in truth-value, not however because it is indeterminate what (one or both of) these terms denote, but because each determinately denotes a vague object. Then it must be a fact about the vague object *a*, i.e. a property of the vague object *a*, that it is indeterminate whether it is identical with the vague object *b*. But, of course, the vague object *b*, like everything else, is determinately self-identical, and so does not possess this property. Hence since *b* lacks a property *a* possesses, by Leibniz's Law (the principle that if *a* is identical with *b* everything true of *a* must be true of *b*), they must be distinct. Consequently the identity statement '*a* = b' cannot be merely indeterminate in truth-value, but must actually be *false*.

Asked to formulate an account of indefinite identity, conceived as a relation obtaining between objects with fuzzy boundaries, I think that one's first thought would be something like this: '*a* = b' is definitely true just in case any predicate definitely true of *a* is definitely true of *b*, while '*a* = b' is definitely false just in case there is some predicate definitely true of *a* whose negation is definitely true of *b*. If '*a* = b' is indeterminate in truth-value, then, because the relation of indefinite identity obtains between the vague objects *a* and *b*, there will be no predicate definitely true of *a* whose negation is definitely true of *b*, but it will not be the case that any predicate definitely true of *a* will also be definitely true of *b*; rather there will be predicates definitely true of *a* which are neither true nor false of *b*.

What the Evans–Salmon argument demonstrates is that indefinite identity, so conceived, can have no application; in the case in which '*a* = b' is indeterminate in truth-value (if this is not merely due to a vagueness in the *expressions* '*a*' and '*b*'), just as in the case in which it is definitely false, there will be a predicate 'it is indeterminate whether $x = b$' definitely true of a, whose negation is definitely true of b.

The other objection to the idea that indeterminacy in statements of identity over time may be explained by appeal to the idea that there are vague objects is simply that far from clarifying matters it makes things even more obscure.

To see this, let us follow through the treatment of Parfit's example of the club which the 'vague object' conception of indeterminate identity dictates.

If 'the earlier club is identical with the later club' is indeterminate in truth-value, then the statement 'the earlier club lasted for at most five years' will also be indeterminate in truth-value. Hence if the 'vague object' proposal is correct, the predicate 'lasted for at most five years' will be neither determinately true nor determinately false of the vague object determinately denoted by the description 'the earlier club' (for if the identity were *true* that predicate would be false of the earlier club, and if it were *false* that predicate would be true of the earlier club). Similarly, the predicate 'lasted for at least twenty-five years' will be neither determinately true nor determinately false of the earlier club (for if the identity were true that predicate would be true of it, and if the identity were false it would be false of it). On the other hand, the predicate 'lasted for at most five years or lasted for at least twenty-five years' must be determinately true of the earlier club (for the object determinately denoted by 'the earlier club', on the 'vague object' proposal, has certainly lasted for at least five years, and there is no other longer-lived entity, apart from the later club – which has lasted for at least twenty-five years – with which it might be identical, so its lifespan must either be a maximum of five, or a minimum of twenty-five years). The earlier club, then, on the 'vague object' proposal, must be an object which determinately satisfies the predicate 'lasted for at most five years or lasted for at least twenty-five years' but neither determinately satisfies the predicate 'lasted for at most five years' nor determinately satisfies the predicate 'lasted for at least twenty-five years'. But I do not understand how there can be such an object.

My difficulty is not that I do not understand how an object can determinately satisfy a disjunctive predicate while determinately satisfying neither disjunct. I have no difficulty with the idea of an object which is determinately either orange or red, but neither determinately orange nor determinately red. Similarly, I have no difficulty with the idea of a person who is determinately either a child or a young man, but neither determinately a child nor determinately a young man. But what we have been led to by applying the 'vague object' proposal to Parfit's example of the reconvened club is different from this: it is more akin to the idea of a person who is determinately either a child or a senior citizen but is neither determinately a child nor determinately a senior citizen – and *is* determinately neither a young man nor a middle-aged man (still more akin, of course, is the idea of a person who *at death* is determinately either a child or senior citizen, but is neither determinately a child nor determinately a senior citizen and is determinately neither a young man nor a middle-aged man). And this is an idea which I do *not* understand.

I conclude that the only account of indeterminacy in statements of identity which makes sense is that according to which such indeterminacy is a consequence of semantic indecision. For the idea of objects which are *themselves* vague or fuzzy in their boundaries is one we can do nothing with. So whatever might be thought to be the implausibility of the ontological commitments involved in regarding indeterminacy in statements of diachronic identity as due to semantic indecision, they must none the less be accepted as necessary commitments of the only coherent account of such indeterminacy available to us.

With this point established we can now take a closer look at the two types of possible borderline cases of personal identity distinguished above.

6.7 Indeterminacy and brain transplants

Consider first the case of the only partially successful brain transplant. Let us follow Shoemaker and call the brain donor 'Brown', the body donor 'Robinson' and the recipient 'Brownson'. Then if we wish to say that the identity statements, 'Brownson = Brown' and 'Brownson = Robinson' are indeterminate in truth-value, and if we wish to explain this indeterminacy as arising from semantic indecision, we are committed to the existence of at least the following four entities, each of which is a borderline case of personhood, i.e. would be a person under at least one acceptable sharpening of the meaning of the term 'person': (1) an entity which is located where Brown is located before the brain transplant but does not exist thereafter, (2) an entity which is located where Brown is located before the brain transplant and where Brownson is located thereafter, (3) an entity which is located where Robinson is located before the brain transplant but does not exist thereafter, (4) an entity which is located where Robinson is located before the brain transplant and where Brownson is located thereafter. In addition, if it is said that another possibility left open by the facts is that *neither* Brown *nor* Robinson is Brownson we must also acknowledge the existence of a fifth entity which does not exist before the brain transplant but is located where Brownson is located thereafter.

Of these entities (1) and (2) are candidates for the denotation of 'Brown', (3) and (4) are candidates for the denotation of 'Robinson' and (2) and (4) (and the fifth entity, if its existence is acknowledged) are candidates for the denotation of 'Brownson', i.e. each would be the denotation of the relevant name on an acceptable sharpening of the meaning of 'person', and the consequent elimination of the indeterminacy in the description fixing its denotation.

Thus 'Brown', uttered before the brain transplant is an expression without determinate denotation, so is 'the man over there' (said pointing to Brown), so is 'you' (said speaking to Brown), and so is 'I' said *by* Brown. This last point is the most important. If it is accepted that it is indeterminate whether Brownson is Brown in this case, and if the indeterminacy is explained as due to semantic indecision, then it must be accepted that an utterance of 'I' before the transplant by the person then in Brown's shoes will be without a determinate denotation. It will be definitely true, that is, that there is just one person who is located where Brown is located (because this will be true under all sharpenings of the word 'person'), and definitely true that the person located where Brown is located is saying 'I' (because this will also be true under all sharpenings), but there will be no one of whom it is definitely true that *he* is the denotation of the 'I'-utterance in question.

Of course, this conclusion goes against deeply engrained intuitions that we all have about the guaranteed denotation of 'I'. For all I know, I might be in Brown's situation myself. The techniques of brain-transplantation the case involves may be not science-fictional, but merely future, and it might be that I will be subject to such a brain transplant in twenty-five years' time. If so my present utterances of 'I' are without a determinate denotation; that is, there is more than one object which, consistently with all the facts (semantic and non-semantic) *could* be their denotation.

6.8 Indeterminacy and Methuselah

Let us now look more closely at David Lewis's case of Methuselah.

Let us suppose that Methuselah (*qua* spatio-temporally continuous living organism) is located in a place L, and each year a dubbing takes place in which the person located in L is given a name. In the first year this name is '$M1$', in the second '$M2$', and so on up to '$M900$'. Now on Lewis's view of the Methuselah case, on which it is analogous to the case of the gradually transformed artefact, '$M1$ = $M900$' is definitely false, but no one of the statements '$M1$ = $M2$', '$M2$ = $M3$', . . . '$M899$ = $M900$' is definitely false, because the changes in Methuselah's psychological make-up are only gradual. But these statements cannot all be definitely true, so at least one must be indeterminate in truth-value.

Our first conclusion about the Methuselah case, then, must be that at least one of the names '$M1$', . . ., '$M900$' must be indeterminate in denotation, and so, in at least one of the years 1 to 900 there must be present in L two distinct objects, each of which is a person under at least one acceptable sharpening of the vague sortal term 'person'.

So far this conclusion is in line with what was said about the Brown/Brownson brain-transplant case in the last section. But in the case of Methuselah we can go further.

Given the transitivity of identity, we cannot accept that each of the series of identity claims '$M1$ = $M2$' . . . is definitely true. But there is a series of weaker claims, entailed by these, which we *can*, and in this case surely must, accept, namely, the series of claims asserting of each pair of successive years in the life of Methuselah that a single person is located in L in both these years, i.e. the series of claims (1) 'There is a single person in L both in year 1 and in year 2', (2) 'There is a single person in L both in year 2 and year 3', . . . (899) 'There is a single person in L both in year 899 and year 900'. But if these claims are all definitely true, and it is also definitely true that *no* single person is located in L both in year 1 and in year 900, it follows that it is definitely true that at some moment or other during the lifespan of Methuselah two *people* (i.e. not merely two borderline cases of personhood) are simultaneously present in *L*. (For there is a person in place *L* in year 1. Now suppose that this person does not cease to exist until after year 899, then in year 899 both it and a person who by claim (899) exists both in year 899 and year 900 are simultaneously present in *L*. The same argument applies whenever, after year 1, we suppose the person we start out with to cease to exist.)

Thus if we regard the case of Methuselah as Lewis proposes that we should, and if we regard the consequent indeterminacy as arising from semantic indecision, we are committed to regarding the case, not merely as one in which there is a multiplicity of borderline candidates for personhood, but also as one in which, at some time or other, two entities which *definitely* qualify as persons are located in the same place, are thinking the same thoughts, etc. In other words, so understood, the case must be regarded as an instance of the Multiple Occupancy Thesis introduced in Chapter 1.

6.9 The determinacy thesis and personal perdurance

By now it should be perfectly evident why I claimed, at the beginning of this chapter, that the two topics introduced there were related.

The key point is that the only way to make comprehensible the idea that statements of identity can be indeterminate in truth-value is by appeal to the idea of semantic indecision. But in order to apply this idea to the explanation of indeterminacy in statements of identity over time one has to acknowledge ontological commitments which fit more comfortably with the four-dimensional theorist's framework than with its rejection. This is true not only when the indeterminate statements of diachronic identity in question are concerned with entities other than persons, but also, and especially, when they are statements of diachronic personal identity.

To bring this last point home consider again the Brown/ Brownson case. If it is indeterminate whether Brownson is Brown then, as we saw in section 6.7, there must be two candidates for the denotation of 'Brown': one which survives the brain transplant and one which does not. Now if the identity statements 'Brown is Brownson' and 'Robinson is Brownson' are indeterminate in truth-value, one possible way of making our language more precise would render the former statement true and the latter false, and another possible way of making our language precise would make the latter statement true and the former false. Suppose that, in fact, the language develops in this second way. Then, of the two entities which were previously rival candidates for the denotation of 'Brown', the one which does *not* survive the brain transplant is now determinately describable as a person, whilst the one which does survive the brain transplant is an entity it is now *definitely incorrect* to describe as a person, but which is spatially coincident with the person Brown during his lifetime and with the person Brownson (= Robinson) subsequently. But that the speakers of this more precise version of English must acknowledge the existence of such an entity even if they do not think of persons as four-dimensional perdurers seems absurd, as absurd as my having to acknowledge the existence of an entity which is spatially coincident with me throughout my lifetime and spatially coincident with my son subsequently, but is not merely a four-dimensional summation of some of my temporal parts and some of my son's. Yet it is this apparent absurdity to which the opponent of the thesis that persons perdure is committed if he accepts the possibility of indeterminate cases of diachronic personal identity structurally equivalent to the Brown/Brownson case.

Other things being equal, then, it seems plain that, given the ontological commitments he must take on board, an opponent of the Determinacy Thesis concerning personal identity has a strong reason for regarding persons as four-dimensional perdurers. And since any Complex theorist is bound to deny the Determinacy Thesis, the previous sentence remains true if we replace 'opponent of the Determinacy Thesis' by 'Complex theorist'. This is not, of course, to say that the Complex theorist is *logically committed* to acceptance of the four-dimensional framework, but only that, unless he has conclusive arguments against it, acceptance of it would seem to suit his philosophical purposes far better than rejection.

The question naturally arises then whether there are, in fact, any conclusive arguments against the four-dimensional conception of persons as perdurers. I shall discuss four candidates.

6.10 Objections to personal perdurance

First, it is sometimes said that persons and suchlike persistents just *are* things that can exist in their entirety throughout an interval of

time. Whenever a person is present he is *wholly* present. For his only
parts are spatial parts. But this seems more like an outright denial of
the thesis that persons are four-dimensional perdurers than an argument against it. Certainly, given the motive that we have seen he has
for regarding persons as perdurers it ought to leave the Complex
theorist unmoved.

A second objection to the thesis that persons perdure is that it
involves an unnecessary ontological commitment. Apparent references to person-stages can always be paraphrased away in favour of
talk of the tensed properties of genuine, i.e. enduring, persons. So
we do not *need* to posit the existence of person-stages, and considerations of ontological economy dictate that we do not. There are two
replies to this objection. First, it is not clear why it should be considered more of an economy in ontology to deny the existence of person-stages and to posit the existence of enduring persons than to
posit the existence of person-stages and summations thereof and to
deny the existence of enduring persons. For, of course, to maintain
that persons perdure is not to say that *in addition* to our familiar
enduring persons there are person-stages and summations thereof; it
is to say that there are *only* person-stages and summations thereof.
And if the thought is that the objectionable feature of the ontology
of the proponent of personal perduring is his acknowledgement of
the existence as *bona fide* entities of summations of person-stages
whose parts belong to *different* persons, then we have seen that an
ontological commitment to entities with just such a spatio-temporal
spread must also be part of the Complex theorist's position, given
that he is committed to the possibility of borderline cases of personal
identity over time. Second, arguments to the effect that A's do not
exist since talk about A's is paraphraseable as talk about B's are
anyway invalid. Talk about nations, to refer to an example from the
last chapter, is paraphraseable as talk about persons and their relationships (setting aside the question whether a finite translation is
possible), but this hardly shows that nations do not exist. Sometimes
it is said that the availability of such paraphrases shows that facts
about A's are nothing 'over and above' facts about B's. But the
proponent of personal perduring need not claim that facts about
person-stages are facts over and above facts about persons. After
all, unless he regards it as a contingent fact that persons have stages,
which would be a very curious view, he must must accept that the
existence of person-stages is *entailed* by the existence of persons. But

if so he can hardly regard person-stages as *additional* entities over and above persons.

A third objection to the thesis that persons perdure is that it is inconsistent with our ordinary moral thinking. We ordinarily think that persons can be held responsible for their past misdeeds. But for a person to be held responsible for a past action, he must be the very same person as performed that past action (this was a central element, of course, in Locke's conception of 'person' as a forensic term). That is, responsibility presupposes that a person is an *enduring* entity persisting through change. But this is what the thesis denies. So if the thesis is correct, no one can be held responsible for anything. A vigorous statement of this argument is given by D.H. Mellor (1981:106). I quote:

> The first prerequisite for moral and legal responsibility is identity through time. Nothing and no one can be held responsible for an earlier action unless he, she or it is identical with whoever or whatever did that earlier action. . . . Now whatever identity through time may call for elsewhere, here it evidently requires the self-same entity to be wholly present both when the deed was done and later when being held accountable for it . . .

But the difficulty with this argument is that it assumes what it sets out to prove. Commonsensically the proposition that the first pre-requisite for moral and legal responsibility is identity through time is correct. But to endorse it, one does not need to deny that persons perdure. For all this proposition says is that a man can only be punished for what *he himself* – not someone else – did. And the proponent of personal perduring can agree with *that*. It is just that, in his view, for a person to have done anything in the past there had to be a past stage of him which did the deed. But the past stage is not *someone else*. The same response serves as an answer to Mellor's second premiss. Certainly no one can be held responsible for a past action unless he is identical with its doer. But to accept that persons perdure is not to deny that persons are identical over time; it is simply to say what it *is* for them to be identical over time.

The fourth objection to the thesis that persons perdure needs more extensive discussion.

This objection, which a variety of philosophers have recently brought to bear against the four-dimensional framework (e.g.,

Thompson 1983, Wiggins 1980, and Kripke unpublished), rests on an appeal to Leibniz's Law. Applied to persons (it can be equally well, and often is, applied to other persisting things) it asserts that persons have different properties, in particular, different modal properties, from the summations of person-stages with which the proponent of personal perduring identifies them, and so, by Leibniz's Law, this identification must be mistaken. As David Wiggins states the argument: 'Anything that is part of a Lesniewskian sum is necessarily part of it. But no person or normal material object is *necessarily* in the total state that will correspond to the person- or object-moment postulated by the theory under discussion' (1980:168). To elaborate a little: I might have died when I was 5 years old. But that maximal summation of person-stages related pairwise by personal unity which, according to the thesis that persons perdure, *is* me, and has a temporal extent of at least 36 years, could not have had a temporal extent of a mere 5 years. So I cannot be such a summation of temporal parts.

Evidently, the premises of this argument are undeniable, so how is the proponent of personal perduring to reply to it? Let us first set out the argument more formally (in what follows 'A' abbreviates 'the summation of person-stages which is me if I perdure'):

(1) I could have had a temporal extent of only 5 years.
(2) It is not true that *A* could have had a temporal extent of only 5 years.

So

(3) I am not identical with *A*.

Here (1) is a *de re* modal assertion saying that I possess a certain modal property (technically expressed, the pronoun 'I' has wide scope relative to the modal operator), and (2) is the denial of a *de re* modal assertion saying that *A* possesses a certain modal property. So there is no hope of faulting the argument by suggesting that 'I' and '*A*' alter their denotations between the premises and the conclusion (e.g., by suggesting that in the premises they stand for their Fregean senses). But one can still reply to the argument by denying that the modal *predicate* stands for the same property in its two occurrences. For one can suggest that the denotation of a modal predicate is *inconstant*, i.e. is dependent on the linguistic context in which it occurs, and, in particular, on the meaning of the singular term to which it is attached. And one can maintain that the difference in meaning between 'I' and '*A*' is sufficient to determine that different properties are denoted by modal predicates when attached to singular terms of these different kinds.

6.11 Inconstancy in modal predication

This may seem a wholly *ad hoc*, and in consequence quite unconvincing response to the fourth objection to the thesis that persons are perdurers. But in fact it is not *ad hoc* at all, for the thesis that the denotation of a modal predicate is inconstant in the way postulated is one which there is good independent reason for accepting. For the alternative to accepting it is to accept the highly implausible proposition that *purely material entities, like statues and lumps of clay, of admittedly identical material constitution at all times may none the less be distinct, though distinguished only by modal, dispositional or counterfactual properties*.

Any one of a number of examples from the fast-growing literature on contingent identity can be used to illustrate this point. But one of the earliest and best is provided by Allan Gibbard. Gibbard writes:

> a clay statue ordinarily begins to exist after its piece of clay does. In such cases, it seems reasonable to say, the statue is a temporal segment of the piece of clay – a segment which extends for the period of time during which the piece of clay keeps a particular statuesque shape. Here, then, is a systematic account of the relation between a statue and its piece of clay. By that account, however, there will be cases in which a clay statue is identical with its piece of clay. For, in some cases, the very temporal segment of the piece of clay which constitutes the statue exists for the entire life of the piece of clay. In such a case, the segment is that piece of clay in its entire extent: the statue and the piece of clay are identical.
>
> (1975:192)

Gibbard goes on to employ the term 'Goliath' to designate a certain statue, and the term 'Lumpl' to designate the clay out of which (as we might ordinarily say) Goliath is composed. We are asked to imagine that Goliath and Lumpl coincide in their spatio-temporal extent. If we follow Gibbard, then, we must say that they are identical. But it will be true of the piece of clay Lumpl that it might never have had the shape possessed by both it and Goliath or that it might have been squeezed into a ball and not destroyed. These things cannot be true of the statue Goliath. Given the identity of Goliath and Lumpl, Leibniz's Law then forces us to conclude that the modal predicate 'might have been squeezed into a ball and not destroyed' cannot denote the same property in the *true* proposition 'Lumpl might have been squeezed into a ball and not destroyed' and the *false* proposition 'Goliath might have been squeezed into a ball and not destroyed'. Hence it cannot be generally true that the denotation of a modal predicate is independent of the linguistic context in which it occurs – or else it must be allowed, *pace* Gibbard, that entities like Goliath and Lumpl, of admittedly identical material constitution at all times, may none the less be distinct.

As I said, Gibbard's example is just one of a variety which would have served to make this point. Another is provided by Denis Robinson (1982:317–41). He first draws attention to the possibility of a cloak consisting of a single piece of cloth and a button. He goes on: 'If the button falls in the fire and is consumed, people will then say: this cloak has no button.' Then he imagines a cloak like the first except that it never has a button (due, say, to a mishap on the production line). It is identical with the piece of cloth constituting it, but unlike the cloth, might have had a button as a part.

These examples and the point they illustrate are anticipated by David Lewis's famous paper (1971). As a materialist who accepts a temporal part metaphysic but wants to allow for the possibility of bodily interchange of the type imagined in the literature on personal identity, Lewis is forced to conclude that an ordinary person who occupies a single body throughout his life, though identical with that body, is only *contingently* identical with it. To make sense of this he revises his Counterpart Theory by introducing a variety of counterpart relations. Contingent identity then makes sense, for 'I and my body are such that we might not have been identical' now translates into Counterpart Theory as 'There is a possible world W, a unique personal counterpart X in W of me, and a unique bodily counterpart Y in W of my body, such that X and Y are not identical.'

The details of Lewis's Counterpart Theory and of its revision in his 1971 paper are not our concern, but the point to note is that it implies the inconstancy of denotation of such modal predicates as 'might have been a disembodied spirit'. For example, in the sentence 'I might have been a disembodied spirit' it denotes the property a thing has if it has a disembodied spirit as a *personal* counterpart, but in the sentence 'My body might have been a disembodied spirit' it denotes the property a thing has if it has a disembodied spirit as a *bodily* counterpart, and these, according to Lewis's theory, are distinct properties.

Thus Lewis's revision of Counterpart Theory is a way of putting flesh on the bare bones of the idea that modal predicates can denote different properties in different contexts. But I want to stress (as Lewis himself emphasizes in his latest book (1984)) that it is only to the skeletal idea and not to Counterpart Theory that one is committed if one maintains that persons perdure (or merely maintains that purely material entities of identical material constitution at all times cannot be distinct).

Perhaps it will suffice to drive this point home if I make the following comparison. Consider Quine's old example 'Giorgione was so-called because of his size' (1961). Clearly, what one must say of the predicate 'was so-called because of his size' is that its denotation when attached to a singular term is determined by the singular term to which it is attached, so that it stands for the property 'being called "Giorgione" because of his size' when attached to 'Giorgione' and the property 'being called "Barbarelli" because of his size' when attached to 'Barbarelli'. The view of modal predicates to which I am suggesting that the proponent of personal perdurance is committed is similar to this evidently correct view of Quine's predicate: the denotation of a modal predicate shifts from context to context and when attached to a singular term is determined by a feature of the singular term to which it is attached. The difference between modal predicates, understood in accordance with this view, and Quine's predicate, is simply that the feature of the singular term to which the latter is attached which determines its denotation is its *spelling*, whereas the feature of the singular term to which a modal predicate is attached which determines the denotation of that predicate is a component of its meaning (it is this difference which accounts for the fact that modal predicates, unlike Quine's predicate, make sense in combination with quantifier phrases as well as with singular terms).

I submit, then, that the proponent of personal perduring is not refuted, as the fourth objection in section 6.10 suggests, by the failure of substitutivity *salva veritate* in *de re* modal contexts of ordinary designations of persons and those designations he would claim to be co-referential with them. For such failure of substitutivity is to be expected if modal predicates are inconstant in denotation, and, I have argued, we have good independent reason to accept that this is so.

6.12 Conclusion

The purpose of this chapter has been to get clearer about what is at issue between those who maintain and those who deny that border-line cases of personal identity are conceivable. In summary I have argued that to make sense of this one must regard the indeterminacy involved as a consequence of semantic indecision. But in order to do so one must take on ontological commitments which are more congenial to the proponent of personal perduring than to his opponent. In the latter part of the chapter I have considered and rejected four objections to the thesis that persons perdure, and developed, in response to the last of them, a conception of modal predicates as inconstant in denotation which, I have claimed, the proponent of personal perduring is committed to accepting.

I turn, in the next chapter, to another topic which has been central to recent debate about personal identity, namely, Bernard Williams's famous Reduplication Argument.

CHAPTER 7

The Reduplication Problem

7.1 Introduction: The generality of the argument

It can be fairly said that after the classic initial discussion of the problem of personal identity by John Locke, and the responses to that discussion by Butler, Reid and Hume (Leibniz's insightful response going largely unremarked) the shape of the controversy was fixed for the next 200 years. Of course, later philosophers had new things to say, and new ways to say old things, but the framework of their discussion of the problem remained the one determined by the writings of Locke, Butler, Reid and Hume. There was the issue between materialists and their opponents; the question whether the self was a simple substance, or something whose identity consisted in a set of relations between successive substances; the controversy between proponents and opponents of the Humean 'bundle theory' of the self. The framework for the discussion of the problem was fixed and remained so until as late as 1956. In that year, however, Bernard Williams published his seminal paper, 'Personal identity and individuation' (1956–7), in which he put forward his famous Reduplication Argument. This argument transformed subsequent discussion of the problem and led philosophers to the formulation of positions which were wholly new. Most notably, as a result of his reflection on Williams's argument (mediated by Wiggins's discussion of fission, Wiggins 1967) Parfit came to the statement of his famous and wholly original thesis 'identity is not what matters in survival'. This has been one of the main foci of interest in the debate over personal identity since its formulation. In addition, as we saw in Chapter 1, the Reduplication Argument has seemed to many of the defenders of the Simple View to be a new and powerful argument in favour of their position (an emphasis to be found particularly in Richard Swinburne's writings), and in consequence in recent years there has been a considerable revival of interest in the Simple View.

Williams's paper (1956–7), and in particular the (actually rather small) section of that paper devoted to the Reduplication Argument, must thus be regarded as a major event in the history of the debate over personal identity. But, in fact, Williams's own original hopes for the Reduplication Argument were relatively modest. He saw it merely as an objection to a version of the Psychological Continuity Criterion of personal identity. However, the reason that it attracted such interest and the explanation of its enormous influence on subsequent debate was that it was quickly seen by proponents of such accounts that its force was considerably more general. As John Perry puts the point: 'the Reduplication Argument is not the compelling refutation of one particular account of personal identity that Williams intends it to be. Nevertheless, Williams has posed an embarrassment for *any* account that uses as a criterion of identity a conceivably duplicable relation' (1976:428, my italics).

The case for this view of the argument was summarized in Chapter 1. First, it seems that even if we insist on identity of the whole body as a necessary condition of personal identity, it is not impossible to imagine a situation in which we are confronted by two bodies, either of which, but for the existence of the other, we would be happy to identify with a certain earlier body (it seems possible to imagine, that is, a situation which we would be tempted to describe as 'a man walking off in two directions'). And second, if we pass on to versions of the view that personal identity requires physical persistence which allow the identification of Shoemaker's Brownson with Brown – as any adequate criterion of personal identity surely must – then it seems impossible to find a plausible stopping point before we reach a version which is clearly vulnerable to the Reduplication Argument. For if Brownson is Brown in Shoemaker's original case he must also be Brown when he has only *half* of Brown's brain which nevertheless carries with it full psychological continuity. But any version of the view that personal identity requires physical persistence which licenses the identification in this case is wide open to the Reduplication Argument.

Williams himself, however, remains resistant to this view of the scope of his argument. His reply to it, in support of his claim that the Reduplication Argument bears specifically on psychological criteria of personal identity, is given in Williams (1973). 'Of course,' he writes,

> Smith's brain might be split, and it is imaginable that exactly the same character and memory-traits should go with the implanting of each half, as go with the implanting of the whole. This is fundamentally no different from the possibility attached to a criterion based on the identity of the whole body, that the whole body should, amoeba-like, split: this is a logical possibility to which all material bodies are heir. This possibility does not show, however, that criteria based on the continuity of material things (whether whole bodies or whole brains) are in absolutely no different case with regard to the reduplication problem than are other criteria not so based. For the reduplication problem arises if a supposed criterion of identity allows there to be two distinct items B and C, each of which satisfies the criterion in just the way it would if the other did not exist. But this is not so with bodily continuity: what is true of B when it is in the ordinary way continuous with A is just not the same as what is true of it when, together with C, it has been produced from A by fission.
>
> (1973:77–8)

And a little later he adds 'the difference between being straightforwardly continuous with A, and being a fission product of A, is a genuine difference in the history of B' (1973:78). Thus, Williams is saying, even if we allow that Brownson is Brown in virtue of possessing Brown's brain, we need not be embarrassed by the split-brain transplant case. For what is true of Brownson in Shoemaker's case, namely that his brain is 'straightforwardly continuous' with Brown's, is not true of either fission product in the split-brain transplant case; neither has a brain which is straightforwardly continuous with that of the original, since each has only one of the original person's brain hemispheres. But then what of the case in which half of Brown's brain is destroyed and the other half transplanted into Robinson's body with consequent transfer of memory and character traits? Either Brownson in this case is identical with Brown or he is not. If Williams says the latter he is wrong (given that Brownson is Brown in Shoemaker's original case). But if he allows that Brownson is Brown in this case he is refuted, for what is true of Brownson in this case, namely that he has a brain which is *not* straightforwardly continuous with that of Brown, being only half of Brown's original brain, is *precisely* what is true of each of the fission products in the split-brain transplant case, and there need be *no* genuine difference between the history of Brownson in this case, and that of the recipient of the relevant brain hemisphere in the split-brain transplant case.

Despite Williams's attempted counter-argument, then, it seems clear that his opponents are correct. It is not only the possibility of a non-bodily criterion of personal identity, but the possibility of any criterion of personal identity *at all*, which is brought into question by the Reduplication Argument.

7.2 The Only x and y principle

In this chapter therefore, we shall be looking more closely at the Reduplication Argument, and, in particular, at the fundamental principle upon which it relies – the Only x and y principle. This is the principle that whether a later individual y is identical with an earlier individual x can depend only on facts about x and y and the relationships between them: it cannot depend upon facts about any individuals other than x or y. Otherwise put, what the principle asserts is that whether x is identical with y can only depend upon the *intrinsic* relationship between them, it cannot be determined *extrinsically*. The intent of the principle is to rule out 'best candidate' theories of identity over time, according to which whether a later individual y is identical with an earlier individual x *can* depend upon whether there is any better candidate than y around at the later time for identity with x. One version of this 'best candidate' approach to personal identity, in fact, the most sophisticated version in the literature, is, as noted previously, Robert Nozick's 'closest continuer' theory. A brief statement of Nozick's theory will be useful at this point.

According to the simplest version of the closest continuer theory, which Nozick calls the 'local' version, the successor under identity of an item of a certain kind is *that* item of the kind which has the highest degree of spatio-temporal and qualitative continuity with the original item, where qualitative continuity includes, for Nozick, the existence of causal links between the qualities possessed by successive temporal stages of the item, i.e. the qualities of a succeeding stage must have developed out of those of a preceding stage in such a way that the succeeding stage would not have been the way it was (for the same reason) if the preceding stage had been different. The type of qualitative continuity required, Nozick allows, may depend on the kind of item in question – the kind may determine the relative weights qualities have in determining identity. (Thus the closest continuer theory of *personal* identity lays great weight on *psychological* continuity.) If there is no item with a sufficient degree of continuity with the original to be that item in the absence of competitors, i.e. there is no sufficiently close continuer, then the original has *no* successor under identity, i.e. it no longer exists. If there is more than one sufficiently close continuer, but none is significantly closer than the rest, then again the original item no longer exists.

A more complicated version of the closest continuer theory is the 'global' version. According to the local version of the theory the closest continuer of an item *is* that item. So if an item has two continuers, each sufficiently close to qualify as that item's successor under identity, but one is significantly closer than the other, then *that* is the item, even if it is substantially shorter-lived than the other close continuer. According to the global version of the theory there is a bias in favour of longevity. The successor under identity of an item is that longest-lived item which, as a whole, is a sufficiently close continuer of the original item, and significantly closer than any comparable long-lived entity – even if some initial temporal part of that item is a significantly less close continuer of the original than some other contemporaneous item of comparable duration (the motivation for the global version, Nozick says (1981:43), is that 'it seems so unfair for a person to be doomed by an echo of his former self').

Now, as I said, the intent behind the formulation given above of the Only *x* and *y* principle is to rule out such 'best candidate' theories of identity over time as Nozick's 'closest continuer' theory. But unfortunately, it does not do so. Whether later *y* is identical with earlier *x*, it says, must depend only on facts about *x* and *y* and the intrinsic relations between them; it cannot depend upon facts about any other individuals. But now suppose that Nozick's closest continuer theory of identity is correct, *y* is, in fact, *x*, because *y* is the closest continuer of *x*, but in another possible situation, in which a closer continuer *z* exists, it is rather *z* that is *x*. The Only *x* and *y* principle ought to entail that this situation is impossible, but as so far formulated it is not clear how it can do so. For if *z is x* in the possible situation envisaged, as the closest continuer theory entails, then facts about z are *not* facts about something *other than x* or y, as they would have to be if they were to be certified irrelevant to the question whether $x = y$ by the Only x and y principle.

Of course, this does not mean that, after all, the Only x and y principle *is* compatible with the 'best candidate' approach to identity over time. It simply means that we need a more careful formulation than the one above (which is based on statements by Williams and Parfit), if we are to be faithful to the obvious intent of its defenders.

Let us see if we can find one.

7.3 The ship of Theseus

I shall proceed by first of all considering some objections to the 'best candidate' approach to identity over time. Reflection on these will allow us to see more clearly what is at stake between proponents and opponents of the Only x and y principle, and the formulation of this principle which we are seeking will then emerge in the course of considering a possible rejoinder by a 'best candidate' theorist to one of these objections.

The first objection to the 'best candidate' approach I shall consider is put forward by David Wiggins (1980:95), who calls it his 'most fundamental' objection to this approach. I shall argue that this objection fails, but that it leads on to another which succeeds.

Wiggins presents his objection to the 'best candidate' approach in connection with the famous puzzle case of the ship of Theseus described by Hobbes. It is in fact this case above all which has made a 'best candidate' approach to identity over time seem plausible, and reflection on it will bring out exactly what that involves.

Following Hobbes's depiction of the story of the ship of Theseus, let us imagine that Theseus has a ship which he thinks to be in need of major repairs. He puts it into dry dock for a year and rebuilds it piece by piece until by the end of the year every plank, bolt and beam is replaced. But what has happened to the old planks? In fact a rival of Theseus has kept them as they have been replaced and hoarded them away, and has now put them together again in the same order to make a second ship. The two ships are now floating side by side on the water and an argument is raging (via megaphone) between

Theseus and the plank-hoarder about which ship is the *original* ship of Theseus: Theseus claiming this title for the one he is standing on (the continuously repaired ship) and the plank-hoarder claiming if for the one *he* is standing on. Whom should we believe?

Now, in this case, it does seem plausible to say that the continuously repaired ship is the original ship of Theseus (hereafter just 'the ship of Theseus'), but that the plank-hoarder's ship is a candidate, too, and would have been the ship of Theseus if its competitor – the continuously repaired ship – had not existed. To insist that the plank-hoarder's ship is not the ship of Theseus even when its competitor does not exist seems absurd – for ships can certainly undergo dismantling and reconstruction. While to insist that it is still the ship of Theseus when its competitor does exist seems implausible. But even if a case could be made out for saying the latter (perhaps by reference to the antiquarian interest of the ship of Theseus), it is clear that any considerations in favour of the plank-hoarder's ship can lend it plausibility at best, so that even if it is not definitely true that the continuously repaired ship is the ship of Theseus in the situation Hobbes describes it is not definitely false either. The identity statement in question is at worst indeterminate in truth-value.

But if this is so it follows that we could revise our language in such a way as to render it definitely true (if it is not so already) that the continuously repaired ship is the ship of Theseus in the situation described by Hobbes, while continuing, of course, to treat it as definitely true that the plank-hoarder's ship is the ship of Theseus when *it* is the only candidate. However, the acknowledgement of this possibility must evidently be as difficult for the defender of the Only x and y principle as the acknowledgement that the continuously repaired ship is determinately the ship of Theseus in the situation described by Hobbes, while the plank-hoarder's ship is determinately the ship of Theseus when it alone exists. For to accept the Only x and y principle, of course, commits one to claiming, not merely that it is not definitely false, but that it is definitely true.

Moreover, even if he could produce a conclusive argument that the plank-hoarder's ship was the ship of Theseus both in the situation in which it alone exists and in that in which its continuously repaired competitor exists too, the defender of the Only x and y principle would still be in apparent danger of refutation by the puzzle of the ship of Theseus. For this would be compatible with the plank-hoarder's ship merely being, in both situations, the *best candidate* for identity with the ship of Theseus, and the defender of the Only *x* and *y* principle would still appear to have a problem on his hands so long as it seemed plausible that the continuously repaired ship would have been the ship of Theseus if the plank-hoarder's ship had not existed.

So much, then, for the way in which the puzzle of the ship of Theseus lends plausibility to the 'best candidate' approach to identity over time. Now, however, we need to look at the consequences of adopting this approach to the puzzle.

7.4 Wiggins's argument

We can picture the three relevant situations as follows.

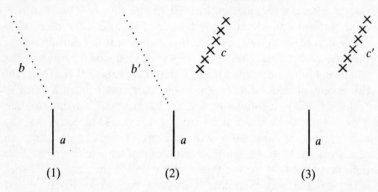

Here the second situation is the one described by Hobbes. The first situation is that in which the ship of Theseus undergoes repair and replacement of parts, but the replaced planks are simply discarded or destroyed, and the third situation is that in which no repair or replacement work takes place, but the ship of Theseus is dismantled plank by plank and later reconstructed.

In each drawing the continuous line represents the history of the ship of Theseus before repair and replacement work begins. The line of dots in drawings 1 and 2 represents the history of the continuously repaired ship, and the line of crosses in drawings 2 and 3 represents the history of the ship reconstituted from the original planks of the ship of Theseus, i.e. the plank-hoarder's ship.

If we designate the ship originally referred to in all three situations as 'the ship of Theseus' by '*a*', the ship undergoing continuous repair in situation 1 by '*b*', the ship undergoing continuous repair in situation 2 by '*b'*', the ship reconstituted from the original planks in situation 2 by '*c*', and the ship reconstituted from the original planks in situation 3 by '*c'*', then if we reject the Only *x* and *y* principle we can, in conformity with the plausible view that both the continuously repaired ship and the plank-hoarder's ship are candidates for identity with the ship of Theseus, though the former has the stronger claim, assert that in situation 1, a = b, in situation 2, a = b' and not: a' = c, and in situation 3, a = c'. These assertions are compatible with the necessity of identity if it is not the case that c = c', otherwise not. But is a 'best candidate' theorist committed to holding the c = c'? Wiggins assumes that he is, and this is the basis of his rejection of the 'best candidate' approach. He writes:

> The most fundamental objection to the 'best candidate' approach is that it licenses the following as a possibility: we could walk up to the antiquarian's ship [i.e. *c*], seen as a candidate to be Theseus' ship, and say that, but for the existence of its rival, i.e. the distinct coincidence candidate that is the constantly maintained working ship plying once yearly to Delos [*b'*], it would veritably have coincided as a ship with Theseus' original ship. But the idea that *in that* case it would have been Theseus' original ship seems to be absurd. There is a temptation to add as a *step* in this argument: nothing might have been a different entity from the entity it actually is. But the temptation is to be resisted. We are discovering in this argument, which for what it is worth is complete as it stands, the real intuitive grounds for doubting that anything might have been a numerically different entity from the one it actually is. The doubt is not a premiss or a step, but something brought to light by the argument; and it is grounded in the violence the contrary supposition does to the understanding of ' = ' that is implicit in everything we think and say about identity (at least when we are not struggling with paradoxical cases). It *underlines* the impossibility of conceiving of an entity's not being identical with that with which it *is*, in fact, identical.
>
> (1980:95)

But, in fact, the 'best candidate' theorist need not accept that c = c'. Of course, he has to accept this if he takes the candidates he is concerned with to be the two later ships, and takes it that what they

are candidates for is literally *identity* with the (one and only) original
ship of Theseus (for then, if *c* is distinct from *c'*, *c* is in *no* situation
identical with *a*, and so it cannot be that it is not identical with *a* in
situation 2 *only because* the better candidate *b'* is also present there).
But he need not take this view, and 'best candidate' theorists who
have their wits about them do not.

For example, Robert Nozick, who regards enduring entities as
'four-dimensional worms', composed of temporal parts or stages,
takes the competing candidates in this case to be not ships but
ship-stages. And what they are candidates for, on his view, is not
identity with the original ship of Theseus, but rather *being at the
later time the stage (temporal part) of the ship of Theseus occurring
then*. The ship-stage present in situation 3 at the location of ship *c'*
possesses this property there, but only contingently if in situation 2 *a*
= *b'* and not: *a* = *c*, for then, while still existing in situation 2, it
does not possess it there. But it does not follow that there is any *ship*
which exists both in situation 2 and in situation 3 and is identical
with the ship of Theseus in situation 3, but distinct from it in situation 2. For despite appearances, the ship *c*, not being identical with
the ship *c'*, is not present in situation 3 at all (see Nozick 1981:656ff.).

Nor does the 'best candidate' theorist need to be a four-
dimensional metaphysician in order to deny the identification of *c*
with *c'*. Consistently with the rejection of a temporal worm
metaphysics he can, for example, take Nathan Salmon's line, deny
that *c* = *c'* and take the rival candidates involved in the case to be,
neither ships nor ship-stages, but rather the *hunks of matter*
constituting *b'* and *c*. Then he can say that what these are rival
candidates for is, again, not identity with the original ship of
Theseus, but rather: *being at the later time the hunk of matter
constituting the ship of Theseus then*. The hunk of matter
constituting *c'* in situation 3 possesses this property there, but only
contingently if in situation 2 *a* = *b'* and not: *a* = *c*, since then,
though it certainly exists in situation 2 (where it constitutes *c*) it does
not possess it there. But it does not follow that there is any *ship* in
situation 3 which is identical with the one and only ship of Theseus
there, but distinct from it in situation 2, for this contingency of
constitution is distinct from the contingency of identity, and does
not entail it, and despite appearances ship *c* is not present in situation 3 at all (see Salmon 1982: Appendix I).

Wiggins is thus mistaken in assuming that it is essential to the 'best candidate' approach to the case of the ship of Theseus that c be identified with c' and the necessity of identity be abandoned; this would indeed be the case if the 'best candidate' theorist was obliged to regard the ships b' and c as the competing candidates involved in case 2 and to regard them as candidates for *identity* with the ship of Theseus, but he is not so obliged. The 'best candidate' theorist, has, indeed, to choose between rejecting the identification of c with c' and abandoning the necessity of identity, but both courses are open to him, and as we have seen, two actual 'best candidate' theorists have opted for the former.

7.5 An alternative argument

Actually, however, to adopt this course is merely to jump out of the frying pan into the fire. For the objection to the 'best candidate' theorist's taking this course should be obvious. We can put it in a form reminiscent of Wiggins's objection. I have stressed that if the 'best candidate' theorist denies that $c = c'$ he must acknowledge that, despite appearances, c is not present in situation 3 at all. He must, then, acknowledge that the following is a possibility: we could walk up to the plank-hoarder's ship in situation 2, seen as a candidate to be Theseus's ship, and say truly that, but for the existence of its rival, the constantly maintained working ship plying once yearly to Delos, it would never have existed *at all*. Similarly, if he takes the same line in the case of personal identity, then, if he accepts a memory or psychological continuity criterion of personal identity which entails that Bernard Williams's Charles *is* Guy Fawkes in the absence of a rival claimant, the 'best candidate' theorist is not committed, as Wiggins suggests (1980:208), to maintaining that it is true of Charles in the reduplication situation that but for the existence of Robert he *would have been* Guy Fawkes. But to avoid this commitment he must acknowledge that we could walk up to Charles in the reduplication situation and, speaking of Robert, say to him, 'You should consider yourself fortunate that that other fellow seems to be as good as you are at reminiscing about attempts to blow up the Palace of Westminster – if he hadn't been you would never have existed.' But it seems obvious that in making these acknowledgements the 'best candidate' theorist would be committing himself to self-evident absurdities.

In case it may be said that the absurdity in the latter case is not one that derives from the 'best candidate' theory as such, but merely from the mentalistic theory of personal identity required to license the identification of the (non-duplicated) Charles with Guy Fawkes in the absence of any possible causal connection between them, let me refer again to the split-brain transplant case. If the 'best candidate' theorist adopts the line of reply to Wiggins presently being considered he must acknowledge that in this case one could say to either of the fission products: 'You should consider yourself fortunate that the other fellow's brain transplant went so well – if it hadn't you would never have existed.' The absurdity seems just as great.

7.6 Further objections

I think that this argument is by itself conclusive against the 'best · candidate' approach to identity over time for artefacts or persons. But there are other implausible consequences of the 'best candidate' approach to be noted, and by reflecting on these we will be able to arrive at a more satisfactory formulation of the Only x and y principle.

Consider again the example of the ship of Theseus. As I said, if we adopt the 'best candidate' approach to identity over time for artefact identity we can, in conformity with the plausible view that both the continuously repaired ship and the plank-hoarder's ship are candidates for identity with the ship of Theseus, though the former is the stronger claimant, assert that in situation 1, a = b, in situation 2, a = b' and not: a = c, and in situation 3 a = c'. We are then committed to saying that, whether or not c = c', the events which constitute the origin of c in situation 2, i.e. the reassembly of the hoarded planks into a ship, do not constitute the origin of that, or any, ship, in situation 3, since, whether or not c = c', c' = a, which came into existence much earlier. This illustrates the next absurd consequence of the 'best candidate' approach to which I wish to draw attention: *events which constitute the origin of some entity of a certain kind in one situation, may not constitute the origin of that, or any entity of the kind, in a second situation, even though all the events constituting the history of that entity in the first situation remain present in the second.*

Again, if we go along with the 'best candidate' approach and accept the statement given in the last paragraph of the identities and non-identities obtaining among *a*, *b*, *b'*, *c* and *c'* in the case of the ship of Theseus, we are committed to saying that two events in the history of ship *c'*, i.e. ship *a*, in situation 3, one occurring before the disassembly and reconstruction of the ship, and one occurring after, will fail to be common parts of the history of that, or any single ship, in situation 2, even though both they, and all the events which were parts of the history of ship *c'* in situation 3, remain present in situation 2. This illustrates another absurd consequence of the 'best candidate' approach: *two events may be part of the history of a single entity in some situation, but may fail to be parts of the history of that, or any single entity of the kind, in a second situation in which both they, and all the events which were parts of the history of the entity in the first situation, remain present.*

7.7 A counter-argument countered

At this point, however, a defender of the 'best candidate' approach to artefact identity may object that while these italicized propositions are admittedly absurd, he is not committed to them. For, in supposing that he is, I have just *assumed* that one can decide whether an event which is part of the history of some entity in one situation is present in another, without first deciding whether that entity itself is present in the second situation. But event identity is tied up with object identity in such a way as to render this impossible. Whether the events in the history of the plank-hoarder's ship in situation 3 (represented by the line of crosses) are also present in situation 2 can therefore not be decided prior to deciding whether the plank-hoarder's ship in situation 3 is the same ship as the plank-hoarder's ship in situation 2. Consequently, the italicized propositions, whilst admittedly absurd, are not consequences of the 'best candidate' approach, since the 'best candidate' theorist, consonantly with his denial that the *same ship* is the plank-hoarder's ship in situations 2 and 3, can simply deny that the *same events* are represented by the line of crosses in the diagrams representing situations 2 and 3.

However, I do not find this a plausible reply, because I do not see that event identity is tied up with object identity in the way this objection claims. Not only are the events in the history of the plank-hoarder's ship in situation 2 qualitatively identical with the events in the history of the plank-hoarder's ship in situation 3, the plank-hoarder's ship in situation 2 is built of exactly the same planks, manned by exactly the same crew and sails over exactly the same seas as the plank-hoarder's ship in situation 3. Moreover, the 'additional' events in situation 2, i.e. those, represented by the line of dots, which do not have even qualitative counterparts in situation 3, have no *causal* effect whatsoever on the events in the history of the plank-hoarder's ship in that situation (this is part of the description of situation 2). Given all this, it seems that while there may be *a* notion of event identity in accordance with which to determine whether the events in the history of the plank-hoarder's ship in situation 3 are identical with the events in the history of the plank-hoarder's ship in situation 2 one must first decide whether the plank-hoarder's ship in situation 3 is identical with the plank-hoarder's ship in situation 2, such a notion can hardly be our everyday notion of event identity.

7.8 Cambridge change

At this point it is helpful to introduce Peter Geach's distinction between real and 'mere Cambridge' change (Geach 1972:321ff.). An object 'undergoes' a Cambridge change just in case a proposition about it changes in truth-value (Geach's reason for this terminology, incidentally, is that this was the criterion of change employed by the great Cambridge philosophers Russell and McTaggart). But this need not involve any change in the object itself. Thus, to take Geach's example, Theatetus underwent a Cambridge change when he grew taller than Socrates, and so did Socrates. But the change in Theatetus was a real one, for his height actually altered, whereas the change in Socrates was a *mere* Cambridge change, a mere change in his relations to other things. Again, that five ceases to be the number of John's children is a Cambridge change in five, but it is not a real change in five, that a politician or a pop star gains or loses in popularity is a Cambridge change in him, but it is not a real change in him. In the Cambridge sense, objects which are not spatio-temporal at all, like numbers, can change, and so can spatio-temporal objects which do not exist at the time in question, as when the activities of a historical figure become a focus of renewed controversy amongst historians. But none of these changes is a real one, they are *mere* Cambridge changes.

Mere Cambridge changes, then, are Cambridge changes which are not real ones, and though the distinction between real and non-real changes is hard to define, our grasp of it, as this is manifest in non-collusive agreement on examples, seems sufficiently firm to make the notion of a mere Cambridge change a useful tool in philosophical argument. (But perhaps, as suggested by Shoemaker (1984:220), it can be defined in an epistemological way. To verify in the most direct way that an object has undergone a *real* change at a certain place and time one must make observations and tests in the vicinity of that place and time, whereas to verify in the most direct way that an object has undergone a mere Cambridge change at a certain place and time it will be necessary to make observations and tests remote from that place and time, and observations made at that place and time will either be irrelevant or insufficient.)

Now given the notion of a mere Cambridge change, one can evidently define a family of related notions. Thus a mere Cambridge *property* is one that can be gained or lost by a mere Cambridge change. Two objects are *similar* in a mere Cambridge way if they share a mere Cambridge property. Two objects *differ* in a mere Cambridge way if one possesses a mere Cambridge property the other lacks. Finally we can define the notion of *two possible situations differing in a mere Cambridge way with respect to what happens in a certain location*. This will be so in the case of two situations S and S', with respect to what happens at location L, just in case the only changes occurring at L in either situation not occurring there in the other are mere Cambridge changes and the only properties instantiated at L in either situation not instantiated there in the other are mere Cambridge properties.

With this notion defined I can now put the point about our ordinary notion of event identity that I was making at the end of the previous section in a different way: namely, that with respect to what happens at the location of the plank-hoarder's ship in situations 2 and 3 the difference between the two situations is a mere Cambridge difference, but our ordinary notion of event identity is such that it is a *sufficient* condition of the events occurring at a certain location being identical in two situations that, with respect to what happens at that location, there is a mere Cambridge difference between the two situations (a simpler way to put this is perhaps to say that we do not ordinarily regard mere Cambridge changes as *events*). But if this is our ordinary notion of event identity, it follows that the 'best candidate' theorist's envisaged rejoinder to my argument fails.

7.9 The Only x and y principle reformulated

I can now provide the reformulation of the Only x and y principle I promised earlier, a reformulation which for me, at least, reveals much more clearly than its original formulation the intuitive force of this principle.

Let us call the sufficient condition of event identity stated at the end of the previous paragraph 'the Cambridge criterion' of event identity. Then the Only x and y principle can be reformulated as follows: *if two events are parts of the history of a single entity of a kind in one situation then they must also be parts of the history of a single entity of the kind in any second situation in which, as judged by the Cambridge criterion, both they, and all the events which are parts of the history of the entity in the first situation, remain present.*

This formulation of the Only x and y principle is not vulnerable to the criticism made of the original version. Unlike the latter it states a condition which, for any kind of entity, is inconsistent with the identity over time of entities of that kind possessing a 'best candidate' structure. And yet, I submit, thought of as applied to artefact identity, personal identity, or the identity of any familiar type of physical object, it is undeniable.

7.10 The multiple occupancy thesis

But what now of the Reduplication Argument? I have argued that the Only x and y principle is an undeniable constraint on personal identity. But, as we saw, the Only x and y principle is the fundamental assumption to which the Reduplication Argument appeals. So if we cannot fault the Only x and y principle must we also accept the Reduplication Argument? And, if so, in view of the argument of section 7.1 for the generality of that argument, how can we stop short of the conclusion that only the Simple View of personal identity can be correct?

These are the questions to which we must now turn.

Consider again the case of the ship of Theseus. Common sense tells us that in situation 1 there is just one ship, which undergoes repair replacement of parts and that in situation 3 there is just one ship, which undergoes dismantling and reassembly. But how can *both* these common-sense views be retained consistently with the Only *x* and *y* principle?

The answer to this question can be arrived at quite straightforwardly by deducing what must be true of situations 1, 2 and 3 if *both* these views *and* the Only *x* and *y* principle are maintained.

If one accepts the Only *x* and *y* principle one has to deny that *c* in situation 2 and *c'* in situation 3 have different origins, or indeed that *c* in situation 2 has a history which is anything other than that of *c'* in situation 3. That is to say, either *c'* in situation 3 did not come into existence until the hoarded planks were reassembled into a ship, or *c* in situation 2 came into existence when the ship of Theseus was originally built. The first alternative is incompatible with the common-sense view that in situation 3 there are not two ships but just one, which is first disassembled and later reconstructed. So we are left with the second alternative. Similarly, with regard to *b* and *b'*, we have to say either that *b* in situation 1 did not come into existence until some time after the repair and replacement work began, or that *b'* in situation 2 came into existence with the original construction of the ship of Theseus. Again, the first alternative is incompatible with the common-sense view that in situation 1 there are not two ships but just one, which some time after it is built begins to undergo repair and replacement work. So we must accept the second alternative. If we are not to describe situations 1 and 3 in obviously mistaken ways, then, the acceptance of the Only *x* and *y* principle forces us to say that in situation 2 the ships *b'* and *c*, which later on are manifestly distinct, share the same origin and an initial part of their history. (Whether they then count as being a single ship or whether they instead qualify as a counter-example to Locke's principle that 'two things of the same kind cannot occupy the same place at the same time' I shall not discuss, but see p. 167 for relevant comment.) This is an instance of *the Multiple Occupancy Thesis* introduced in Chapter 1.

But if *b* and *b'* have exactly the same history and *c* and *c'* have exactly the same history, nothing stands in the way of concluding that b = b' and c = c', and this is obviously what a defender of the Only x and y principle must conclude. But since b' (or b) is distinct from c (or c'), it follows that it cannot be true both that a = b in situation 1 and a = c' in situation 3. Whence we have to conclude that drawings 1 to 3 have been mislabelled: 'a' was introduced as the name of *the* ship originally referred to in all three situations as 'the ship of Theseus', but in situation 1 that is b (b'), and situation 3 c' (= c), and it is not the case that b = c'. What one has to say, if one accepts the Only x and y principle and does not wish to describe situations 1 and 3 in obviously mistaken ways then, is that as used in situation 1 the name 'the ship of Theseus' designates *one* ship, namely b (= b'), and as used in situation 3 it designates *another*, namely c' (= c). Which ship it designates in situation 2 depends on which of b (b') and c (c') has the best claim to the title.

This discussion should make it clear how acceptance of the Only x and y principle is consistent with the rejection of the conclusion that the Reduplication Argument is intended to yield. Consider the case of the double-brain transplant again, i.e. the case in which a brain is divided and its two halves transplanted into different bodies with consequent transference of memory and character traits. Application of the Reduplication Argument would yield the conclusion that since in this case *both* the fission products cannot be identical with the original person, even if only *one* brain hemisphere was transplanted personal identity would not be preserved. And this is inconsistent with the Physical and Psychological Criteria of personal identity. But we can now see that it is, in fact, consistent for a proponent of one of these Criteria to accept the Only x and y principle. In order to do so, however, he must accept the Multiple Occupancy Thesis and say that before the double-brain transplant there were, in fact, two people occupying a single body, and thinking the same thoughts, who later became spatially distinct. The reasoning which establishes this is entirely parallel to that just gone through with reference to the case of the ship of Theseus.

It may be objected at this point, however, that whatever the considerations in its favour this view of the double transplant case must be mistaken. For it is an undeniable datum of common sense that in this case there is only one person present before the brain transplant, whereas the multiple occupancy analysis proposed entails that this is not so.

The first point I wish to make in response to this objection is just that it is not clear to me that the proposed 'undeniable datum of common sense' is so undeniable. It is certainly tempting to describe this case, and the similar ones that are imagined in the literature on personal identity, as cases in which 'one person becomes two'. But is it not also in *some* degree tempting to describe them as cases in which two people were present all along, though this did not become obvious until after the brain transplant? I submit that it is.

But actually, whatever the truth about this matter is, it is of little importance. For the fact is that a defender of the multiple occupancy analysis of the double transplant case is not committed to denying the common-sense view (supposing it to be so) that just one person is present before the brain transplant.

To see this point it is necessary to reflect a little on what is involved in counting. It is a deeply engrained conviction in many philosophical circles that if x is an F and y is an F and x and y are not identical then x and y cannot legitimately be counted as *one F*. According to this philosophical view, when counting F's one must count them as one if and only if they are identical. But, in fact, it is perfectly possible to count by a relation weaker than, i.e. not entailing, identity. Suppose R is a relation weaker than identity which holds among F's and which sorts the F's into equivalence classes (as, for example, the relation *being the same height as* sorts men into equivalence classes in respect of their height) then one can count F's according to the rule that F's x and y are to be counted as one just in case xRy. To do so one assigns the number *one* to any F and to any F which bears R to that F, and to no other F, one assigns the number *two* to any F to which a number has not been assigned, to any F which bears R to it and to no other F, and so on. The number finally arrived at will be the count of F's in the domain under consideration when counting by R, and if it can be true that xRy even if x is not identical with y this number may obviously be smaller than the number arrived at when counting by identity.

What a proponent of the multiple occupancy analysis of the double transplant case can say then (and what, in fact, such proponents of this analysis as Lewis (1976) and Robinson (1985) do say) is that when the common-sense man says that only one person is present before the transplant he is reporting the result of counting not by identity, but by some weaker relation – say *spatio-temporal coincidence at all times before the transplant* – and so the common-sense report, properly understood, is consistent with the multiple occupancy analysis. The appearance of inconsistency derives from failing to distinguish the common-sense way of counting, according to which x and y may be counted as one even if they are not identical, and the strict philosophical way of counting, according to which this is impermissible.

Moreover, he might add, it is perfectly obvious *why* common sense does not count by identity in such cases. Only facts about the future make it true that, counting philosophically, two people are present before the brain transplants, but we do not know the future and it is anyway irrelevant to most of the practical purposes which everyday synchronic counting is usually required to serve. There is no need prior to the brain transplant to treat the (counting by identity) *two* original persons any differently from any *one* person whose future one knows nothing of (for, as Robinson nicely puts it, they are not merely as alike as two peas in a pod, they are as alike as one pea in a pod), and unless one insists on counting by identity one need not speak as if there is.

7.11 Conclusion

Thus the proponent of the Multiple Occupancy Thesis can defend his position against the charge that it is straightforwardly in conflict with common sense by claiming that, contrary to long-standing philosophical opinion, common-sense counting is not always in accordance with identity. But there is no doubt that the Multiple Occupancy Thesis is counter-intuitive. Nevertheless, I submit that the Reduplication Argument demonstrates that unless we wish to embrace the Simple View of personal identity we have no choice but to accept it. For the Only x and y principle, in its final formulation, is an undeniable constraint on our concept of personal identity. This conclusion will be confirmed in Chapter 9, where an argument of Parfit's against the Only x and y principle will be shown to be mistaken, and in the final chapter an account of personal identity compatible with the Only x and y principle will be elaborated and defended (in fact, as we shall see, there is more than one account of personal identity compatible with the Only x and y principle – we shall have to compare them).

Chapter 8
Quasi-Memory

8.1 Introduction

We have seen that there are two main lines of objection to the theory that personal identity can be defined in terms of psychological continuity. The first was the Reduplication Argument. The second is the *vicious circularity* objection: the objection that any account of personal identity in terms of memory will necessarily be viciously circular, since memory presupposes personal identity and, therefore, cannot be used to define it. Since any account of personal identity in psychological terms must be at least *in part* in terms of memory, if this is a good objection to the straightforward Memory Criterion of personal identity it will be equally forceful as an objection to the more general psychological continuity account.

This second objection is generally regarded as originating in Butler's critique of Locke. But as we saw in Chapter 3, it is doubtful whether Butler had anything so sophisticated in mind, and anyway, considered as an objection to Locke's position the circularity objection is unconvincing. However, this is because of a feature of Locke's position, namely, his insistence on a tripartite ontology of persons, men and thinking substances, which few (if any) present-day defenders of psychological continuity accounts of personal identity would be willing to accept. In recent years the most popular response to the vicious circularity objection has been to appeal to the notion of 'quasi-memory' which was introduced by Shoemaker (1970). This is the notion I wish to examine in this chapter.

Our memories are our most direct source of knowledge of the past, and the region of the past to which they provide us with access is, in the first place, *our own* past, that is, our own past experiences, actions and thoughts, and past events to which we have been

169

witnesses. Someone who had a faculty of quasi-memory would have a capacity for knowledge of the past which was essentially like that provided to us by memory, except that it was not thus restricted in its range to his own past.

Shoemaker argues that such a concept of quasi-memory is intelligible, and that using it one can give an account of personal identity which is not vulnerable to the vicious circularity objection. One might think that if this is correct the special access which we in fact have in memory to our own pasts will be revealed as a mere contingency. But Shoemaker argues that this is not so. Even if there was quasi-remembering which was not remembering, he argues, there would remain a sense in which a person had a special access to his own past, and hence a sense in which a person's knowledge of his own identity over time was radically unlike his knowledge of the identity over time of other persons and things.

In what follows I shall be arguing that though they contain an element of truth, these latter claims of Shoemaker's cannot be sustained. In fact, there are *two* notions of quasi-memory. One of them is clearly incapable of yielding a definition of personal identity by itself but *can* enter, without circularity, into a more general account of personal identity in terms of psychological continuity. If such an account of personal identity is correct, however, it *is* a mere contingency that memory gives us a special access to our own pasts and it is a fact merely about *this* world but not all *possible* worlds that our knowledge of our own identity over time is radically different, in the way Shoemaker emphasizes, from our knowledge of the identity over time of other persons and things.

The other notion of quasi-memory is the one with which Shoemaker operates. It is a more restrictive notion than the former and so, at first sight, looks more likely to yield, by itself, i.e. without appeal to any other type of psychological continuity, an adequate definition of personal identity. But the feature of this notion of quasi-memory which makes this seem likely, and which also suggests that such a definition would be consistent with the idea that a subject has a special access of his own past, also guarantees that any such definition would be viciously circular.

With this preliminary statement of the aims of this chapter let us now turn to details. We can begin with a closer look at the vicious circularity objection.

8.2 The circularity objection

The heart of this objection is that memory *presupposes* personal identity, and so cannot be used, without circularity, to define it. But what exactly does this amount to?

In general we speak of a definition as circular when it takes for granted an understanding of the very notion being defined. In some cases the application of this idea is straightforward. Thus, suppose that you are explaining to a non-English speaker what a bachelor is. You say that a bachelor is an unmarried man. But it turns out that your friend is not familiar with the word 'unmarried'. So you explain it to him: you say that to be unmarried is to be (an adult who is) a bachelor or a spinster. Clearly you have come round in a circle and your explanation is useless, for your friend will understand it only if he already understands the word 'bachelor', but his trouble is precisely that he does not.

This is a clear case of vicious circularity in definition. But, of course, the circularity entered only at the second stage, when the word 'unmarried' was explained. There was no circularity in the original definition of a bachelor as an unmarried man, taken by itself.

Since this is so, however, the example does not help us to see what is viciously circular about defining personal identity in terms of memory, for, obviously, no one with his wits about him would give such a definition and then go on to define memory in terms of personal identity.

Sometimes it is said that the reason why it is unacceptably circular to define personal identity in terms of memory is that memory *implies* or *logically entails* personal identity. That is, for example, '*S* remembers performing action *A*', implies '*S* performed action *A*', which in turn implies '*S* is the very same person as the one who performed action *A*.'

But this cannot be right. For far from this implication being inconsistent with the definability of personal identity in terms of memory, it is, of course, something that *must* obtain if such a definition is to be correct; definitions must at least give sufficient conditions.

The sense in which it is circular to define personal identity in terms of memory is thus not as obvious as might have been thought. But I believe that the following statement of the objection by Shoemaker brings out the crucial point:

while someone's remembering a past event is a sufficient
condition of his being a witness to that event, we cannot use
the former as a criterion for the latter, since in order to establish
that a person really does remember a given past event we have
to establish that he, that very person, was a witness to the
event. And, if that is so, the formula 'If S remembers E, S is
identical with someone who witnessed E' will be circular if
offered as a partial analysis of the concept of personal identity.

(1970:281)

What the vicious circularity objection comes to, then, is this. To
establish that someone not only *thinks* that he remembers, or *seems*
to remember, but actually *does* remember doing or experiencing
something, we have first to establish that he, that very same person,
did indeed do or experience it. The point is not that remembering
doing or experiencing so-and-so implies or logically entails being the
very same person as the one who did or experienced it. That would
not be an objection to an analysis of personal identity in terms of
memory. The point is rather that the *conclusive verification* of the
proposition that someone remembers doing so-and-so would have
to involve checking that he did indeed do it. To *know* that someone
remembers doing so-and-so you would have to *know* that he did it
(whereas, of course, in many other cases a proposition P implies or
logically entails a proposition Q, without *knowledge* of P entailing
knowledge of Q). But this means that someone must already have
the concept of personal identity if he is to have the concept of
memory, and recognition of the applicability of the latter concept
must rest on recognition of the applicability of the former. In short,
the concept of personal identity is *epistemologically prior* to that of
memory, and so cannot be defined in terms of it.

But why is this so?

A plausible explanation goes as follows. We have not only the
concept of veridical memory, but also that of non-veridical, or
seeming memory, and we accept without difficulty the idea that
people can seem (to themselves) to remember doing things which
they did not do, but were, in fact, done by others. But how can this
distinction be made if not by an appeal to the notion of personal
identity? If I remember performing a past action or undergoing a
past experience then at least two conditions must hold: (1) I must
presently be in a state *as of* remembering it, and (2) the content of

this state must match in an appropriate way the nature of the past action or experience. But these two conditions are not sufficient. I do not remember your first toothache just because I remember mine, and mine was indistinguishable from yours. Nor do I remember some past action or experience of yours if a hypnotist produces in me a state of seeming to remember it intrinsically indistinguishable from your present veridical recollection of it. It is an obvious thought that what must be added to conditions (1) and (2) to distinguish veridical from non-veridical recollection is condition (3): if I am to count as remembering performing an action or having an experience this must have been *my own* past action or experience (this is a special case of what Shoemaker calls 'the strong previous awareness condition' for memory). But if appeal to this condition really is the *only* way to mark off genuine cases of memory then, of course, it becomes trivially analytic that if I have a genuine memory of performing an action or undergoing an experience I must be the same person as the one who performed the action or underwent the experience. But if this is the case we cannot, without circularity, employ the notion of (veridical) memory as a constituent in an account of personal identity.

8.3 Quasi-memory

Shoemaker's reply to this is to accept that it refutes the idea that personal identity can be defined in terms of memory (thought of as satisfying the strong previous awareness condition), but to maintain that we can retain the spirit, if not the letter, of the position of memory theorists by introducing the concept of quasi-memory, where this is in all other essential respects identical with the concept of memory, but does not satisfy the strong previous awareness condition. The Memory Criterion, or the Psychological Continuity Criterion, of personal identity can then be rendered safe from the vicious circularity objection by the simple device of replacing all references to 'memory' by references to 'quasi-memory'.

But, as I said, there are, in fact, two notions of quasi-memory. The first, which I shall call quasi-memory (*G*), can be explained as follows. We have in memory a capacity for *direct* or *non-inferential* knowledge of the past, i.e. knowledge of the past not based on indications after the event, whether evidence or testimony. However, the region of the past to which this gives us access is restricted to that of which we ourselves have had experience (the strong previous awareness condition). Someone with a faculty of quasi-memory (*G*) would have a similar capacity for non-inferential knowledge of the past, but the region of the past to which he had access would *not* be restricted to that which he had himself experienced; it could not be the whole of the past, experienced or unexperienced, nor could it even be the whole of the experienced past (see Shoemaker 1970 for the argument for this), but it might be, for example, the whole of the past experienced by his parents, or by his ancestors for five generations back, or the whole of the past experienced by the people present when he was born.

Quasi-memory thus understood seems a clearly intelligible idea (albeit the stuff of fantasy and science fiction) and one I shall be returning to later. But for now I want to contrast it with the second more restrictive notion of quasi-memory which is the one Shoemaker employs. I shall call this quasi-memory (*R*).

The easiest way to acquire an understanding of this is to note, first of all, that conditions (1) to (3) above are not, in fact, sufficient to define veridical memory. Suppose that I have completely forgotten some past action or experience, but a hypnotist produces in me an apparent memory of that past action or experience which is intrinsically indistinguishable from the state I would be in if I had had a veridical recollection of it. Let us suppose further that it is pure coincidence that he does so (his *intention* was to produce in me, say, a state intrinsically indistinguishable from *your* present veridical recollection of your first toothache, but since your experience of your first toothache was, quite coincidentally, quite indistinguishable from mine, the apparent memory he produces in me is consequently also intrinsically indistinguishable from the state I would be in if I now had a veridical recollection of mine). And let us suppose finally that the apparent memory the hypnotist induces in me is all his own work, that is, he does not bring to the surface any latent memory of the action or experience, and his success is in no way dependent on its actual occurrence.

Then in this case conditions (1) to (3) are satisfied, yet my apparent memory is not veridical.

What this brings out is that memory is a *causal* notion. I have a veridical memory of performing a past action or undergoing an experience only if my present apparent memory of doing so is causally and counter-factually dependent upon the state of awareness of the action or experience which existed in me at the time.

However, not all causal links between a past action or experience and a present ostensible recollection of it are of the type required for memory.

Let us suppose, varying the story just told, that the hypnotist met me many years before, and in sessions now long forgotten extracted from me immensely detailed accounts of my earlier life and experiences. And let us suppose that the content of the apparent memory he now produces in me is derived from the knowledge of my past life he then acquired. In this case there is a causal link between my present apparent memory and the past event to which it corresponds, but it still does not qualify as a veridical memory of that event, since the causal connection is of the wrong sort.

Shoemaker calls the type of causal connection that links a past action or experience to a veridical memory of it 'an *M*-type causal chain'. Employing this terminology we can now say that for veridical memory, in addition to conditions (1) to (3), we also need condition (4): my present apparent memory must be linked by an *M*-type causal chain to the past action or experience in question.

But now we can define Shoemaker's notion of quasi-memory (*R*) simply by omitting condition (3) from this list. Specifically, one can say that I quasi-remember (*R*) performing a past action or undergoing a past experience (which may or may not have been my own) just in case:

(1) I am presently in a state (which may be dispositional) *as of* remembering it.
(2) The content of this state matches in an appropriate way the nature of the past action or experience.
(4) This state is linked by an *M*-type causal chain to that past action or experience.

Thus the notion of quasi-memory (*R*) Shoemaker employs is just the notion of memory, 'stripped' of the identity-presupposing element in the latter notion.

But if we define quasi-memory (*R*) in this way, what of the cases of non-veridical memory that condition (3) was originally brought in to exclude. Do they now qualify as cases of quasi-memory?

A glance back at the details of these examples will confirm that they do not. For they do not involve an M-type causal chain between the apparent memory and the earlier event. In fact, in the world as we know it quasi-memory (R), thus defined, just like quasi-memory (G), extends no further than memory.

But, Shoemaker argues, even though this is so, with the notion of quasi-memory (R) defined in this way it is certainly *intelligible* that someone should quasi-remember (R) an action, experience or event of which he himself had no previous knowledge; and consequently the notion of quasi-memory (R) cannot *presuppose* that of personal identity, as that of memory does, because it does not even *imply* or *logically entail* it.

In order to establish this Shoemaker appeals to cases of fission and fusion. These provide us with cases of quasi-remembering (R) which are not cases of remembering if there is no personal identity between the products of these processes and the originals involved, and Shoemaker, rejecting the Only x and y principle, is happy to maintain that this is so.

But then, he argues, there can be no objection to defining personal identity in terms of quasi-memory (R) and this he therefore does, proposing, in particular, as a sufficient condition of personal identity: *having a quasi-memory which is linked by a NON-BRANCHING M-type causal chain with a cognitive and sensory state of* (cases of branching, of course, just being cases of fission and fusion).

We shall come back to this proposal and its consequences in a moment, but for now I just want to explain the distinction between the notion of quasi-memory (R), and that of quasi-memory (G). One difference is that the notion of quasi-memory (R) is explicitly a causal notion, whereas the notion of quasi-memory (G) is not. Of course, the notion of quasi-memory (G) is the notion of a capacity for *knowledge* of the past, and it is plausible to suppose that this in itself imports the idea of causality. But it is at least not a mere *definitional* consequence of the explanation given of quasi-memory (G) that that notion is a causal one. More importantly, nothing in the explanation of quasi-memory (G) implies that one can only quasi-remember (G) events with which one is linked by an M-type causal chain – unless, that is, we take the notion of an M-type causal chain to be such that it *suffices* for a causal chain between present knowledge and a past event to be of this type that the present knowledge is based neither on evidence nor testimony concerning the event. However, it is clear that this explanation of the notion of an *M*-type causal chain could not serve Shoemaker's purposes, for it would not then be at all plausible that a non-branching *M*-type causal chain, by itself, would provide a sufficient condition of personal identity. Thus, just as something could be conceivably a case of quasi-memory (*R*), as Shoemaker explains it, without being a case of memory (so long, that is, as the Only *x* and *y* principle is set aside), so something could be a case of quasi-memory (*G*) without being a case of quasi-memory (*R*).

8.4 Quasi-memory and privileged access

But let us now return to Shoemaker's proposed criterion of personal identity and what he takes to be its consequences. I have emphasized earlier that he maintains that the privileged access we have in memory to our own past histories would remain, albeit in a weaker form, in a world in which there was quasi-remembering (*R*) which was not remembering. Essentially his thought is that this is so because such cases of *mere* quasi-memory (*R*) could only occur if there was branching of *M*-type causal chains. For, whilst the possibility of such branching would create the possibility of error through misidentification in first-person memory claims, the type of error involved would be radically unlike that involved in third-person misidentification and its correction could involve no procedure happily describable as 'the application to one's own case of a *criterion* of personal identity'.

Let us now look at the details.

As things are, as Shoemaker explains, an important class of first-person memory claims is in a certain sense immune to error through misidentification. If it seems to me that I was having dinner in a certain restaurant last night I can, of course, be mistaken. But my error cannot consist *merely* in my thinking that it was I who was in the restaurant last night when, in fact, it was someone else. I cannot be right about everything except my identity with the person who was in the restaurant last night. By contrast if I believe, on the basis of what I recall, that *you* were in the restaurant last night, my memory might be wholly accurate, and yet I might still be mistaken – for the person who was in the restaurant might have been your twin brother. I might have mistaken him for you at the time and (as Shoemaker puts it) preserved this misidentification in memory, or alternatively, if, for example, I had never met you before today, I might have made the misidentification subsequently on the basis of the (accurately) remembered appearance of your twin. Obviously no such misidentification can occur if what I recall is that *I* was in the restaurant last night, for it makes no sense to say that either last night or subsequently, I took myself to be my twin brother, deceived by the likeness between us. Thus my memory claim 'I dined in that restaurant last night', made on the basis of an accurate recollection of the occasion, is immune to error through misidentification with respect to 'I'.

The immunity to error through misidentification with respect to 'I' of such memory claims is, of course, one of the main sources of the temptation to say that we have in memory a special access to our own past, and it provides an explanation of the evident absurdity of the idea of attempting to apply a criterion of personal identity to one's own case to determine whether one is identical with a person whose actions one remembers performing. But, as Shoemaker points out, immunity to error through misidentification is *not* preserved in quasi-memory (R). If I claim on the basis of a quasi-memory (R) that I was in a certain restaurant last night this claim might involve an error through misidentification, for it may be that I am reporting 'from the inside' an experience of someone other than myself.

However, Shoemaker argues, even though immunity to error through misidentification is not preserved in quasi-memory (R) it remains that there is a significant sense in which the possessor of a faculty of quasi-memory (R) has a special access to his own past history. In a world in which there is no branching of M-type causal chains all M-connected mental states will be co-personal; whilst even in a world in which branching of M-type causal chains does occur M-connected mental states will be co-personal *unless* the M-type causal chain linking them has branched at some time during the interval between them. But, Shoemaker argues, this implies that even in a world in which there is branching of M-type causal chains, if one quasi-remembers (R) performing an action one is *entitled to presume* that one is identical with the agent of that action, and that the quasi-memory (R) is a memory. This is so, Shoemaker argues, even in worlds in which there is 'unequal' branching, i.e. some of the

offshoots of a past person are 'better candidates', in respect of
M-connectedness, for identity with him, than are others. For,
Shoemaker argues, even in such a world it will still be the case that in
any total mental state the memories, i.e. the quasi-memories (*R*)
produced by the past history of the person whose total mental state it
is, must outnumber the quasi-memories (*R*) produced by the past
history of any other person. For if the latter outnumbered the former surely *he* would be the later person, and not the other. But this
implies that if a person quasi-remembers (*R*) performing an action
then, in the absence of any evidence to the contrary, he is entitled to
regard it as more likely that the action was done by him than by any
other given person. And this, Shoemaker says, gives us a sense in
which quasi-memory (*R*) can be said to provide the quasi-
rememberer (*R*) with a 'special access' to his own past history. And
in this sense it will be true in any possible world, and not merely in
ours, that people have a special access to their own past histories.

What these arguments of Shoemaker's establish, I think, is that if
personal identity can be defined, in the way he thinks, in terms of
quasi-memory (*R*) then quasi-memories (*R*) will have a certain *a
priori* evidential status relative to claims of personal identity. That *S*
quasi-remembers (*R*) an event *E* (doing an action *A*) will necessarily
be evidence, albeit defeasible evidence, that *S* is one of the witnesses
of *E* (the person who did *A*) and so if it is known both that *S* does
quasi-remember (*R*) *E* (doing *A*) *and* that nothing else relevant is
known, then it should be regarded as more likely than not that *S* is
someone who witnessed *E* (did *A*).

But there is also another respect, Shoemaker argues, in which a
possessor of a faculty of quasi-memory (*R*) would retain a special
access to his own past history. Namely, that the knowledge of his
own past provided to him by his capacity for quasi-memory (*R*)
would be, in essence, *non-criterial*.

Given the strong previous awareness constraint on memory I cannot sensibly ask whether some action or experience I remember
'from the inside' was mine, and *a fortiori* I cannot set out to determine the answer to such a question on the basis of a criterion of
personal identity. However, in a world in which there was quasi-
remembering (*R*) which was not remembering it obviously would
make sense for me, quasi-remembering (*R*) performing an action or
undergoing experience, to ask myself whether the action or experience was my own or someone else's; and at first sight there is no

difficulty in the idea that I should attempt to answer this question on the basis of a criterion of personal identity. But Shoemaker argues that this is not so. When I enquire whether a quasi-remembered (R) action is mine or someone else's the only question I can be asking is whether there has been any branching of the M-type causal chains leading from the action to the quasi-memory (R). If I go on to verify that there was no branching, I thereby establish that a sufficient criterion of personal identity is satisfied. But an important part of what the satisfaction of this condition consists in, namely my quasi-remembering (R) performing the past action, is not something I establish, but something I necessarily presuppose. In cases where one quasi-remembers (R) performing a past action, and knows of it only on that basis, one cannot significantly enquire concerning it whether one does quasi-remember (R) it. For there is no way of knowing the past which stands to quasi-remembering (R) as quasi-remembering (R) stands to remembering, i.e. is such that one can know of a past event in this way and regard it as an open question whether in so knowing of it one is quasi-remembering (R) it. So in such cases the satisfaction of this part of the memory criterion of personal identity is a precondition of one's being able to raise the question of identity, and cannot be something one establishes in attempting to answer that question.

This is Shoemaker's case for his thesis that even in worlds in which there was quasi-remembering (R) which was not remembering one would retain a special access to, and essentially non-criterial knowledge of, one's own past. The case rests upon two assumptions: first, that quasi-memory (R) can be used without circularity to provide a sufficient condition of personal identity, and second, that there is no way of knowing the past which stands to quasi-memory (R) as quasi-memory (R) stands to memory. I shall be arguing that the intelligibility of the concept of quasi-memory (G) undermines both these assumptions.

8.5 *The content of quasi-memory*

Before turning to these arguments, however, I need to consider a different criticism of Shoemaker's position. I need to consider this because, if correct, it would also go against my own position. For it would refute the claim that quasi-memory (G) can be employed without vicious circularity as one of the components in an account of personal identity in terms of psychological continuity. The objection comes from Evans (1982:248ff.).

To quasi-remember performing an action is, by definition, to have an apparent memory of performing that action. This holds whether we are talking of quasi-memory (*G*) or quasi-memory (*R*). But is not '*S* apparently remembers *F*-ing' simply elliptical for '*S* apparently remembers himself *F*-ing'? If so, if I have a quasi-memory of *F*-ing, and, therefore, an apparent memory of *F*-ing, I must have an apparent memory of *myself F*-ing: a full and honest report of the content of my quasi-memory must consequently take the first-person form: 'I *F*-ed'. That is, to generalize, quasi-memories must necessarily present themselves to their subjects in the first-person mode, as apparent memories of their own actions, experiences and witnessings.

But since 'I *F*-ed' is equivalent in content to 'I am the same person as one who *F*-ed' (since the concept of a person is just the concept of an object of first-person reference) it follows that any account of personal identity in terms of quasi-memory will be circular. The circle will indeed not be the same as that involved in defining '*P*' in terms of 'knowledge that *P*', but it will be just as unacceptable – for it will be the same as that involved in defining '*P*' in terms of '*belief* that *P*'.

As Evans points out, many philosophers have taken the intelligibility of the idea of quasi-remembering which is not remembering as establishing

> the possibility of a faculty which is both like our memory in
> giving subjects knowledge of the past, and unlike it in that the
> content of the memory states in no way encroaches upon the
> question of *whose* past is concerned. The informational states
> of a quasi-memory faculty announce themselves, so to speak,
> as *merely* quasi-memories, so that it seems to the subject that
> someone or other F-ed without its in any way seeming to him
> that *he* F-ed.

> (1982:248)

It is just such a notion of quasi-memory which has to be defended if the objection now being considered is to be met.

However, as Evans insists, the possibility of such a faculty is not established by the mere intelligibility of the notion of quasi-memory, defined as I have defined it (following Shoemaker). I can equally easily introduce the notion of quasi-perception in such a way that a subject can be said to quasi-perceive a tree provided that he seems to see a tree as a causal result of a process which takes that tree as input, whether or not that tree is where the subject is disposed to locate it either in space or time. But, by this purely linguistic manoeuvre, I have not shown the intelligibility of a faculty of quasi-perception: in the sense of one which involves informational states whose content is simply of the existence, somewhere in space and time, of such and such a kind of tree. The manoeuvre does not show the possibility of its perceptually seeming to the subject that there is a tree without its seeming to him that there is a tree where he is (see Evans 1982:248). The same points hold *mutatis mutandis* for the notion of quasi-memory.

Thus answering the circularity objection we are presently considering is not a trivial task. Nevertheless, I think, the objection *can* be answered; for though it is not a mere matter of definition that in a world in which there is quasi-remembering which is not remembering a subject's quasi-memories will announce themselves (as Evans puts it) as *mere* quasi-memories, in some (though not all) such worlds, this *will* be so; subjects in such worlds will indeed have a faculty which is like memory in giving them knowledge of the past, but unlike it in that the content of their quasi-memory states in no way encroaches upon the question of *whose* past is concerned.

To see what such a world must be like let us first consider a world which is *not* like this, although it is a world in which there is quasi-remembering which is not remembering. This is the world imagined by Parfit in his story of 'Jane and Paul' (1984:221), a world in which there is surgical transplantation of memory traces from one person to another.

> Jane has agreed to have created in her brain copies of Paul's memory traces. After she recovers consciousness in the post-surgery room, she has a new set of vivid apparent memories. She seems to remember walking on the marble paving of a square, hearing the flapping of flying pigeons, and the cries of gulls and seeing light sparkling on green water.

It might be disputed whether these apparent memories are genuine quasi-memories, given that we have defined a faculty of quasi-memory as providing its possessor with a capacity for *non-inferential* knowledge of the past (it can be admitted without difficulty, of course, by someone pressing this point, that if Jane knows that her apparent memories are systematically correlated with Paul's experiences then she can *infer* from the occurrence of an apparent memory to the existence of a corresponding past experience and thereby *acquire* knowledge of the past), but this point is not our concern at present. What does seem undeniable, however, is that Jane's quasi-memories of Paul's experiences, allowing them to be such, will present themselves to her in the first-person mode. Of course, given that she knows what has been going on, they will not automatically give rise to *beliefs* about what her own past experiences were, but her spontaneous reports of her apparent memories of actions and experiences, if she does not inhibit them, will none the less take the first-person form 'I *F*-ed in the past'; and she will not be able to report the *content* of her apparent memories faithfully except in this way, for even though she knows it to be false, what seems to her to be the case will precisely be that *she* once walked on the marble paving of a square, hearing the flapping of flying pigeons, etc., etc.

A world in which there was quasi-remembering which was not remembering and in which quasi-memories did not come labelled as apparent memories of their possessors' own pasts, then, would at least have to be a world in which spontaneous, uninhibited reports of quasi-memory were not first-personal in form. But to imagine such a world it seems that we must imagine a world in which quasi-memory is a natural phenomenon 'underwritten by evolution' as Evans puts it (1982), and not merely the result of surgical advances.

Let us imagine, then, a world in which when children learn to talk they are able spontaneously to report on events in the past lives of their parents, just as we are able spontaneously to report on events in our own past lives. The reason why our reports of our memories of experiences and actions are spontaneously first-personal is that this is how we were brought up, trained, to report them by our elders, who themselves spontaneously reported their memories of their own experiences and actions in the same way. But in the imagined world, if the capacity to report an event in the lives of one's parents is a natural phenomenon, adults will not habitually employ such first-personal reports in giving expression to their quasi-memories (just as Jane, in Parfit's case, will learn to refrain from doing so), they will use a less committed form of words (which need not be translatable into our language). And so the children will do so, too. First-person reports of apparent memories will be regarded as justified only when there is evidence – from its content or some other source – that the quasi-memory in question is, in fact, a genuine memory, and children who make first-person memory reports in the absence of such evidence will be corrected by their elders.

In our imagined community of quasi-rememberers, then, spontaneous reports of quasi-memories of actions and experiences will not be first-personal. But if so this greatly reduces the plausibility of the claim that the content of these quasi-memories can only be faithfully reported in this manner. For to insist on this is to insist that the members of this community refrain, in their spontaneous reports of their quasi-memories, from telling the whole truth about how things seem to them. But how could we possibly convince them of this? And if we could not, what is the objective content of the claim that, none the less, it *is* so?

However, if it is allowed that in this community, in which quasi-memory 'from the inside' of the actions and experiences of others is a natural phenomenon, someone can have an apparent memory of *F*-ing without thereby having an apparent memory as of *himself* *F*-ing, then it seems to follow that the content of an apparent memory is not determined by its intrinsic features but by its causal role – in particular, by the contents of the belief it tends to produce in its subject. For it seems impossible to deny that a member of this community might have an apparent memory which is indistinguishable in respect of its intrinsic nature from one of ours. Either the notion of the intrinsic features of a memory state makes no sense, then, or identity of content of such states is not guaranteed by identity of intrinsic features.

I believe that these considerations provide good reasons for denying that an apparent memory of *F*-ing must necessarily be an apparent memory of *oneself* F-ing. Initially this might seem to be true merely as a matter of grammar. But equally it might initially seem to be a mere matter of grammar that imagining *F*-ing is the same as imagining *that* one is *F*-ing or imagining *oneself* F-ing. This latter equation is incorrect, however; one can imagine seeing a tree without imagining *that one* is seeing a tree or *one's* seeing a tree, and in general one can imagine a situation from a point of view which, if the situation were actual, would be that of a participant in it, without imagining oneself to *be* a participant in the situation (see Williams 1973:26–45). Equally one can have an apparent memory of *F*-ing (in possible worlds of the type imagined above) without having an apparent memory *that one* is *F*-ing or an apparent memory of *oneself F*-ing. All that we can say, in general, about imagining *F*-ing is that to imagine *F*-ing is to imagine *F*-ing from the point of view of a *subject*, whose identity with someone existing outside this particular imaginative activity (whether this be oneself, or another actual person, or a creature of legend or fiction or myth) may, or may not, be part of what is imagined. Similarly, all that is necessarily true of apparently remembering, is that an apparent memory of *F*-ing is an apparent memory of *F*-ing from *a* point of view. This point of view may be that of one's actual empirical self, or as in the case of a quasi-memory which is not a memory, it may be that of some other subject. But the identity of this subject need be no part of the content of the apparent memory, just as it need be no part of what is imagined when one imagines *F*-ing.

I conclude that the circularity objection considered in this section, which if valid would undermine my own views as well as those of Shoemaker, can be met. I turn now to my own objection to Shoemaker's position.

8.6 *M-connectedness and personal identity*

A faculty of quasi-memory is meant to provide its possessor with a capacity for *knowledge* of the past and Shoemaker is able to demonstrate that this condition can only be satisfied if the region of the past to which the quasi-rememberer has access is significantly restricted; a capacity for 'knowledge' of the past which was too extensive would simply fail to yield any knowledge at all (Shoemaker 1970). Shoemaker suggests that we can impose the necessary restriction by adding to the notion of quasi-memory (*G*) as already characterized a further element which he thinks is present in the ordinary notion of memory – namely that if I remember being *F* then my cognitive state is partly caused by my earlier being *F*. So we get a stipulation on a stronger notion of quasi-memory, namely that if I quasi-remember (someone's) being *F* then my cognitive state must be partly caused by someone's earlier being *F*. If, as is generally assumed, causal chains must follow spatio-temporally continuous paths, this condition preserves the notion of quasi-memory as a faculty capable of yielding knowledge of the past.

So far, I think, so good. As his argument convincingly establishes, in requiring this causal constraint Shoemaker is not just imposing an arbitrary restriction on the notion of quasi-memory, but merely drawing out what was already implicit in the initial characterization of the notion.

But so far, of course, we have not got to Shoemaker's own notion of quasi-memory, i.e. quasi-memory (R), for no mention has yet been made of M-type causal chains.

That the knowledge of the past provided by a faculty of quasi-memory should be non-inferential, of course, imposes *some* contraints on the type of (spatio-temporally continuous) causal chain which can link a quasi-memory to the event of which it is the memory, but obviously Shoemaker intends further restrictions to be implied by the notion of an 'M-type' causal chain. For his intention is that quasi-memory (R) should be as much like memory *as possible*, consistently with the possibility of people sometimes quasi-remembering events they did not witness, and so M-type causal chains should resemble as much as possible the causal chains that are responsible for actual remembering, i.e. should remember them as much as is compatible with their sometimes linking mental states belonging to different persons (1970:278).

But why does Shoemaker impose this further condition on quasi-memory? The reason is simply that it enables him to go on to define personal identity in terms of quasi-memory, and specifically, to offer as a sufficient condition of personal identity *having a quasi-memory which is linked by a non-branching M-type causal chain with a cognitive and sensory state of*. In short quasi-memory (R) is restricted as it is *for no other reason* than to enable personal identity to be defined in terms of it.

But now the suspicion naturally arises that the notion of an M-type causal chain, and hence the notion of quasi-memory (R), can *only* be characterized using the notion of personal identity, in which case the whole enterprise turns out, after all, to be hopelessly circular.

Shoemaker puts his finger on the crucial issue here in a footnote:

> if quasi-remembering is to be as much like remembering as
> possible then not just any causal chain linking a past cognitive
> and sensory state with a subsequent quasi-memory can be

allowed to count as an M-type causal chain. For . . . there are
. . . cases in which a man's knowledge of a past event is
causally due to his previous experiences of it but in which the
causal connection is obviously not of the right kind to permit
us to say that he remembers the event. . . . *The notion of an
M-type causal chain would, of course, be completely useless if
it were impossible to determine in any particular case whether
the causal connection is 'of the right kind' without already
having determined that the case is one of remembering* – but I
shall argue in Section V that this is not impossible.

(1970:278, my italics)

Let us look, then, at the argument Shoemaker offers us in his
section V. What he says is this:

let us take 'remember-W' to be synonymous with 'quasi-
remember'. Clearly to establish that S remembers-W an event
E it is not necessary to establish that S himself witnessed E, for
it will be enough if S is the offshoot of someone who witnessed
E. And while one cannot claim that statements about what
events or actions a man remembers-W logically entail
statements about his identity and past history, this does not
prevent the truth of the former being criterial evidence for, and
partly constitutive of, the truth of the latter. For we can still
assert as a logical truth that if S remembers-W event E, and *if*
there has been no branching of M-type causal chains during
the relevant stretch of S's history then S is one of the witnesses
of E. Here we avoid the circularity that Butler and others have
thought to be involved in any attempt to give an account of
personal identity, and of the criteria of personal identity in
terms of memory.

(1970:281)

The first point to note about this response to the difficulty is that
it rests squarely on a rejection of the Only *x* and *y* principle. For on
the account of personal identity being proposed a quasi-memory
will fail to be a memory only when there has been a branching of
M-type causal chains and all that will prevent a quasi-rememberer in
such a case from being a rememberer is that he is only one of several
rival candidates for identity with the original person or (as in a case
of fusion) that there are several rival candidates for identity with

him. If, then, as I have argued in Chapter 7, the Only x and y principle should be accepted, Shoemaker's defence of his definition against the charge of circularity fails.

But I think that it fails anyway, even if the Only x and y principle is set aside. In that case, as Shoemaker intends, there will be possible cases of quasi-memory which are not cases of memory so long as branching of M-type causal chains is a possibility. In particular, when in a fission case an offshoot of an original person quasi-remembers some event which was witnessed by that person this will not be a case of memory. But now, how is one to decide that someone is an offshoot of a previous person? It is not sufficient that his cognitive states should be causally connected to cognitive and sensory states of the previous person, nor is it sufficient that he should in consequence have the capacity to inform us of events in the life of the previous person of which he has encountered no later indications in the form of evidence or testimony. For all this will not guarantee the presence of an M-link, the type of link involved in memory. But then how *is* this to be determined? I think it is clear what one must do to determine that someone is an offshoot of a past person – that the kind of causal link between their mental states is an M-link. One must ask what is wrong with identifying him with the past person – what is lacking that such an identification requires. Suppose one can find nothing wrong and is forced to say that all that speaks against the identification is the existence of another candidate, equally good or better, and that if the present person had been thus related to the past person without any other candidate existing he would have *been* that person. *Then* the link is an M-link and the present person is an offshoot of the past person. Otherwise not.

But if this right one can determine that someone is quasi-remembering only by employing the concept of personal identity. For one can determine that someone is quasi-remembering only by determining that he is (at least) an *offshoot* of the person whose life he apparently remembers (for brevity I ignore the possibility of fusion), and one can determine that this is so only by considering the applicability of the concept of personal identity to the (possibly counterfactual) situation in which no competing candidate for identity with that earlier person is available.

Evidently, then, whether or not the Only x and y principle is accepted Shoemaker's attempt to answer the circularity objection to his account of personal identity fails. For like the concept of memory itself the concept of quasi-memory (R), which he employs, defined via the notion of an M-type causal chain, is epistemologically posterior to the concept of personal identity.

This point can be driven home by thinking again about the possible world considered earlier in which quasi-memory, i.e. quasi-memory (G), is a natural phenomenon. This might be a world in which children have quasi-memories of events in the lives of their mothers before they were born. Now the details of such a world might be imagined in various ways. But let us suppose that, in fact, such quasi-memories are a fairly infrequent phenomenon (though under hypnotic suggestion, say, children who have never done so spontaneously can be brought to make accurate quasi-memory claims), and that there is no Lamarckian inheritance of abilities or character traits, etc. Then in such a world, I take it, it would be incorrect to regard mother and child as one person.

Of course, in many cases this would be entirely in conformity with Shoemaker's account of personal identity. For whenever the mother did not die in childbirth she would be a rival (and superior) candidate for identity with her earlier self, and whenever she had several children these would be competing candidates. So in all these cases Shoemaker's account of personal identity would yield the intuitively correct result.

However, it would not do so in a case in which the mother *did* die in childbirth and only *one* child was born – unless it was claimed that in this case there was no M-link between the child's apparent memories and the mother's experiences, so that the child's apparent memories were not after all quasi-memories (R). But, of course, one would have no reason in such a case, independently of one's prior conviction that the mother and child were *not* one person, to deny that the causal link in question was an M-link. Once again the point that emerges is the epistemological priority of the notion of personal identity to that of M-connectedness or quasi-memory (R).

Of course, this still leaves us with quasi-memory (G), and nothing I have said shows that there is anything wrong with the proposal that this notion of quasi-memory can be used as one of the ingredients in a more general psychological continuity criterion of personal identity.

But what, then, becomes of Shoemaker's claims about the special access a subject necessarily has to his own past?

Shoemaker's first point was that quasi-memories have an *a priori* evidential status relative to claims of personal identity, so that when reflecting on the question whether one is identical with a quasi-remembered self (i.e. a person of whom one has quasi-memories 'from the inside') one is necessarily committed to acknowledging that one has, at least, *one* piece of evidence in favour of the identity, albeit a defeasible one. In the context of a more general psychological continuity account of personal identity this point remains valid. I cannot simultaneously query the status of my apparent quasi-memories (G) and raise the question of my identity with the quasi-remembered self; so in raising the question I must accept the apparent quasi-memories as genuine and hence accept that I have some evidence in favour of the identity. And this point does bring out a significant difference between my knowledge of my own identity over time and my knowledge of the identity over time of others. For I can, of course, raise the question whether *you* are identical with a person I (quasi-)remember without thinking myself to have any evidence in favour of the identity claim.

A related point is that I can raise the question of your identity with a person I (quasi-)remember without presupposing that *your* present psychological states have any causal links with his, and, therefore, without presupposing that *you* have any knowledge of his life, but I cannot raise the question of my own identity with a quasi-remembered self whilst remaining agnostic about my possession of knowledge of his life or about the existence of causal dependencies between my psychological states and his. (This point, it should be noted, holds even if a purely physicalistic account of personal identity is correct.)

These points, I believe, constitute what I referred to earlier as the element of truth in Shoemaker's insistence on the thesis that a subject necessarily has a special access to his own past history. But Shoemaker goes beyond them, and I believe, goes too far, when he insists that even in a world in which there is quasi-memory which is not memory, a subject's knowledge of his own identity cannot be grounded in criteria of personal identity.

Shoemaker's thought is that, if one quasi-remembers someone's life 'from the inside' one can only fail to be identical with him if there has been a branching of M-type causal chains, but to determine that there has been no such branching is radically unlike applying a criterion of personal identity to determine whether someone other than oneself is identical with someone one remembers. But, of course, this point lapses if, as I have argued, there can be quasi-remembering which is not remembering even in the absence of branching. And in a world in which this possibility was realized determining one's identity with a quasi-remembered self would be very much akin to determining the identity of a third person with someone of whom one had a quasi-memory: it would be appropriate to take into account the similarity of the quasi-remembered self to one's present self; the likelihood of the similarity being a mere coincidence; the richness and variety of the causal dependencies between one's present psychological states and his, etc.

In fact, as things are, our knowledge of our own past is non-criterial and we do have in memory a special access to our own past histories. But the lesson to be learned from this discussion of quasi-memory is that these things are so only because of *contingent* facts of human nature. In other possible worlds, to which our concept of a person still has unproblematic application, these things are otherwise.

And so, I suggest, notwithstanding the ineffectiveness of the circularity objection, the memory theorist is refuted. David Wiggins writes:

> If one defines a person in Locke's manner, and if one also attaches so much importance to the self-recording faculty of experiential memory that active exercise of the faculty becomes a criterial property for being a person, then it will be very natural to expect that, by virtue of being counted as part of the condition of existence and persistence, this active exercise will register upon the identity conditions for persons. This will seem to follow from certain truths that are now very familiar . . . about the intimate relation holding between an account of *what a thing is* and the elucidation of the identity condition for members of its kind. In the end, though, this natural expectation is disappointed. Memory registers only faintly on identity conditions . . . though experiential memory is one component in an inner nucleus of conceptual constituents of what it is for a person to continue to exist . . . there is no strictly necessary or sufficient condition of survival that one can formulate in its terms.
>
> (1980:151)

That, I submit, is exactly right.

CHAPTER 9
Parfit and What Matters in Survival

9.1 Introduction

In his first paper on the subject of personal identity Derek Parfit (1971) formulated his famous thesis 'identity is not what matters in survival'. In his book *Reasons and Persons* (1984) he returns to the defence of this thesis.

Parfit also argues for a version of the Psychological Continuity Criterion of personal identity according to which personal identity has a 'best candidate' structure, and explicitly rejects the Only x and y principle. In fact, his rejection of this principle is a crucial component of his argument for his thesis that identity is not what matters in survival.

It is this thesis which is the topic of this chapter. The first task is to get clear about what it means.

9.2 Identity and survival

What Parfit means by his claim that identity is not what matters in survival is that one's concern for one's own future existence and well-being is a derivative concern: a concern not for an end but for a means to an end. What this end is, is the existence and well-being of a future person (or future persons) related to oneself by certain relations of psychological continuity and connectedness. Let us call such people one's 'Parfitian survivors'. Then, Parfit claims, that one has a *Parfitian* survivor at a future time does not entail that one has a *literal* survivor at that time, i.e. that one *exists* at that time, that one of the people alive at that time is *identical* with oneself; and so, in certain conceivable, and perhaps merely future, circumstances (in which *Star Trek* technology, brain transplants, etc., were possible) one would be able to ensure a Parfitian survivor for oneself without ensuring one's literal survival. In such circumstances, given the guarantee of a Parfitian survivor, one would have *no* reason to seek to ensure one's literal survival, and it would be positively irrational to do so if any price had to be paid, i.e. if one could only do so by reducing, even marginally, one's present level of well-being. But as things are this is not so. Given the actual state of present medical technology the *only* way that one can ensure that one has a Parfitian survivor is by ensuring one's *literal* survival, and so one does have a reason to seek the latter. But this is merely a derivative reason, even though most of us do not realize this because we do not reflect enough on puzzle cases about personal identity.

Parfit uses an analogy to illustrate this claim. Most of us value our eyes, but we do so, plausibly, only as a means to various ends and not as ends in themselves. We value our eyes as providing us with information about the world and as a source of a variety of pleasurable visual experiences. But if our eyes could be replaced by artificial devices which served as well in these respects we would not regard the prospect with horror (just as people do not now regard the prospect of false teeth with horror). At a time when medical technology was less advanced we might have found this idea hard to grasp. But given the present state of medical technology it is fairly obvious. By contrast the kind of medical technology which could create a state of affairs in which one had a Parfitian survivor who was other than oneself is still wildly science-fictional. Nevertheless, Parfit claims, when we reflect on cases in which we imagine such technology to be available we can see that our concern for our literal survival has, in fact, the same derivative status as our concern for our natural eyes or teeth.

Of course, this claim of Parfit's is deeply counter-intuitive. As I explained in Chapter 1, we would ordinarily think that a community of people who used *Star Trek* teletransportation as an alternative to travel believed the process to be identity preserving. If they explained to us that this was not so we would regard their use of the teletransporter as an indication that they were quite mad, or anyhow, wholly alien. But according to Parfit we would be quite wrong to do so. For far from being mad these people would be acting exactly as it would be rational for us to act, given our present desires and concerns, if we were given the opportunity to use the teletransporter. It would be quite irrational for us, according to Parfit, given these desires and concerns, to refuse to use the teletransporter on the ground that teletransportation was not an identity-preserving process. For this could only be relevant if, over and above our interest in *Parfitian* survival, we also had an interest in *literal* survival. But, Parfit's thesis is, we do not.

9.3 What does matter

So much for an initial statement of Parfit's thesis. But before turning to his argument for it, let us look at it a little more closely.

First, it should be noted that the thesis in fact has two components: a negative component and a positive component. The negative component is that our interest in *literal* survival is merely a derivative interest. The positive component is that what this is derivative from is an interest in *Parfitian* survival. The content of this latter component of the thesis is obviously crucially dependent on the precise explanation of the notion of 'Parfitian survival'. So far in explaining this I have merely referred vaguely to psychological continuity and connectedness. But, as we shall see, Parfit himself distinguishes various forms of psychological continuity and connectedness in terms of the types of causation involved, and argues that only one of these (what he calls connectedness/continuity in the 'widest sense') deserves to be regarded as what really matters in survival. Obviously, then, one could agree with the negative component of Parfit's thesis whilst disagreeing with its positive component.

An additional complication is that the negative component of Parfit's thesis is itself complex. In fact it is a conjunction. What it says is that *neither* our literal survival *nor* our own future well-being (as opposed to that of our Parfitian survivors) is of non-derivative concern to us. In short, *all* self-concern is derivative. But the two conjuncts are separable. Another view might be that though our concern for our literal survival has a derivative status, this is not true of our concern for our own future well-being. In fact, this is Nozick's view (1981).

The difference between these views is that, according to Nozick's view, if I knew that I was going to have a Parfitian survivor but (for whatever reason) that I was not going to survive in the literal non-

Parfitian sense, then I would have no reason to worry. And for me to spend a great deal of money (or even a little money) in such circumstances to try to ensure my literal survival would be wholly irrational. But if I was informed that I was going to survive, in the literal sense, but was going to be horribly tortured tomorrow, then it would be rational for me to try to prevent this – even if I knew that all I could hope for instead was a situation in which I did not exist but the occupant of the torture chamber was my (perhaps only) Parfitian survivor. According to Parfit's view, by contrast, in such circumstances the only rational thing for me to do would be to resign myself to my fate. For it could rationally be of no comfort to me to know that not I myself, but merely one of my Parfitian survivors, was to be tortured tomorrow.

However, this disagreement between Nozick and Parfit is not of great importance to us at present (though it will become so). We shall return to it later.

9.4 Fission and survival

Parfit's basic argument for his thesis was explained in Chapter 1. It begins from a reflection about fission. Parfit argues (a) that a fission case such as the familiar split-brain transplant case must be described as a case in which the original person ceases to exist, but would not have done so if only one of the fission products had come into being, but (b) that it would be quite irrational, if you were the original in the case, to be concerned about the impending fission in the same way as you would be concerned about your impending death, or to think that you could gain anything by preventing the fission, e.g. by bribing a nurse to destroy one of the brain hemispheres before the transplant – thus reducing the number of fission products to one. But these conclusions, he notes, are apparently in conflict. For according to the first, whether the original person lives or dies depends crucially on whether there is one fission product or two, whilst according to the second it must be a matter of total indifference to the original person whether there is one fission product or two. However, Parfit claims, this appearance of conflict can be explained away by rejecting the common-sense view that our literal survival is a matter of non-derivative concern to us and accepting in its stead his thesis that what we really care about is merely non-literal, Parfitian survival, and since this is the *only* way to explain away the apparent conflict, this is what we should do.

9.5 *Assessment of the argument*

As we have seen, there are various views about the correct way to describe fission cases. The description Parfit endorses entails that one person ceases to exist at the fission, no one survives it (in the literal sense) and two new people come into being in consequence of it, and is straightforwardly inconsistent with the Only *x* and *y* principle (naturally, since it is a consequence of a 'best candidate' Psychological Continuity Criterion of personal identity). And if it is accepted, the conclusion Parfit draws seems virtually self-evident. For to accept this description of the fission case is to accept that one's identity or non-identity with a later person is something that can be determined extrinsically, by the existence or non-existence of a rival candidate. But it seems perfectly evident (and this is the source of the plausibility of contention (b)) that whether I stand in the relations that matter in survival to a future person cannot be something that is determined by anything other than the *intrinsic* relations between us.

Parfit's argument thus does establish, I believe, that one cannot *both* maintain a criterion of personal identity which conflicts with the Only *x* and *y* principle *and* maintain the common-sense view that our concern for our literal survival is non-derivative. But, of course, this is not enough for his purposes. For it leaves open the option of embracing the Only *x* and *y* principle and rejecting his thesis.

One way of doing this has been developed by David Lewis (1976), who puts forward an account of personal identity in conformity with the Only *x* and *y* principle according to which *no one* ceases to exist when the fission takes place, so that *of course* it is absurd to regard it as death. But Lewis's account of personal identity is not the only one consistent with the Only *x* and *y* principle, and another, whilst equally enabling us to reject Parfit's argument, might be preferable on other grounds. In fact, I think that this is so, and I will be developing such an account later. But for now the point I wish to stress is merely that Parfit's argument, as so far described, is inconclusive: it establishes that one cannot *both* regard personal identity as something which is of non-derivative importance *and* regard it as determinable by extrinsic facts, but it gives no reason why one should not retain the common-sense view that personal identity is *both* of non-derivative importance *and* intrinsically determined.

And, in fact, such a response would not be merely *ad hoc*, as we saw earlier. For there are very strong arguments for the Only *x* and *y* principle, as a constraint not just on personal identity, but on identity over time far more generally. Nor is there any logical objection to an account of personal identity in conformity with the Only *x* and *y* principle: it is just that any such account, applied to a fission case, must entail the Multiple Occupancy Thesis, the thesis that two or more persons may be at a given time the co-occupants of a certain body and the joint thinkers of certain thoughts. But whilst the Multiple Occupancy Thesis is undeniably counter-intuitive, it is certainly no more counter-intuitive than Parfit's thesis.

Parfit does make an attempt to explain away the plausibility of the Only *x* and *y* principle, but there are two respects in which this attempt is inadequate. According to Parfit the reason why we find the Only *x* and *y* principle plausible is that we mistakenly believe that identity *is* the relation that matters in survival, i.e. we mistakenly believe that we do have a non-derivative concern for our survival in the literal sense. Because we make this mistake we illegitimately ascribe properties of the relations that do matter to identity. Now it is the case that whether *these* relations (namely, psychological continuity and connectedness) hold between an earlier person and a later one cannot be determined extrinsically, and so we find it plausible to say the same of identity.

But in the present context, of course, this attempt to explain away the plausibility of the Only *x* and *y* principle is entirely question-begging: for what is at issue is precisely whether we are *mistaken* in ascribing to ourselves a non-derivative concern for our survival in the literal sense. And we have seen that unless we have prior reason to reject the Only *x* and *y* principle Parfit's argument provides no reason at all to think that this is so.

The second defect in Parfit's proposal is that it can at best explain away our finding the Only *x* and *y* principle plausible as a constraint on *personal identity*. Neither it, nor any analogous proposal, can explain why we find the Only *x* and *y* principle plausible more generally. For, of course, there is no plausibility at all in the suggestion, which would be crucial to any such proposal, that we misconceive the nature of our interest in things other than persons, i.e. that we think, mistakenly, that the literal survival of such things is of non-derivative concern to us. For me to think this would be for me to believe, for example, that I have a non-derivative interest in the literal survival, i.e. continuing existence, of this computer. But I know that I do not. I know that I value this computer merely as a locus of utilizable characteristics and would have it replaced by another such locus without any compunction whatsoever. And, of course, in this regard I am no different from anyone else. We all value things other than persons (and, perhaps, some animals) merely as loci of useful or pleasing or otherwise desirable characteristics, and yet, quite inexplicably, if Parfit is right in his diagnosis of our adherence to it, we *still* find the Only *x* and *y* principle plausible as a constraint on their identity over time. The plausibility of this principle must thus lie deeper than Parfit suggests.

9.6 Anti-Parfit

So far, then, I have argued that Parfit's argument for his thesis that identity does not matter in survival ought not to convince an advocate of the Only *x* and *y* principle, who can retain the common-sense view of its non-derivative importance so long as he is prepared to accept an account of fission which allows for multiple occupancy, and I have argued that Parfit fails to explain away in a satisfactory manner why the Only *x* and *y* principle does seem so plausible. But nothing I have said so far provides a positive argument *against* Parfit's position. However, I believe that there is such an argument, which I owe to Nozick.

The fundamental point of this argument is that there is only one way in which Parfit can explain the derivativeness of our self-concern, namely as derivative from our concern for the future existence and well-being of our Parfitian survivors. But this is not in accordance with other intuitions we have, which are as worthy of attention as those on which Parfit's argument relies.

To see this point one must recall that the most plausible version of the Revised Psychological Continuity Criterion of personal identity (and, in fact, the one accepted by Parfit) is the 'best candidate' version, according to which a *sufficient* condition of a later person's identity with an earlier person is that he be, in respect of psychological continuity and/or connectedness a *better candidate*, or to use

Nozick's terminology, since it is his argument which is to be expounded, a *closer continuer*, than any other contemporary person.

According to the Revised Psychological Continuity Criterion, so understood, then, a multiplicity of later candidates for identity with an earlier person does not automatically mean that the earlier person no longer exists at the later time: this will be so only if there is no *best* candidate, no *closest* continuer, but instead, as Nozick puts it, a tie for first place.

The sort of case to which it is tempting to apply this type of account of personal identity is vividly illustrated by Parfit. He first refers to the familiar *Star Trek* notion of teletransportation, and then introduces the *Branch Line Case*:

> I am often teletransported. I am now . . . ready for another trip to Mars. But this time, when I press the green button, I do not lose consciousness. . . . I say to the attendant 'It's not working. What did I do wrong?' 'It's working', he replies, handing me a printed card. This reads: 'The New Scanner records your blueprint without destroying your brain and body. We hope that you will welcome the opportunities which this technical advance offers.' The attendant tells me that I am one of the first people to use the New Scanner. He adds that if I stay for an hour, I can use the Intercom to see and talk to myself on Mars. 'Wait a minute', I reply. 'If I'm here I can't also be on Mars.' . . . a white-coated man asks to speak to me in private. . . . Then he says: 'I'm afraid that we're having problems with the New Scanner. It records your blueprint just as accurately, as you will see when you talk to yourself on Mars. But it seems to be damaging the cardiac system which it scans. Judging from the results so far, though you will be quite healthy on Mars, here on Earth you must expect cardiac failure within the next few days.' The attendant later calls me to the Intercom. On the screen I see myself just as I do in the mirror every morning. But there are two differences. On the screen I am not left-right reversed. And while I stand here speechless I can see and hear myself, in the study, on Mars, starting to speak.
>
> (1984:199)

When one thinks of this sort of case, the 'best candidate' approach to personal identity over time can seem very plausible. The person left on Earth is the best candidate for identity with the original person and so *is* the original person, but if he had not existed (in which case we would have had a case of what Parfit calls *Simple Teletransportation*) then the person on Mars would have been the original person, since he would then have been the best (indeed, the only) candidate.

However, if a version of the Revised Psychological Continuity Criterion of personal identity which gives these results is accepted a problem now arises for Parfit. For reflection on the Branch Line Case in conjunction with the Case of Simple Teletransportation strongly suggests that when there *is* a best candidate, or closest continuer, I will care especially about it in a way that is not determined by and does not merely reflect, its additional degree of closeness. The person on Mars is psychologically continuous and connected with the original person to just the same degree in both the Branch Line Case and the Case of Simple Teletransportation, but in the former case he is a *mere* Parfitian survivor, a *mere* continuer, whereas in the latter case he is the *closest* continuer of that person, and so *is* that person. If I imagine myself to be the original person in these two cases and try to think about how I should view the future it seems to me that looking ahead in the Branch Line Case I should have some concern for the Parfitian survivor on Mars, but not as much as I should have for the closest continuer left on Earth – the news of whose imminent heart attack will fill me with fear and trembling. On the other hand looking ahead in the case of Simple Teletransportation I should care more about the fate of the person on Mars then I should in the Branch Line case, and in fact should be as concerned about his fate as I am about my own future fate in *any* situation, including that of the Branch Line Case.

But, if this is right, degree of care is *not* directly proportional to, or determined by, degree of closeness of continuity, as Parfit's account of the derivativeness of our self-concern implies. My concern for the fate of the person who I believe will, in some anticipated situation, be me, is a special one, and it is not simply explicable as concern for someone who is continuous with me to a certain degree.

This argument against Parfit is, as I said, Nozick's. But in presenting it Nozick makes a mistake which the statement just given avoids, and causes Parfit, in his discussion of Nozick, to miss the point (1984:477ff.).

According to Nozick, the reason why degree of care is not directly proportional to degree of closeness is that the degree of care one has for one's closest continuer, i.e. for oneself, is a *constant*, which is independent of degree of closeness. As he expresses it: 'Let $c(x,y)$ be the amount of care that x has for y as x's closest continuer, the care which is especially for the closest continuer *qua* closest continuer. When y is not x's closest continuer then $c(x,y) = 0$' (1981:63). However, when y is x's closest continuer, then, irrespective of the degree of closeness of y to x, care (x,y) equals $c(x,y)$. That is, the special degree of care one has for one's closest continuer *qua* closest continuer is not added on to an existing care proportional to the degree of closeness. Rather, the degree of care one has for one's closest continuer is equal across situations in which its degree of closeness varies, and is always greater than any degree of care for any (temporally equidistant) continuer that is not closest (Nozick 1981:63–4).

But this is implausible, as Parfit points out (1984:478). When one thinks of cases like that of his Combined Spectrum it seems clear that one's degree of care for a future self will not be independent of its degree of closeness to oneself. This is also evident from the Methuselah case. Parfit is right to criticize Nozick on this point. But the argument against Parfit's position as I have stated it does not need Nozick's implausible assumption. All it requires is that the original person's concern for his continuer on Mars in the Case of Simple Teletransportation should be *greater* than his concern for him in the Branch Line Case, and this seems undeniable. (Actually, though, although not needed by the argument, it does seem intuitively correct that it should be *as great* in the Case of Simple Teletransportation as his concern for the person left on Earth in the Branch Line Case: but this is not in conflict with the anti-Nozickian intuitions about the Combined Spectrum and Methuselah just noted, since it is only in respect of physical continuity and the under-lying cause of the psychological continuity that the continuer on Mars in the Branch Line Case is inferior to his counterpart on Earth.)

9.7 The Only x and y principle revisited

Let us now take stock. What we have seen is that there are two sorts of intuition about puzzle cases to explain. First of all there are the intuitions about fission upon which Parfit rests his argument that identity cannot matter in survival. Most importantly, the intuition that the original person could gain nothing of value to him by ensuring that he had only one Parfitian survivor, and thus would be wholly irrational to sacrifice anything to ensure such uniqueness, But second, there are the intuitions, just discussed in the last section, which make it apparent that our self-concern has aspects which are not explicable if it is taken to be merely derivative from a concern of our Parfitian survivors.

I have claimed that Parfit's argument for the derivativeness of our self-concern, which is based on the first of these sets of intuitions, begs the question against proponents of the Only *x* and *y* principle. But I have acknowledged that if a 'best candidate' version of the Psychological Continuity Criterion of personal identity (or, in fact, any account of personal identity inconsistent with the Only *x* and *y* principle) is accepted, then our intuitions about fission must be regarded as inconsistent with the common-sense view that it is identity that matters in survival. However, I have argued that in the context of any such 'best candidate' or 'closest continuer' theory of personal identity Parfit's thesis that what really concerns us is solely Parfitian survival and the well-being of our Parfitian survivors is inconsistent with the second set of intuitions which were discussed in the last section. Thus any hope of providing a *comprehensive* account of our intuitions rests on rejecting Parfit's position. The distinction noted earlier between Parfit's position and Nozick's now becomes relevant. For, of course, it is his own position that Nozick intends the argument outlined in the last section to support.

Now Nozick's position, like Parfit's, involves a denial of the Only *x* and *y* principle, and, like Parfit's, it claims that our concern for our literal *survival* is derivative from a concern for Parfitian survival. But unlike Parfit's position it claims that our concern for our future *well-being* is *not* merely derivative from a concern for the well-being of our Parfitian survivors. Thus it appears that it might be capable of providing the comprehensive account of our intuitions that Parfit's position cannot. The argument of the last section, though it refutes Parfit's position, thus cannot be taken as a demonstration of the correctness of the common-sense view that identity is what matters in survival, for the crucial question now becomes whether Nozick's position is satisfactory. I believe, however, and will argue in the last chapter, that it is not. In fact, quite apart from the fact that it conflicts with the Only x and y principle, which is, I think, in itself a sufficient reason to reject it, it is as incapable as Parfit's position of explaining the intuitions to which Nozick draws attention. These intuitions *can* be explained, I believe, but only in the context of a position which accords with common sense *both* in regarding personal identity as what matters in survival *and* in regarding it as intrinsically determined.

However, these remarks are by the way, the important point to keep hold of for present purposes is that whatever may be said about Nozick's position, Parfit's at least is refuted.

9.8 Parfitian survival and trivial facts

Another line of argument to this same conclusion, which will deepen our understanding of what is at issue between Parfit and common sense, can start from a closer examination of what was earlier described as the positive component of Parfit's thesis.

According to this what does have non-derivative importance in survival is the obtaining of what Parfit calls 'relation R' – psychological continuity and connectedness *with any cause*, or what Parfit calls psychological continuity/connectedness 'in the widest sense'. Whether the cause is the normal one, or even a reliable one, is completely irrelevant, for any cause is as good as any other, since it is solely the *effect* that matters (1984:286). Thus I have a survivor, in the non-literal, Parfitian sense, at some future time t just in case (a) there is a person at t who is psychologically continuous and/or connected with me, and (b) this person's psychological states at t are *in some way or other* causally derivative from my present psychological states. And *I myself* will be in existence at t, according to Parfit's 'best candidate' version of the Revised Psychological Continuity Criterion of personal identity, if (a) and (b) are both satisfied and, in addition, the Parfitian survivor in question is the best (or only) candidate for identity with me existing at t.

To make the implications of this vivid, let us imagine the following. At time t, which is sometime after what would ordinarily be referred to as 'my death', you fall into the hands of a lunatic brain scientist. This person has studied my history intensively and for perverse reasons of his own has come up with a plan to 'resurrect' me. What he intends to do is to use his various techniques to transform you into a psychological replica of me. In fact, the man's theories about how to do this are as mad as he is, but by one in a million chance he succeeds. After he has finished with you, you think, act and talk like me, and you think you *are* me.

Now, according to Parfit's proposal, you may be right. Certainly you qualify as one of my Parfitian survivors at *t*. Unless I have another Parfitian survivor at *t*, then, according to Parfit, you *are* me. And whether or not this is so, the fact that you exist at *t*, thus transformed, is enough to ensure that whatever fears I had on my death-bed (relating, that is, to my imminent permanent departure from the scene of things rather than to any pain I might suffer, or the prospect of a possibly unpleasant after-life) were ill-founded. For what I desired then, whether I knew it or not, was merely the future existence of a Parfitian survivor, and that *you* are.

This story makes it clear how radical Parfit's proposal is. Before Parfit wrote, it was generally accepted by philosophers that whether a later person counted as 'psychologically continuous' with an earlier person in a sense relevant to personal identity would depend greatly upon the nature of the causal dependence of his psychological states on those of the earlier person. Parfit denies that this is so – *any* type of causal dependence will do.

Suppose, then, that I claim to remember some incident in my childhood, say, cutting open my head when I was 4 and being taken to hospital to have it stitched up. In fact, this never happened to me, but it did happen to my brother, who later told me all about it. The incident preyed on my mind and so deeply impressed me that somehow my knowledge of it transformed itself into a seeming memory of having undergone the ordeal myself. Now, according to Parfit, since I have this apparent recollection of the incident, and it is causally dependent (via his telling me of it) on my brother's experience then I *am* to some extent psychologically continuous with my brother in a way that is relevant to my being his Parfitian survivor. Of course, I am only continuous with him to a small degree, and I am far from being the best candidate for identity with him. But, none the less, the relation that holds between myself and my brother in virtue of his telling me of his experience is *of the right sort*, according to Parfit, to be one of the elements of relation *R* which in the absence of branching will constitute personal identity.

Intuitively, however, one wants to protest that this is quite wrong. The *provenance* of an apparent memory is crucially relevant to whether it qualifies as an element in psychological continuity, thought of as relevant to personal identity, and the provenance of this apparent memory, going as it does by way of the verbal recounting of the incident by its original subject, is quite inappropriate.

That Parfit is wrong to think that just any kind of causal dependence is enough for psychological continuity and/or connectedness can also be brought out by considering the application of his proposal to purported cases of reincarnation. In such a case the reincarnation claimant typically manifests knowledge of the life and history of a deceased person which, we are tempted to say, he had no way, in the normal course of events, of acquiring. Now investigators into such cases typically regard reincarnation as one hypothesis among many. And this is so even if they discount fraud. In particular, another hypothesis they will consider will be cryptomnesia, or 'hidden memory'. This occurs when someone, usually a child, gets information about a deceased person in the normal way, or at least, from normal sources, such as newspapers, history books, encyclopedias, overheard conversations, etc., but then forgets the source and remembers the information as if he were remembering events or incidents he himself witnessed. But according to Parfit's proposal it is a mistake to regard the cryptomnesia hypothesis as distinct from the survival hypothesis. If, say, a child reads the autobiography of a historical figure, Napoleon or whoever, and subsequently becomes deranged and imagines that he *is* the person in question, and acts and talks like him, etc., then, so long as no better candidate is around he *is* that person. This case might be very different from one in which a child begins to act like this who has had no exposure whatsoever to French history, but, according to Parfit, this difference cannot be relevant to whether the child *is* Napoleon: to answer that question we need only ask (a) whether there is a (sufficient degree of) psychological continuity, (b) whether this is causally grounded, and (c) whether it is non-branching. If all three are the case then there is personal identity however different the causal grounding of the psychological continuity from that in everyday cases of personal identity. Thus, if Parfit is right, the cryptomnesia hypothesis is not an *alternative* to the survival hypothesis in cases of claimed reincarnation, rather cryptomnesia is, essentially, merely one way in which survival might occur.

This is, I take it, a *reductio ad absurdum* of Parfit's position on personal identity. But Parfit might not be too concerned given his view of the intrinsic unimportance of personal identity. However, the point can be pressed further.

The essence of Parfit's argument for the merely derivative importance of identity in survival is that what matters non-derivatively in survival cannot depend on trivial facts, but whether identity obtains can depend on an extrinsic and hence trivial fact, and so identity itself cannot be of non-derivative importance. Hence since, according to Parfit, what *is* of non-derivative importance is the obtaining of relation *R*, he is committed to saying that whether *this* relation obtains cannot depend upon a trivial fact: the difference between a case in which it obtains and one in which it does not must be, to use one of his favourite expressions, *a deep difference*.

However, it seems that this will not necessarily be so. Consider the following series of science-fiction cases (taken from Ehring 1987).

(a) Future medical technology makes it possible to record on tape information giving the entire structure of a person's brain. It has become common in old age to arrange a transfer of one's memories and personality traits to a new body by way of this process. After the information is recorded the original body is destroyed and a new brain in a new body is restructured in accordance with the information on the tape. If we call the person with the old body *A* and the person with the new body *B* then we can suppose that *B* seems to remember having experiences which *A* had and that these apparent memories are causally dependent in some way on the experiences of *A*. There exists, then, both psychological connectedness and/or continuity between *A* and *B* and a causal dependence of *B*'s psychological states on those of *A*, i.e. *B* is a Parfitian survivor of *A*. The result then, on Parfit's view, should be regarded by *A*, looking forward, as being as good as literal survival.

(b) In this case an unlikely causal sequence occurs. After the information giving the state of *A*'s brain is recorded and *A*'s body is destroyed, the tape is accidentally dropped onto another recording machine. As a result the tape is damaged beyond repair. However, the tape hitting the machine causes it to malfunction, with the highly improbable outcome that this machine produces another tape exactly similar to the original. Although the original tape plays a causal role in the production of the new tape, the latter is not a *copy* of the former. A pre-prepared brain is restructured in accordance with the information on the new tape. The resulting person *B* is psychologically continuous and/or connected with A and there is a causal link between his psychological states and those of A. Consequently he is a Parfitian survivor of A. Once more, then, on Parfit's view, A, looking forward, should view the case as as good as literal survival.

(c) In this final case, just as in case (b) the original tape is dropped into another recording machine and is damaged beyond repair. However, in this case the dropping of the tape has no effect on the machine. None the less the machine produces an entirely similar tape at just that moment as a result of a causally unrelated accident. A pre-prepared brain is reconstructed in accordance with the information on this tape as before. The resultant person B seems to remember A's life, and is identical with him in character and personality just as in the previous two cases, but his psychological states are *not* causally linked to those of A. Hence he is not a Parfitian survivor of A on Parfit's view, and so the case should not be regarded as as good as literal survival by A, looking forward.

Now it seems clear that Parfit is right about case (c). It might be a comfort to me on my death-bed somehow to know that as a result of an amazing coincidence a psychological replica of me was going to be created centuries hence. It might equally be a comfort if I knew that a monument in my honour was in process of construction. However, if I were now given the opportunity of a very expensive, but possibly life-saving operation, neither piece of knowledge would make it rational for me to pass it by. Yet if the future psychological replica of me was linked to me by the relations that mattered in survival it *would* be rational for me, knowing that it was going to be created, to pass the life-saving operation by.

Parfit's view of case (c) thus seems to be correct. But, according to Parfit, case (b) is very different. Looking forward in case (c) A ought to regard what is to happen with despair. But looking forward in case (b) just as in case (a), he ought to be quite content. For in case (b) there is a causal link between his psychological states and those of B, albeit one of a highly accidental kind. But this difference between cases (c) and (b) is surely trivial. If A views case (c) with pessimism it is impossible to see why he should view case (b) differently – given the nature of the causal facts in the two cases. Of course, A *might* view the cases differently if he has a view of personal identity according to which he survives, in the literal sense, in case (b), but not in case (c). Such a view of personal identity, according to which non-branching psychological continuity and/or connectedness with *any* cause is all that is requisite for personal identity I have argued to be quite untenable. But whether this is so or not, it would be quite inappropriate for a defender of Parfit's position to appeal to it; for according to that position, the importance of personal identity is merely derivative. But if so, unless the difference between the causal structure of case (b) and case (c) can be seen to be of significance *without appeal* to its bearing on the issue of personal identity, it can have no significance at all.

And, in fact, I believe, this is actually the logical terminus of Parfit's own position. To see this let us look at the argument he gives that any type of causal grounding for psychological continuity is enough to ensure the presence of what matters in survival. The argument is actually an appeal to an analogy:

> Suppose there is an unreliable treatment for some disease. In most cases the treatment achieves nothing. But in a few cases it completely cures the disease. In these few cases only the effect matters. The effect is just as good, even though its cause was unreliable. We should claim the same about relation R. . . . In our concern about our own future, *what fundamentally matters is relation R* with any cause.
>
> (1984:287)

Certainly, if I am suffering from a life-threatening disease and I am then cured I will be indifferent to whether the treatment which cured me was a generally reliable one (except, as Parfit notes, for reasons irrelevant to his argument, e.g. I might want to sue the doctor for using me as a guinea-pig without my permission). But equally, I will be indifferent to whether my recovery had *any* assignable cause. All that will matter to me will be that I am well again. By parallel reasoning then if, as Parfit claims, I ought to be indifferent to whether a future psychological replica of me is going to be produced by a reliable causal process or by an unreliable causal process, I ought also to be indifferent to whether his psychological states are in *any way* causally linked to mine. In each of the three situations in question – exemplified by cases (a), (b) and (c) – the effect will be the existence of a person who is my psychological replica. If it is only the effect that matters, then, as in the disease case, the differences between these three cases must be irrelevant. However, if certain of these differences, namely those between (b) and (c), do matter, then it is not *just* the effect that matters, and in that case the analogy with the disease case fails at the crucial point.

Thus, I suggest, Parfit's quoted argument is question-begging, but if it is accepted it must be taken further. Then, however, it will yield results that even Parfit cannot swallow.

Nevertheless, there is some plausibility in Parfit's position: if identity is of no intrinsic importance in survival how can it matter whether a psychological replica of oneself is produced by a reliable causal process or by an unreliable one? It is an implication of Parfit's disease case analogy, I suggested, that if we consider the differences between cases (b) and (c) *without* taking into account their possible bearing on the issue of personal identity it is impossible to regard them as of any significance. But if we consider the difference between case (a) and case (b) under the same restriction, is not the same true? Simply considered as sequences of events in the world with a certain outcome it is impossible to see any important difference between (a) and (b). But if personal identity is merely of derivative importance, as Parfit says, this is how they *must* be viewed. It would merely be confusion, on his view, for someone who held a theory of personal identity which yielded the result that *A* was *B* in case (a) but not in case (b), to argue that *this* difference was an important one between the cases.

Thus, if Parfit is right that identity is merely of derivative importance in survival then there is no way of avoiding the conclusion that to *A*, looking forward in each of the cases (a), (b) and (c), they should seem to be equivalent. But, of course, this conclusion ceases to be compelling if Parfit's view is rejected. For then *A*, if his theory of personal identity entails, say, that he survives in the literal sense in case (a), but not in case (b) or (c), can rationally appeal to this fact to explain why the difference between case (a), and cases (b) and (c), is important. He can rationally answer the question: 'Why do you prefer (a) to (b) or (c)?' by saying: 'Because in (a) I survive (in the literal sense), but in (b) and (c) I do not.' And if pressed to say why *that* is a reason for preferring (a) he need have no answer; in fact, if the importance of identity is non-derivative, he *must* have no answer.

I conclude, then, as at the end of the previous section, that Parfit's thesis of the merely derivative importance of identity in survival must be rejected. There my argument was that if we took into account the *totality* of intuitions to be explained and not just that subset appealed to by Parfit, it was clear that no explanation of Parfit's type was adequate. Here the point is the same: we do recognize significant differences between cases which, considered merely as sequences of events in the world, have the same outcome. If Parfit's thesis is correct it is impossible to explain how we can do so. Once again the only way forward is to reject this thesis, a thesis for which, I have anyway argued, Parfit has no non-question-begging argument.

CHAPTER 10
The Self and the Future

10.1 Introduction

In this chapter we will be concerned with the arguments of Bernard Williams's well-known and influential paper, 'The self and the future' (1970). What Williams does in this paper is to present proponents of the Complex View with a conundrum. He does this by putting forward two arguments, each by itself at first sight wholly convincing, one an argument for a psychological continuity account of personal identity, and the other an argument for a bodily continuity account of personal identity. The implication of the paper is that there is nothing straightforwardly *wrong* with either argument, despite their conflicting conclusions, and hence that there is some sort of conflict or antimony at the heart of our concept of personal identity.

Williams's arguments have been much discussed, and have elicited a variety of responses.

One response, which has been elaborated in most detail by Robert Nozick (1981), and will be discussed further in Chapter 11, is to take Williams's paper as merely another demonstration of the way in which adherence to the Only *x* and *y* principle leads to irresoluble perplexities about personal identity. For, as Williams himself makes perfectly clear, the Only *x* and *y* principle is as much a premiss of his argument in 'The self and the future' as it is of his earlier Reduplication Argument, so if it is rejected, the conundrum is solved.

Another response, by some Simple Theorists (e.g., Swinburne in Shoemaker and Swinburne 1984, and G. Madell 1981), has been to take the conundrum as establishing that *Complex* theorists are indeed committed to inconsistent views, and thus as establishing that the only sustainable account of personal identity is that given by the Simple View. It need hardly be said, of course, that this is far from being the conclusion Williams would himself wish to see drawn from his arguments.

Finally, a third response to the conundrum has recently been elaborated by Mark Johnston (1987). Williams's arguments in 'The self and the future' rely heavily on an appeal to our intuitions about imaginary science-fictional puzzle cases – in the manner which is, of course, perfectly standard in discussions of personal identity. Johnston suggests that we take Williams's conundrum as revealing the bankruptcy of this standard way of debating problems of personal identity – what he calls 'the method of cases'.

In what follows I shall argue that none of these responses is necessary or appropriate, for Williams's arguments, despite their ingenuity, contain straightforwardly identifiable flaws, and so do not create the crisis he supposes. Let us now get down to details.

10.2 Two puzzle cases

The strategy of Williams's paper is as follows. First, he sets out what are apparently two different puzzle cases and argues that the correct description of one of them coincides with that which would be given by a proponent of the Psychological Continuity Criterion of personal identity, i.e. that a person has exchanged bodies, whilst the correct description of the other coincides with that which would be given by a proponent of the Bodily Criterion of personal identity, i.e. that a person has undergone a radical psychological change, involving loss of memory, transformation of character, etc. So far this seems to establish only that there are circumstances in which bodily identity is not necessary for survival and circumstances in which psychological continuity is not necessary for survival, which leaves open as an obvious option the view that personal identity is essentially a disjunctive concept with at least two distinct sufficient conditions. But Williams now argues that what he first presented as *two* puzzle cases are, in fact, nothing of the kind; they are, rather, the *same* puzzle case with irrelevant differences in presentation. If so, however, the easy option of regarding personal identity as a disjunctive concept is not available after all, and the room for manoeuvre begins to look very limited.

An immediate response is to say that all that this brings out is the familiar point that personal identity can be indeterminate; that is, cases are possible in which several conflicting descriptions are equally plausible, and so no answer is unambiguously correct. But Williams anticipates this reaction and argues against it. His conclusion is that we are left with a conundrum.

There are two presentations of the imagined [case] each of which carries conviction, and which lead to contrary conclusions. The idea that the situation is conceptually undecidable in the relevant respects seems not to assist, but rather to increase the puzzlement; while the idea (so often appealed to in these matters) that it is conventionally decidable is even worse. Following all that, I am not in the least clear which [conclusion] it would be wise to [accept]. I find that rather disturbing.

(1970, p.168)

Let us now turn to the details of Williams's arguments.

The first case Williams describes, designed to encourage the view that body-switching is a possibility for persons, is the following. Two persons, A and B, are made to enter a fabulous machine. This machine produces the sort of psychological transformation which would be produced by transposing brains. When the machine is turned on it records all features of the brains of A and B relevant to the determination of dispositional and occurrent mentality. It then alters the A-brain so that it ceases to have associated with it the dispositional and occurrent mentality of A and comes to have associated with it instead what appears to be the continuation of B's dispositional and occurrent mentality. The A-body person thus emerges with what appear to be B's memories, character traits, projects and the like. *Mutatis mutandis* for the B-brain. The B-body person thus emerges from the machine with what appear to be A's memories, character traits, projects and the like. Standardly, in science-fiction stories, and in the literature on personal identity, such a transformation is regarded as an exchange of bodies, and Williams argues strongly that this is how the case should be described.

Williams's second puzzle case is apparently quite different. Someone tells me that I am to be tortured tomorrow, but that before the suffering comes I will have changed greatly in memories, character traits, projects, etc., perhaps so greatly as to possess the character, memories, values and knowledge of someone else who is now alive. It is explained to me that this will be done by the use of a fabulous machine which is able to record all the features of my brain relevant to the determination of dispositional and occurrent mentality and reorganize these features so that dispositional and occurrent mental features very different from my present ones will be realized by my brain tomorrow. Then and only then will my body be tortured.

This second case, as Williams presents it, is designed to encourage the belief that bodily continuity is the crucial element in personal identity. For, as he argues, faced with this prospect:

> Fear, surely, would be the proper reaction: and not because one did not know what was going to happen, but because in one vital respect at least one did know what was going to happen – torture, which one can indeed expect to happen to oneself, and to be preceded by certain mental derangements as well.

> (1970)

But, as Williams points out, if this is right the situation now begins to look mysterious. For this second case is, of course, merely one side, differently represented, of the first.

There is nothing to distinguish the fabulous machine referred to in the second case from the fabulous machine referred to in the first, and no justification for regarding what happens to me in the second case as any different from what happens to A in the first case. So the second case simply *is* the first case, looked at from A's point of view, with the omission of any changes to the B-body.

Because of his acceptance of the Only x and y principle Williams regards the descriptions of these two cases for which he argues as genuinely in conflict. For granted that exactly the same things happen to the A-body in the two cases, the only way they *can* be reconciled is by allowing that what happens elsewhere can determine whether or not the A-body continues to be the body of a single person, but only a 'best candidate' theorist can allow this possibility. But the crucial question is whether Williams is right to think that it is obligatory to describe his two puzzle cases as he does. I shall argue that he is wrong, and that consequently there is no genuine conflict even given the Only x and y principle.

10.3 Body-switching?

Let us first look at Williams's argument for describing his first case as one in which bodies are exchanged. This turns on what the A-body person and the B-body person are likely to say, after the fabulous machine has done its work, about the wisdom, assessed from a purely selfish point of view, of choices made earlier by A and B. The sequence of events after which the A-body person and the B-body person are to make their assessment of the choices of A and B, is the process of information transfer by the machine (which Williams refers to as 'the experiment'), followed by the torture of either the A-body person or the B-body person by the experimenter and the handing over of a cheque for \$1,000,000 to the other. The choices made by A and B, before the experiment takes place, concern which of these should get the money and which should get the pain.

Williams's argument is now that what the A-body person and the B-body person are likely to say after the experiment in a series of cases in which A and B make different choices provides strong support for the view that the A-body person is B and the B-body person is A, and hence for the description of the first case yielded by the Psychological Continuity Criterion of personal identity.

Actually, however, this argument is unconvincing. In order to see what is wrong with it one need only notice that the choices of A and B, made in a purely selfish spirit, are bound to reflect their views on personal identity, however inarticulate these views may be: for each is concerned that *he* gets the money and the other gets the pain, and each (Williams is clearly assuming though he does not say) thinks he has reason to believe that his choice will be acted on by the experimenter when he decides whom to reward and whom to punish. But since the A-body person's brain has been wiped clean and reprogrammed to ensure that the A-body person is identical with B in all psychological respects, the A-body person must share B's views on personal identity; similarly the B-body person must share A's views. Furthermore, each can assess the wisdom of the choices of A and B only on the basis of *his own* views on personal identity. Hence each must regard the choice he 'recalls', i.e. the choice made by the person with whom he is psychologically identical, as a wise one, and (whether or not he thinks that the choice he 'recalls' is his own choice) he must regard his own choice as a wise one if and only if it is a choice in accordance with the views on personal identity he presently holds, i.e. the views which are reflected in the choice he 'recalls'. Once this is understood the plausibility of Williams's argument evaporated. For in so far as the A-body person and the B-body person are likely, in the series cases Williams imagines, to make statements that appear to provide support for a psychological criterion of personal identity, this will be so only if they are themselves believers in such a criterion; any criterion of personal identity, no matter how bizarre, could be given a similar appearance of support by imagining what would be said by people crazy enough to accept it. On the other hand, in so far as the A-body person and the B-body person do not accept a psychological criterion of personal identity they will not be likely to make statements which even *appear* to support such a criterion.

To confirm this let us look more closely at Williams's argument (for a more detailed discussion see Noonan 1982a and 1983).

(i) First he supposes that A and B are believers, however inarticulate, in a psychological criterion of personal identity and choose appropriately: A that the A-body person get the pain and the B-body person the money, and B conversely, and after the experiment the experimenter gives the pleasant treatment to the A-body person and the unpleasant treatment to the B-body person. Both the A-body person and the B-body person are now bound to regard the choices he 'recalls' as wise ones, and each is bound to regard the choice he 'recalls' as his own. Each is, therefore, bound to believe that his own choice was a wise one and to make exactly the type of remarks Williams imagines. Namely, 'the B-body person will not only complain of the unpleasant treatment as such but will complain that that was not the outcome he chose' and the A-body person 'will express satisfaction at the fact that the experimenter has chosen to act in the way he, B, so wisely chose' (1970). But contrary to what Williams claims, these facts provide no support at all for a psychological criterion of personal identity, for what the A-body person and the B-body person are likely to say is not determined just by their memories, but also by the views they hold on personal identity.

This becomes clear when we consider the cases where A and B make other choices with regard to the experiment, where Williams is led into inaccuracy in his description of what the A-body person and the B-body person are likely to say.

(ii) Williams next supposes that both A and B make choices

appropriate to a belief in a bodily criterion of personal identity and that after the experiment the experimenter gives the pleasant treatment to the A-body person and the unpleasant treatment to the B-body person. Each is bound to regard the choice he 'recalls' as a wise one and also to regard his own choice as a wise one (for the A-body person can turn to the B-body person and say (and the B-body person will not dissent), 'You're the B-body person and chose money for the B-body person and pain for the A-body person, and I am the A-body person and chose money for the A-body person and pain for the B-body person; from a purely selfish point of view both your choice, which I "recall" though you don't, and my choice, which you "recall" though I don't, were wise ones'). But each is bound to distinguish his own choice from the choice he 'recalls' and to dismiss his 'memory'–impressions as illusory. Hence Williams is wrong when he says that the B-body person will 'naturally express' his acknowledgement that the distribution of pain and pleasure is in accord with A's choice by saying that this is the distribution he chose. Rather, he will merely have a *tendency* to express this acknowledgement in this way (if he had no such tendency he would not have 'memory'–impressions of A's life at all – whether or not illusory), a tendency he will try to supress: his considered statement will be to the effect that the distribution is not the one he chose, but merely the one he has an illusory 'memory'–impression of choosing. Similarly, the A-body person will not, as Williams says, reckon it good luck that the experimenter did not produce the outcome he recalls (minus scare quotes) choosing, but merely reckon it good luck that the experimenter did not produce the outcome he has an illusory 'memory' of choosing, but rather produced the outcome he chose, but knew before the experiment he would have no recollection of choosing.

(iii) Finally, Williams supposes that A chooses in a way appropriate to a believer in a psychological criterion of personal identity and B chooses in a way appropriate to a believer in a bodily criterion of personal identity, and that the experimenter produces the outcome that they both want, namely money for the B-body person and pain for the A-body person. Each of these is now bound to regard the choice he 'recalls' as a wise one, but otherwise they will differ. The B-body person will regard the choice he 'recalls' as his own choice, i.e. a choice he genuinely recalls, and so regard his own choice as a wise one. The A-body person, however, is bound to distinguish the choice he 'recalls' from his own choice, and to regard his own choice as a mistaken one.

Williams is right, then, when he says that in this case the *B*-body person 'likes what he is receiving, recalls choosing it, and congratulates himself on the wisdom of (as he puts it) his choice'; but wrong when he says that the *A*-body person 'does not like what he is receiving, recalls choosing it, and is forced to acknowledge that (as he puts it) his choice was unwise'. Of course, the *A*-body person does not like what he is receiving, but he would not accept that it is what he recalls (minus scare quotes) choosing, nor would he acknowledge that the choice he 'recalls' choosing was unwise, nor would he be prepared to put any comment about the choice he 'recalls' in the form 'My choice . . .'. Once again, the point that emerges is that Williams accurately describes what the *A*-body person or the *B*-body person is likely to say only when that person accepts a psychological criterion of personal identity – when, however, what he says, being expressive of a commitment to such a criterion, cannot, for just that reason, provide more than an appearance of support for it; while whenever the *A*-body person or the *B*-body person accepts a bodily criterion of personal identity Williams is forced to misdescribe what he is likely to say in order to preserve any appearance of cogency for his argument.

This becomes even clearer, if anything, when we look at some subsidiary arguments Williams gives. He now drops the supposition that *A* and *B* are forced to choose how the *A*-body person and the *B*-body person are to be treated after the experiment and assumes a more benevolent character for the experimenter. First he supposes that *A* and *B* are disposed to accept a psychological continuity criterion of personal identity, and that each agrees to the experiment partly, at least, in the hope of exchanging his body for a more attractive one. He then points out what the reader should by now be able to predict, that what the *A*-body person and the *B*-body person are likely to say after the experiment now appears to provide support for a psychological continuity criterion of personal identity. Next he supposes that when the experiment is proposed *A* and *B* think rather of their psychological advantages and disadvantages. *A*'s thoughts turn primarily to certain sorts of anxiety to which he is very prone, while *B* is concerned with the frightful memories he has of past experiences which still distress him. They are each inclined to accept a bodily continuity criterion of personal identity, and so each hopes that the experiment will result in his acquiring a healthier psychological state. A, for example, reasons that, if the experiment comes off, the person who is bodily continuous with him will not have his anxiety and while the other person will no doubt have some anxiety – perhaps in some sense his anxiety – at least that person will not be he. The experiment is performed and the experimenter (to whom A and B previously revealed privately their several difficulties and hopes) asks the A-body person whether he has got rid of his anxiety. Williams now writes 'this person presumably replies that he does not know what the man is talking about; he never had such anxiety, but he did have some very disagreeable memories, and recalls engaging in the experiment to get rid of them, and he is disappointed to discover that he still has them. The B-body person will react in a similar way to questions about his painful memories, pointing out that he still has his anxiety.' But this, as the reader will now appreciate, is wholly mistaken. Since both A and B accepted a bodily continuity criterion of personal identity, so must the A-body person and the B-body person. The A-body person will therefore reply to the experimenter's question by saying something to the effect that since he does not know what the experimenter is talking about he presumes that he has indeed got rid of the anxiety to which he was so prone, and that from his (A's) point of view the experiment has been a complete success. Unfortunately, he will continue, he has acquired instead some illusory 'memories' of B's life of a distinctly unpleasant character, but, he might add, given B's willingness to engage in the experiment in the first place some such outcome was only to be expected. The B-body person will react in a similar way to questions about his painful memories, and say he now realizes why A was so willing to participate in the experiment with him (B). Once again, then, Williams is able to give his argument an appearance of plausibility only by misdescribing what the A-body person and the B-body person are likely to say in the situation he puts them into.

In sum, then, Williams's argument for describing his first case as a case of body-switching is unconvincing. But, of course, it might still be *correct* to describe the case in this way. However, if this is so the only hope for the Complex theorist who does not wish to abandon the Only x and y principle must be to find some flaw in Williams's argument for his apparently conflicting description of his second case, to which I now turn.

10.4 Mind -swapping?

This argument has two parts: a preliminary part, to which I shall return, followed by a challenge to the psychological continuity theorist to draw a line somewhere in the following series of cases, i.e. to say at what point it becomes incorrect to say that the *A*-body person is still *A* after the change described:

(i)   A is subjected to an operation which produces total amnesia,
(ii)   amnesia is produced in A, and other interferences lead to certain changes in his character,
(iii) changes in his character are produced, and at the same time certain illusory memory beliefs are produced in him; these are of a quite fictitious kind and do not fit the life of any actual person,
(iv)   the same as (iii), except that both the character traits and memories are designed to be appropriate to another actual person, B,
(v)   the same as in (iv) except that the result is produced by putting the information into A from the brain of B, by a method which leaves B the same as he was before,
(vi)   the same happens to A as in (v) but B is not left the same, since a similar operation is conducted in the reverse direction.

(1970)

The psychological continuity theorist must say that in (vi) – which is, of course, just Williams's first case – the *A*-body person is no longer *A* after the change described, since the *B*-body person is. But, Williams asserts, he cannot deny that *A* survives the change described in (i). Hence he must draw the line somewhere in between, but this, Williams argues, he cannot do.

Now, a proponent of the 'best candidate' approach will say that a line can be drawn between (v), which, of course, is just Williams's second case, and (vi), but in order to dispute Williams's description of his second case a line must be drawn before this.

Williams argues that this cannot be done, but once again his argument is ultimately unconvincing.

The best way to see its weakness is first to note its intended scope. The process of information transfer referred to in (v) and (vi) is the fabulous process referred to in Williams's earlier argument for the description of his first case yielded by the psychological criterion of personal identity, so the psychological continuity theorist Williams is now explicitly arguing against is one who accepts that such an information transfer constitutes a bodily exchange. But Williams refers at the beginning of his paper to Shoemaker's Brown/ Brownson case and the criterion of personal identity it suggests according to which Brownson is Brown, namely: 'having the brain and in consequence the memory and character traits of', and he clearly intends his argument to be a challenge to this suggestion too. So let us consider how it might apply.

Of course, we now need to consider a somewhat different series of cases: (i) to (iv) can remain the same, but (v) and (vi), in which reference is made to information transfer, need to be replaced by (v') and (vi').

(v')   the same as in (iv), except that the result is produced by dividing B's brain and putting one half into A's skull (A's brain having been removed) leaving the other half in B's skull,

(vi')   the same happens to A as in (v'), except that the result is produced by transferring A's entire brain into B's skull and conducting a similar operation in the reverse direction.

Now Williams's challenge to the psychological continuity theorist is to draw a line in this series, and thereby to show that he can reconcile his philosophical convictions with the familiar commonsense facts about the way people can suffer from amnesia, character change and illusory memories whilst retaining their identity referred to in (i)–(iv). But it seems easy enough for a psychological continuity theorist who endorses the criterion of personal identity stated in the previous paragraph to do so. The line, he should say, must be drawn between (iv) and (v'). Up to (iv) the changes are consistent with A's survival as the A-body person, but with the change in (v') identity of A and the A-body person ceases. Williams objects to the proposal that in the series (i)–(vi) the line can be drawn between (iv) and (v) on two grounds. First, that in the move from (iv) to (v) all we have added is that the 'memory' impressions which result from the change have not only a model, as in (iv), but a model which is also their cause, and he says, it is difficult to see why that, to A looking forward, should make the difference between expecting pain and not expecting pain. Williams's second reason for denying that the line can be drawn between (iv) and (v) is that in (v) the *A*-body person is certainly not *B*, for there we have an undisputed *B* in addition to the *A*-body person, and certainly these two are not the same person. Hence, if the *A*-body person is not *A* in (v), though he is *A* in (iv), this is not because he is *B* in (v), and who else, Williams is implicitly challenging the psychological continuity theorist to explain, might he be?

Neither of these objections to drawing the line between (iv) and (v) applies to drawing the line between (iv) and (v′) in the revised series of cases. The difference between (iv) and (v′) is that in (v′) *A*'s brain has been removed from his skull and replaced by one of *B*'s brain-halves, and in consequence the *A*-body person is psychologically continuous with *B*: that is, the *A*-body person is as he is psychologically because of the way *B* was in the past, and had *B*'s history been different this would have been reflected in differences in the *A*-body person's present psychological state. On the other hand, the *A*-body person's psychological state is not at all dependent on *A*'s past history. It seems absurd to suggest that the outcome of this change, because it can be brought under the very general description 'the *A*-body person has memory-impressions which have not merely a model, but a model which is also their cause', cannot rationally be regarded by *A* as involving his death (if he assumes his own brain to be destroyed) or, at least, his ceasing to have the body he previously had (if he is agnostic about the fate of his own brain). Certainly, the psychological continuity theorist can allow the common-sense facts about survival through amnesia, character change and inducement of illusory memory impressions referred to in (i) to (iv) while maintaining that in (v′), as opposed to (iv), *A* ceases to be the occupant of the body which was previously his, which now comes to house a different person.

But, then, if *A* is no longer the *A*-body person after the changes described in (v′), who is? This brings us to Williams's second objection to drawing the line between (iv) and (v), which again turns out to be no objection to drawing the line between (iv) and (v′) in the revised series of cases. This objection was to the effect that the *A*-body person in (v) cannot be *B*, since there is an undisputed *B* in addition to the *A*-body person in (v); so who *can* the latter be but *A*? In (v′), however, it is not so clear that we should say that there is an undisputed *B* in addition to the *A*-body person. It is only in bodily respects that the *B*-body person is a closer continuer of the original *B* than the *A*-body person, and so – the psychological continuity theorist might well say – what has happened to *B* should be regarded as fission. Now, as we have seen, how to describe a fission case is one of the main points at issue in the debate over personal identity, but none of the competing descriptions involves that just one of the fission products is the *undisputed* claimant to identity with the original person. So if what happens to *B* in (v') is regarded as fission then whilst it is certainly not true that the *A*-body person is *B*, as Williams correctly says, nor is it true that the *B*-body person is *B*; rather, both are offshoots of *B* (however, the notion of 'off-shoots' is to be explicated) and, as for *A*, he is not in the picture at all.

Thus, neither of Williams's two objections to drawing the line between (iv) and (v) carries much conviction when applied to the suggestion that the line be drawn between (iv) and (v') in the revised series of cases and, what is the crucial point, nothing he says makes it seem likely that a psychological continuity theorist who regards psychological continuity grounded in brain-continuity as a sufficient condition of personal identity cannot retain his philosophical convictions whilst allowing for the common-sense facts about survival through amnesia, character change and inducement of illusory memories to which Williams refers.

If we turn to Williams's preliminary argument this conclusion is confirmed. He argues that if someone who had you in his power were to approach you and inform you that you were going to be tortured tomorrow but that when the moment of torture came you would not remember any of the things you were now in a position to remember and would have a quite different set of impressions of your past, then you would be perfectly rational in fearing the torture. And so you would. But this is no argument against someone who regards psychological continuity grounded in brain-continuity as a sufficient condition for personal identity, since he can simply point out that the description given of what is to happen is general enough (once the question-begging repetition of 'you' is ignored) to cover both a situation in which the change described is brought about by a process of, say, brain-washing and hypnosis, which leaves your psychological state at least to some extent counter-factually dependent on your own past history, and a situation in which the change described is brought about by the removal of your brain and its replacement by another. Since, according to the psychological continuity theorist, *one* of these situations will involve your torture it is entirely rational for you, convinced that what is described will happen, to feel fear, even if the other situation, will *not* involve your torture – in just the way that, as Williams later says, fear for yourself is rational if you are informed that 'one of you five – which one we've not decided yet – is to be shot'.

In sum, then, if Williams's argument is intended to cast doubt on the thesis that psychological continuity grounded in brain-continuity is a sufficient condition of personal identity, as he gives us reason to believe at the outset of his paper, then it is an unconvincing objection to that thesis.

But, it may be said, all that this shows is that the scope of Williams's argument is more limited than he perhaps implies: it does not show that it is unsuccessful when used against the type of psychological continuity criterion of personal identity to which he explicitly addresses himself, and, crucially for our purpose, it does not show that Williams has not got a good argument for describing his second case in the way a bodily criterion of personal identity would dictate.

However, once it is seen that Williams's argument is ineffective against the thesis that psychological continuity grounded in brain-continuity is sufficient for personal identity it does not take much more thought to realize that it is equally ineffective against the type of psychological continuity criterion of personal identity he explicitly discusses.

For the process of information transfer referred to in (v) and (vi) of Williams's series is meant to involve the total wiping clean of the brain to which the information is transferred, what Perry refers to in his review of Williams as a 'brain zap' (1976) (it must involve a brain zap otherwise the psychological continuity theorist would not have to accept (vi) as a clear case of bodily interchange); thus in (v) the *A*-body person is not merely in a state of amnesia with respect to *A*'s life, from which he might emerge after a process of treatment or an accidental jolt on the head; his memories of *A*'s life are gone as finally as they are in (v'), where *A*'s brain is gone too. Given this it seems that Williams's objections to drawing the line between (iv) and (v) are as unsuccessful, so regarded, as they are when regarded as objections to drawing the line between (iv) and (v'). For the difference between (iv) and (v) is not merely that in (v) the *A*-body person's memory-impressions have a model which is also their cause, but that they have been induced by a very special causal process which ensures that the brain of A has been wiped clean of all the information it contained and that the A-body person is psychologically identical with B. If the psychological continuity theorist regards *this* difference between (iv) and (v) as a reason for drawing the line between them he would seem to be in no danger of having to deny common-sense facts about survival through amnesia (ordinarily so-called), character change and inducement of illusory memory-impressions. Again, given that both the A-body person and the B-body person in (v) are psychologically identical with B, Williams's claim that we have an undisputed B in addition to the A-body person after the change described seems as open to question as we saw with respect to (v'). Again it seems that the psychological continuity theorist can reasonably adopt the position that what has happened to B is fission and that both the A-body person and the B-body person are offshoots of B.

If we turn to Williams's preliminary argument the same point is applicable: Williams's argument against the psychological continuity criterion of personal identity he is explicitly attacking fails for just the same reason as it does when regarded as an argument against the thesis that psychological continuity grounded in continuity of brain is sufficient for personal identity. For the description of what is going to happen which Williams imagines: 'You will be tortured, and will not remember anything about your present life, but will have a completely false set of memory-impressions', is general enough to describe both a situation in which a brain zap has occurred and a situation in which amnesia as ordinarily understood has set in. Hence fear of torture will be appropriate, the psychological continuity theorist can say, even if the result of a brain zap (without the information being transferred) is death; so the fact that fear would be appropriate in such a situation does not prove a brain zap without information transferral not to be death and does not show that there is anything wrong with the psychological continuity criterion of personal identity under attack.

In sum, then, Williams's argument against a psychological continuity criterion of personal identity and in favour of the description of his second case yielded by the bodily criterion of personal identity is unconvincing. And we have been able to show this both without having to dispute the Only x and y principle and without having to appeal to the possibility of indeterminacy in personal identity. Williams's conundrum, considered as a threat to the Complex View, is thus disarmed.

10.5 Identity and determinacy

However, we are not finished with Williams yet. For though he intends the argument he gives against the possibility of indeterminacy in personal identity (referred to in section 10.2) merely as a response to an attempt to defuse his conundrum, in fact it can stand alone, and, if valid, it is sufficient by itself to refute the Complex View.

We have seen that the idea that there is something especially puzzling about borderline cases of *personal*, as opposed to other types of identity, is historically one of the central components of the Simple View. And it is an idea which has become increasingly prominent in recent defences of that view. But *why* exactly it is that personal identity is thus different from the identity of other things is a question that is seldom asked by proponents of the Simple View. The great merit of Williams's discussion is that he does ask this question and makes a most determined effort to answer it. Let us consider what he says.

Williams's argument is at first sight very persuasive. A reasonable summary of its main points can perhaps be put as follows.

Suppose that I, in the company of others, am in the clutches of a mad scientist. A guard comes to tell me that tomorrow one of the prisoners is to be tortured, leaving it open whether it will be me or someone else. I do not know exactly what to expect, but I know that tomorrow this indeterminacy will be eliminated, and my hopes, fears and imaginings will revolve about the alternative ways in which this might occur. But now suppose instead that the guard comes to tell me that someone will be tortured who (because of the mad scientist's tamperings) will be so related to me as to make it conceptually undecidable whether he is me or not. By contrast to the former case I cannot now regard the indeterminacy in what I have been told to expect as something that will be eliminated when tomorrow comes; and so I cannot think of any future situation in which I am definitely present as one I might live through. But then what I have been told by the guard cannot serve, in the way it could in the former case, as the basis of any hopes, fears or imaginings; and it seems, in fact, that there is absolutely no way I *can* mirror it in my expectations and the emotions to which they give rise. As Williams puts it:

> To be told that a future situation is a borderline case for its being myself that is hurt, that it is conceptually undecidable whether it will be me or not, is something which, it seems, I can do nothing with; because, in particular, it seems to have no comprehensible representation in my expectations and the emotions that go with them.

> (1970)

An opponent of the possibility of borderline cases of personal identity might now suggest that my difficulty has a straightforward explanation. Namely that what I have been told to expect is impossible. So of course it is difficult for me to think about it, and in fact incurably so. To reinforce this point Williams poses a dilemma. Suppose I engage in projective imaginative thinking about how it will be for me in the future situation: then I implicitly answer the necessarily unanswerable question. But suppose instead that I think that I cannot engage in such thinking: then it looks very much as if I also answer it, though in the opposite direction. Perhaps, then, I should just refrain from such thinking, but am I *just* refraining from it, if it is incurably undecidable whether I can or cannot engage in it?

The upshot of all this, Williams thinks, is that the idea that borderline cases of personal identity are unproblematic, popular though it has been, should be rejected. Its only appeal can be to those who wish to hold back from a commitment to definite answers when confronted with puzzles about personal identity, but, in fact, if taken seriously it does not ease, but rather exacerbates, the puzzlement such cases create. And as regards the related idea that it can, and sometimes ought to be, a matter for conventionalist decision whether personal identity obtains in such a case, Williams is still more outspoken:

> This line of talk is the sort of thing appropriate to lawyers deciding the ownership of some property which has just undergone some bewildering set of transformations; they just have to decide, and in each situation, let us suppose, it has to go to somebody, on as reasonable grounds as the facts and the

law permit. But as a line to deal with a person's fears or
expectations about his own future, it seems to have no sense
at all.

(1970)

It seems clear that the last part of this, at any rate, must be correct.
If I am told that someone is going to be tortured tomorrow who will
be neither definitely me nor definitely not me, I might be at a loss to
know what to think. But the idea that being told that from tomorrow on people will *agree to speak* as if that person is (or is not) me
will, or ought to, cause my puzzlement to disappear, is transparently
absurd. Suppose that I am told that from tomorrow on people will
speak as if that person is other than me. Ought I then to breathe a
sigh of relief, and dismiss from my mind any anxiety I might have
been feeling? Or suppose that I am told that from tomorrow on
people will speak as if that person is me. Ought I then to collapse in
terror or attempt suicide if I find the thought of the torture
unbearable? Clearly, it could be absurd for me to react in either way,
for however people choose to talk the facts about my relationship to
the unfortunate person who is to be tortured tomorrow will remain
the same, and if my knowledge of these facts leaves me baffled as to
how to form my emotions when they are presented to me under the
description 'facts which make it indeterminate whether or not you
will be tortured tomorrow', I ought to be as baffled as ever, when, as
a result of a change of language, it becomes possible to present the
same facts under a different description.

But it does not follow from this alone that we ought to go along
with Williams in his rejection of the possibility of conceptually
undecidable cases of personal identity. All we have accepted so far is
that *if* one finds oneself in a situation in which a conceptual shadow
lies over one's identity it would be absurd to let one's emotional
response to that situation be determined by whatever linguistic
refinements or revisions the people around one choose to agree on to
enable them to pigeon-hole the situation in the way that they find
most convenient. The question whether such situations *are* conceptually possible is another matter altogether.

Williams argues that they are not, because there is no way in
which we can think about them. But his argument for this, as stated
above, though at first sight rhetorically effective, looks vulnerable on closer inspection. Consider first the dilemma Williams

presents. The subject in such a situation, he claims, has an incurable difficulty about how to think about what is going to occur; if he engages in projective imaginative thinking about how it will be for him he implicitly answers the necessarily unanswerable question; whilst if he thinks that he cannot engage in such thinking, it looks very much as if he also answers it, though in the opposite direction.

But what if the subject says that he cannot engage in such projective imaginative thinking about how it will be for him, and gives *as his reason* that to do so would be implicitly to answer the necessarily unanswerable question? Why should that commit him, as Williams implies that it would, to the view that he will definitely *not* be present in the future situation?

The conclusion Williams needs is that a situation in which it is indeterminate whether I will be present must in some way be incapable of representation by me. But while it is true that I cannot correctly represent such a situation to myself either as one in which I occur or as one in which I do not that is *all* I cannot do. Williams's conclusion could only follow if a fully adequate representation of the situation would have to eliminate the indeterminacy. But to assume that that was so would simply be to beg the question against proponents of the possibility of conceptually undecidable cases of personal identity.

It may be thought, however, that this reply sidesteps the most telling point in Williams's argument, namely the point about the inability of one who is told that he faces a future in which his identity will be indeterminate to produce any comprehensible *emotional* response to this information.

But why *should* such a response be possible? Surely the correct reply to Williams here is to question the assumption that one must be able to produce an appropriate emotional response to any genuinely possible situation which one can foresee. For if the situation is of a type one has never before encountered there is no reason why this should be so. If what I wish for is that *P*, but what is going to happen will make it neither the case that *P*, nor the case that not-*P*, then relative to my desire that *P* neither elation nor disappointment is an appropriate response to what is going to happen. But if this is the first situation of this borderline type I have encountered I may have no other relevant desire. Then what to think about the situation will simply be an irresoluble problem for me. But that cannot show that situations of this borderline type are impossible.

Nevertheless, I think that Williams does have a point which is not answered by these rejoinders – though it is not a point that establishes the impossibility of borderline cases of personal identity. This point comes out best, however, not in Williams's own exposition, but in a passage from Richard Swinburne (1973–4) inspired, as Swinburne emphasizes, by Williams's discussion. The argument concerns a case in which a person *A* is told that someone whose identity with him will be conceptually shadowed will be tortured tomorrow:

> Has he cause to fear? Presumably less cause than if the person
> to be tortured were fully himself, and more cause than if he
> were not at all himself. But how can an intermediate reaction
> be justified? Each subsequent person will either be tortured or
> not; no half-tortures will be laid on. An intermediate reaction
> would be justified if A did not know who would be tortured,
> i.e. whether it would be himself or someone else. But A has
> been told who will be tortured, i.e. someone who is equally
> well described as A or as not–A. How can any suffering affect
> A unless he suffers it all or suffers part of it? – and neither of
> these alternatives is being suggested here.
>
> (1973–4:237–8)

Perhaps the idea of a borderline case of torture, like the idea of a borderline case of baldness, makes sense, but, as Swinburne rightly indicates, it is irrelevant to our problem. So, setting it aside, supposing, that is, that 'no half-tortures are to be laid on', the people existing at any future time can be divided into two groups: those being tortured then and those not being tortured then. And so the people in existence *now* can similarly be divided into two groups; namely, those being tortured at the future time and the rest (the latter group consisting of those no longer alive then and those alive then but not suffering torture). *Any* presently existing person must fall into one of these latter two groups, it seems, and so how can it be, as proposed, that *A* is in neither?

This, I take it, is the basic perplexity underlying the rhetorical questions of both Williams and Swinburne. And it does establish *something* – but not that borderline cases of personal identity are impossible. What it establishes, in fact, is the impossibility of making sense of the possibility of such borderline cases whilst assuming that the singular terms which occur in their description have a determinate denotation. It is the presupposition that this is so which gives the arguments of Williams and Swinburne their appearance of cogency and makes it seem so difficult to answer their questions. On the other hand once this presupposition is rejected the difficulties disappear. If '*A*', in Swinburne's argument, is a term lacking a determinate denotation then, by the argument of Chapter 6, there must be at least two candidates for its denotation, one which has a tomorrow stage which is being tortured, and one which has not. The first candidate would therefore be entirely justified in feeling fear, and the second candidate would be entirely justified (on selfish grounds) in not doing so. But since these two entities share their present stage neither can have an opinion or think a thought that the other cannot; so it is indeed impossible to say what *A* should think. A similar diagnosis applies to the difficulties Williams's argument brings out. Of course, just as he says, there is 'an obstinate bafflement in mirroring in my expectations a situation in which it is conceptually undecidable whether I occur'. For by the argument of Chapter 6 if such a situation exists in the future it follows that my *present* 'I'-thoughts lack a determinate denotation. That is to say, there are (at least) two candidates for their denotation: one being an entity which does occur in the future situation and the other an entity which does not. The one which does occur in the future situation would be justified in expecting it, whilst the one which does not, of course, would not. But at present neither can form an expectation or think a thought that the other cannot, and so it is impossible to answer the question: 'What should *I* think?'

Thus I conclude, the Swinburne–Williams argument does not after all establish the impossibility of conceptually undecidable cases of personal identity. But what it does do is to drive home the lesson we already learned in Chapter 6, namely that the only way to make sense of the possibility of such borderline cases is by appealing to the idea that the singular terms in their description will lack determinate denotations. What, in addition, Williams and Swinburne bring out, is the very great unnaturalness of this way of thinking, which is nevertheless obligatory if the possibility of borderline cases of personal identity is accepted.

10.6 Conclusion

That completes my discussion of Williams's views in 'The self and the future'. I have argued that despite their ingenuity his arguments fail, and thus that it remains possible both to advocate a version of the Complex View and to accept the Only x and y principle. It remains in the next chapter to develop the version of the Complex View which I wish to recommend.

CHAPTER 11
Against the Closest Continuer Theory

11.1 Introduction

It is now time to pull together the threads of the discussion. As will by now be obvious to the reader the theory of personal identity I favour is a version of the Complex View, and it is a version of the Complex View according to which what is crucial for personal identity is neither identity of body nor brain, but psychological continuity, in the wide sense which includes other continuities as well as continuities of memory. Where I disagree with such psychological continuity theorists as Shoemaker and Parfit is in my adherence to the Only x and y principle, and my consequent rejection of any 'best' or 'no rival candidate' version of a psychological continuity account of personal identity. The crucial difference is that I am committed to saying that *any* sufficiently strong line of psychological continuity represents the history of some person irrespective of what fissions or fusions have taken place, or will take place.

In this final chapter I want to develop this account of personal identity and to attempt to demonstrate its superiority to the 'best candidate' approach. In order to do this I shall proceed by comparing it with Nozick's closest continuer theory of personal identity (1981), which is by far the most sophisticated and strongly defended version of the 'best candidate' approach in the literature. I shall argue that the alternative theory I favour can explain everything Nozick's theory can explain, can explain some things Nozick's theory cannot explain, and does not have the implausible consequences of Nozick's theory. By Nozick's own criterion of theory choice in philosophy (1981: 'Introduction'), then, it should be regarded as definitely preferable to his theory.

233

Apart from the fact that it is the strongest version of the 'best candidate' account available, I have another reason for choosing to discuss Nozick's theory in this chapter, namely some unfinished business left over from Chapter 9. In that chapter, it will be remembered, I argued that Parfit's thesis that identity does not matter in survival could not be sustained in the form he intended – the crucial argument against it, in fact, being one first given by Nozick. But we saw there that a more nuanced form of the thesis, which Nozick proposed, did not seem to be vulnerable to the same considerations. In this final chapter, then, I shall argue that even in this more sophisticated form the thesis that identity is not what matters in survival is unacceptable. In fact the very intuitions which Nozick points to as inexplicable on Parfit's view, are equally inexplicable on his own. The only way to explain them, as we shall see, is *both* to adopt an account of personal identity consistent with the Only x and y principle *and* to accept the primitiveness of our self-concern.

11.2 The Only x and y principle revisited

Before getting into these arguments, however, I want to return for one final time to the Only x and y principle and to consider an objection to it which has not yet been discussed.

Let us recall again the case of the ship of Theseus and the description of it which acceptance of the Only x and y principle entails.

The three relevant situations were originally pictured as follows:

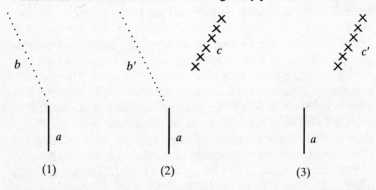

In each diagram the continuous line represents the history of the ship of Theseus before repair and replacement work begins. The line of dots in drawings 1 and 2 represents the history of the continuously repaired ship, and the line of crosses in drawings 2 and 3 represents the history of the ship reconsituted from the original planks of the ship of Theseus, i.e.the plank-hoarder's ship.

The constant '*a*' was introduced to designate the ship originally referred to in all three situations as 'the ship of Theseus', '*b*' was introduced to designate the ship undergoing continuous repair in situation 1, '*b'*' to designate the ship undergoing continuous repair in situation 2, '*c*' to designate the ship reconstituted from the original planks in situation 2, and '*c'*' to designate the ship reconstituted from the original planks in situation 3.

Now we saw that if we accept the Only *x* and *y* principle, and accept that in situation 1 there is exactly *one* ship which undergoes repair and replacement work, while in situation 3 there is exactly *one* ship which is first disassembled and later reconstructed, we must say that in situation 2 the ships *b'* and *c*, which later on are manifestly distinct, share the same origin and an initial part of their history. And in fact we must accept that *b'* in situation 2 has exactly the same history as *b* in situation 1, and *c* in situation 2 has exactly the same history as *c'* in situation 3.

But if *b* and *b'* have exactly the same history and *c* and *c'* have exactly the same history nothing stands in the way of concluding that $b = b'$ and $c = c'$, and this is obviously what a defender of the Only *x* and *y* principle must conclude. But since *b'* (or *b*) is distinct from *c* (or *c'*), it follows that it cannot be true both that $a = b$ in situation 1 and $a = c'$ in situation 3. Whence we have to conclude that drawings 1 to 3 have been mislabelled: '*a*' was introduced as the name of the ship originally referred to in all three situations as 'the ship of Theseus', but in situation 1 that is $b = b'$, and in situation 3 $c' = c$, and it is not the case that $b = c'$. What one has to say if one accepts the Only *x* and *y* principle and does not wish to describe situations 1 and 3 in obviously mistaken ways, is that as used in situation 1, 'the ship of Theseus' designates one ship, namely *b* (= *b'*), and as used in situation 3 it designates another, namely *c'* (= *c*). Which ship it designates in situation 2 depends on which of *b*(*b'*) and *c*(*c'*) has the best claim to the title, and it is to this matter that the intuitions about strongest candidature, which seem to support a 'best candidate' approach, in fact relate.

One can in fact take over Nozick's terminology to describe the situation from the point of view of a defender of the Only *x* and *y* principle. In each of the situations 1 to 3 when the name 'the ship of Theseus' is first introduced it will be introduced to name that ship whose history one follows by tracing the line of closest continuity from the ship-stage present at the baptismal ceremony. This is b in situation 1, c' in situation 3, disputable in situation 2. Similarly, in each situation, someone looking at the brand new ship of Theseus immediately after its launching will use 'that ship' or 'the new ship over there' with the intention of speaking of the ship whose history is traced by following the line of closest continuity from the ship-stage present there and then. Again this is b in situation 1, c' in situation 3, disputable in situation 2. However, *every* line of sufficiently close continuity represents the history of some entity, and the only sense in which the continuously repaired ship and the plank-hoarder's ship are rival candidates for identity with the ship of Theseus is that in different situations (1 and 3) each is the referent of the name 'the ship of Theseus' when that expression has its reference fixed in the way just indicated.

This account explains, as well as Nozick's, or any 'best candidate' account of artefact identity, our common-sense intuitions about the case of the ship of Theseus. We think that in situation 1 the ship of Theseus is the continuously repaired ship, that in situation 3 it is the plank-hoarder's ship, and that in situation 2 it is disputable – though most of us would say, if pressed to answer, that it was the continuously repaired ship. And, indeed, on my own account the reference of 'the ship of Theseus' in situation 1 *is* the continuously repaired ship, in situation 3 it *is* the plank-hoarder's ship, and in situation 2 it *is* disputable – though most of us would say, if pressed, that it was the continuously repaired ship, since we would say that, if either had greater weight, it was spatio-temporal continuity which was a more important factor in continuity *simpliciter* than identity of original parts.

However, there is an argument that a high price must be paid for the adherence to the Only x and y principle which this account allows. This price is not, as might be one's first hasty thought, that the name 'the ship of Theseus' cannot be a Kripkean rigid designator (see Kripke 1980 for this notion). For, of course, though its reference *as used in different possible situations* will be different (given that it is fixed in the same way in each), this does not rule out its having the same reference *with respect to every possible situation*, which is all that is required of a rigid designator. But given that 'the ship of Theseus' as used in situation 1 (or 2, or 3), is in fact a rigid designator, the argument I have in mind goes, it follows from my description of situations 1, 2, and 3 that someone in situation 1 contemplating situation 3 will speak falsely if he says 'The ship of Theseus might have undergone precisely *that* history of disassembly and reconstruction', for that ship, namely *b*, which in situation 1 is rightly called 'the ship of Theseus' is not present in situation 3, and a defender of the Only *x* and *y* principle can hardly maintain that the very history which is the history of *c'* in situation 3 could have been had by *b* instead in some other situation.

However, that the ship of Theseus might have had precisely the history of disassembly and reconstruction present in situation 3 will, of course, be the unhesitating judgement of any non-philosopher in situation 1. So here my alternative to Nozick's account leads me, if this argument is right, into a conflict with common sense at least as great as any involved in the rejection of the Only *x* and *y* principle.

So let us look more closely at this argument. Its crucial step is a move from the premiss, which my account entails, that the ship referred to as 'the ship of Theseus' in situation 1 has in no possible situation the history of disassembly and reconstruction which ship *c'* has in situation 3, to the conclusion that one must speak falsely if one says in situation 1: 'The ship of Theseus might have had precisely the history of disassembly and reconstruction had by ship *c'* in situation 3' – using 'the ship of Theseus' as a rigid designator, or anyway, giving it wider scope than the modal operator. But this move is not uncontentious; for its validity depends on the correct account of the satisfaction conditions of modal predicates of the form '*x* might have *F*'d'. The most obvious way to understand the argument, in fact, is as implicitly assuming a certain account of these satisfaction conditions: namely, that '*x* might have *F*'d' is true just in case there is a possible situation in which *x* does *F*.

But I have tried to show in Chapter 6 that this account of the satisfaction conditions of such modal predicates *must* be incorrect if it is right to regard continuants as four-dimensional perdurers. At the least this means that a defender of the closest continuer theory is awkwardly placed to use this argument as a way of supporting Nozick's account of continuant identity against my alternative. For, of course, Nozick himself accepts the four-dimensional metaphysic. Moreover, as I shall argue in a moment, there is some reason to believe that a defender of the closest continuer theory, or of any 'best candidate' account of identity, if he wishes to recommend it as a *general* theory of continuant identity, might be ill-advised to reject such a metaphysic. But whether or not this is so, a four-dimensional metaphysic is both plausible (as argued in Chapter 6), and widely accepted. So if this argument against my account of continuant identity requires its rejection that in itself is a serious weakness in it.

First, then, let us recall the demonstration in Chapter 6 that if continuants are four-dimensional perdurers the truth condition of 'x might have F'd' cannot just be that in some possible situation (world) x does F.

The argument appealed to Gibbard's (1975) story of Lumpl and Goliath. Lumpl is a piece of clay, and Goliath is the statue which is composed of Lumpl. Lumpl and Goliath, we are asked to imagine, have exactly the same temporal extent – they come into and go out of existence together. Then, on the four-dimensional conception, they have all and only the same temporal parts, and so they are identical. It will, however, be true of the piece of clay that it might never have had the particular shape in fact possessed by both it and Goliath, or that it might have been squeezed into a ball and not destroyed. These things cannot be true of the statue Goliath. Given the identity of Goliath and Lumpl, Leibniz's law then forces us to conclude that a modal predicate like 'might have been squeezed into a ball and not destroyed' cannot stand for the *same* property in the true proposition 'Lumpl might have been squeezed into a ball and not destroyed' and the false proposition 'Goliath might have been squeezed into a ball and not destroyed'. It therefore cannot stand in *both* sentences for the property possessed by a thing if and only if there is a possible situation in which it is squeezed into a ball and not destroyed. So it cannot be generally correct to think that 'x might have F'd' is true just in case in some possible situation x does F.

Of course, this conclusion can be contested by someone who rejects the four-dimensional metaphysic, since he can deny that Goliath and Lumpl are identical, but the four-dimensional theorist cannot take this way out, for it involves accepting that material objects which are always spatially coincident may none the less be distinct: since for the four-dimensional theorist material objects are simply summations of thing-stages and the thing-stages x-at-t and y-at-t are identical just in case x and y coincide at time t he must regard this as an impossibility.

The four-dimensional theorist, then, has no choice but to regard modal predicates either as not standing for properties at all, or as capable of standing for different properties in different sentences, e.g. when attached to different singular terms. But, of course, this option is also available to someone who rejects the four-dimensional metaphysic, and I believe that he, too, ought to accept it. For, as argued in Chapter 6, the only other option available to him is to accept that admittedly purely material entities, like statues and lumps of clay, of admittedly identical material constitution at all times, may none the less be distinct, though distinguished only by modal, dispositional or counterfactual properties. But this is surely an astonishing view.

So much, then, for the argument that an advocate of a four-dimensional metaphysic (or, indeed, anyone who is unwilling to acknowledge that admittedly purely material entities of admittedly identical material constitution at all times may none the less be distinct) cannot accept the account of the satisfaction conditions of predicates of the form 'x might have F'd' which is presupposed by the objection to my account of continuant identity under consideration in this section. I turn now to the promised argument that a defender of the closest continuer theory, or any 'best candidate' account of identity, if he regards that as a *general* theory of continuant identity, might be ill-advised to reject such a metaphysic.

Recall the content given to the notion of rival candidature for the title 'the ship of Theseus' in my alternative to Nozick's account. The rival candidates are simply the ships, the continuously repaired ship and the plank-hoarder's ship, and they are rivals just in the sense that in situations 1 and 3 respectively they are correctly referred to as 'the ship of Theseus', while in situation 2 it is unclear which is the reference of that name. This is not the notion of rival candidature involved in Nozick's account, however. For that account entails that it is the *same ship* which is rightly referred to as 'the ship of Theseus' in situations 1, 2 and 3. The obvious thought is that the rival candidates are still, on Nozick's account, the continuously repaired ship and the plank-hoarder's ship, but that they are not merely rivals for a *title* but rivals for *identity* with the (one and only) original ship of Theseus. But this will not do, of course, unless identity is contingent in a stronger sense than any that can be countenanced, indeed in a sense which is demonstrably absurd (see Chapter 7). So if the defender of the closest continuer theory is disinclined to accept such contingent identity, as he better be, he cannot regard the rival candidates as candidates for *identity* with the (one and only) original ship of Theseus, and so he cannot regard them as being the continuously repaired ship and the plank-hoarder's ship – for there is certainly nothing else these are candidates for. But then he cannot regard the rival candidates as being ships at all.

Another suggestion, put forward by Nathan Salmon in Appendix 1 of his *Reference and Essence* (1982), is that the rival candidates are *hunks of matter* and what they are candidates for is, not identity with, but *constituting* the ship of Theseus at the later time when two ships are floating side by side on the water. Now this suggestion of Salmon's is obviously very interesting, but it evidently cannot provide the notion of rival candidature the closest continuer theorist wants if he wishes to regard his theory as a general account of continuant identity, since hunks of matter are themselves continuants. If the closest continuer theory is to be a general one, and contingent identity is eschewed, the rival candidates whose possibility it must acknowledge cannot be continuants at all. If the defender of the closest continuer theory is a four-dimensional theorist, like Nozick, he can accept this conclusion with equanimity, of course. But what can he do if he is not? It seems that he will then have to regard the rival candidates as *events* in the histories of the relevant continuants. But at the same time he will have to insist that there is a great difference between an event being a stage *in the history of* a continuant and its being a stage *of* that continuant, and claim, in fact, that the latter notion is nonsense. So his position will have to be that there *are* both events and continuants, that the latter category is irreducible to the former, but that an account of our understanding of the identity conditions of items of the latter category requires ineliminable reference to items of the former category. Now I do not say that this is an impossible position to defend, but it is certainly not the position of those who have been most insistent on their rejection of a four-dimensional metaphysic – I am thinking especially of Prior, Geach and Strawson – who have tended to regard events as at best a kind of logical fiction. In adopting such an eclectic position, then, the defender of the closest continuer theory will find himself under attack from all sides, and committed to defending a point of view whose consistency is simply uninvestigated. As I said, then, unless he has a conclusive reason for rejecting it, he might be better advised to follow Nozick in adopting the conception of continuants as four-dimensional perdurers.

So much for the case of the ship of Theseus and some issues arising out of it. I have argued that what we regard it as correct to say about this case is as well explained by my own account of continuant identity, which accords with the Only *x* and *y* principle, as by Nozick's closest continuer theory, and that the objection to the Only *x* and *y* principle considered in this section is unconvincing. But Nozick claims a good deal more evidence for his closest continuer theory than its yielding a plausible description of the ship of Theseus case: in a wide range of cases, he suggests, the closest continuer theory explains and justifies what we think it correct to say, whilst no competing theory has comparable explanatory coverage. Against this claim I shall now argue that there is in fact *no* case Nozick discusses in which his theory is definitely superior in power to my own.

11.3 The Vienna Circle

First, let us look at the case of the Vienna Circle, which Nozick puts forward as a knock-down refutation of the Only *x* and *y* principle.

In actual fact the Vienna Circle was driven out of Austria and Germany by the Nazis; one member, Hans Reichenbach, landed in Istanbul (later he left and went to the USA). Nozick now supposes that there were twenty members of the Circle, of whom three ended up in Istanbul and kept meeting throughout the war years. In 1943 they hear that all the others are dead. On hearing this they proclaim that now *they* are the Vienna Circle, meeting in Istanbul. In 1945, however, they learn that nine other members of the original circle succeeded in reaching the USA, where they continued to meet, discuss philosophy, and so on. The group in Istanbul now happily acknowledge that they were mistaken in 1943 in proclaiming themselves to be the Vienna Circle: it is the group in America which is the Vienna Circle; they are merely its Istanbul offshoot.

Now Nozick is clearly correct in supposing that it would be right for the Istanbul group to react to the pieces of information they receive in 1943 and 1945 in the ways he suggests, but clearly wrong to suppose that this fact provides a knock-down refutation of the Only *x* and *y* principle. For the structural identity with the case of the ship of Theseus should make it obvious that it is equally well explained by my own account of continuant identity. In 1943 the Istanbul group claims a *title* and in 1945 turns out to be wrong in doing so. That is all there is to the case. Nozick's theory entails on the other hand that if we compare the two situations: the possible one envisaged by the Istanbul group in 1943 (situation 1) and the actual one which the Istanbul group became aware of in 1945 (situation 2), then the facts are (a) that some *entity*, the Vienna Circle, travels from Vienna to Istanbul in situation 1, and travels from Vienna to the USA in situation 2, though no *person* who travels from Vienna to Istanbul in situation 1 travels from Vienna to the USA in situation 2, and (b) that some entity comes into being in Istanbul (or on the way from Vienna to Istanbul) in situation 2, which never existed at all in situation 1, though nothing happens on the road to Istanbul or in Istanbul itself in situation 2 which does not happen in situation 1. It seems to me that these consequences of Nozick's account do not correspond with our intuitions about the case as well as my own description of it, which implies that *nothing* travels from Vienna to the USA in situation 2 which travels from Vienna to Istanbul in situation 1 and that the only entity (if any) which never exists at all in situation 1 which exists in situation 2 is there located in the USA, not Istanbul, in 1945.

11.4 The self and the future

Another argument Nozick gives is that the closest continuer theory reconciles and justifies the apparently conflicting intuitions we have about the two puzzle cases described by Bernard Williams in 'The self and the future' (1970), and at the same time provides the materials for a refutation of the argument for a bodily continuity criterion of personal identity which Williams gives in that paper. In fact, however, far from justifying the intuitions Nozick specifies, the closest continuer theory actually entails that one of these intuitions is mistaken. And whilst it does entail that Williams's argument is unsound, since it entails the falsehood of the Only *x* and *y* principle which, as Nozick says, is one of that argument's implicit premisses, this is not much of a point in its favour (even from the point of view of an opponent of the bodily continuity criterion). For Williams's argument is unsound even given the Only *x* and *y* principle, as we saw in the last chapter.

The first of Williams's puzzle cases, it will be recalled, is as follows. Two persons A and B enter some machine: upon leaving, the A-body person has all of (the previous person) B's memories, modes of behaviour and so on. Similarly the B-body person emerges with A's memories, modes of behaviour and so on. When enough details are filled in, Nozick says – and in this he seems to be right – we are prone to say or conclude that the people have switched bodies. If the events were to be described beforehand, and A was to decide solely on selfish grounds to which body something very painful was to be done afterwards, then our intuition is that A should designate the A-body, for *he* will be elsewhere – occupying the B-body – at a later time. And if he knows that something very pleasant will be happening to the B-body person at that later time, then, we are inclined to think not only will he be able to think of the future – in which the A-body person will be undergoing great suffering – without fear, it will even be possible for him, and from a purely sel-fish point of view entirely reasonable for him, to think of it with cheerful anticipation.

Nozick now presents Williams's second puzzle case. You are told that you will undergo terrible suffering. This prospect is frightening. You next receive the information that before this suffering comes you will have changed enormously in psychological traits – perhaps so greatly as to possess the memories, modes of behaviour and so on of someone who is now alive. This would frighten you even more, perhaps. You do not want to lose all your memories and distinctive psychological traits – to lose your identity, as we might say – and afterwards undergo enormous suffering. Yet how does this differ from what happened to A in the first story, which we were inclined to think of as something he could look forward to with calm? Sup-pose you *are A*: then the second case simply *is* the first case with the omission of any change to the B-body. Exactly the same changes happen to the A-body, however, and yet, Nozick suggests, follow-ing Williams, our intuition in this case, unlike the first, is that A continues throughout to be the occupant of the A-body, undergoing successive psychological disintegration, acquisition of a new psy-chology, and torture.

Because of his acceptance of the Only x and y principle Williams regards these intuitions about his two puzzle cases as genuinely in conflict. But Nozick argues that it is a merit of the closest continuer theory that it can justify both. For granted that exactly the same changes happen to the A-body in the two cases, it is entailed by the closest continuer theory that events which happen *elsewhere* can none the less determine whether or not it continues throughout to be the body of a single person: and that, Nozick argues, is precisely what explains the apparent conflict in our intuitions about Williams's two puzzle cases.

However, though Nozick is right that events which happen elsewhere can have such implications according to the closest continuer theory, he is wrong in supposing that it can justify the intuitions about Williams's puzzle cases which he endorses.

To see this we have to notice that in Williams's first case there is a causal process of transmission of information from the *A*-body person to the *B*-body person and conversely, and it is in large part because of this that it is plausible to think of what happens as body-switching. So in the second puzzle case, if everything is the same but for lack of changes to the *B*-body, there must still be a transmission of information from the *B*-body to the *A*-body. Hence at the later time there will be two continuers of the earlier *B*-body person – though one, the one occupying the *B*-body, will be the closest continuer; and there will be two *predecessors* of the later *A*-body person, namely the earlier *A*-body person and the earlier *B*-body person. Now it is part of the closest continuer theory that for a later stage *y* to be part of the same continuing object as an earlier stage *x*, not only must *y* be the closest continuer of *x*, also *x* must be the closest predecessor of *y*. But what makes for closeness in the case of predecessors cannot be different from what makes for closeness in the case of continuers, and Nozick must maintain that psychological continuity is a more important factor in determining degree of closeness of continuity in the case of persons than bodily continuity – otherwise he could not describe Williams's first puzzle case as one of body-switching. It follows that what Nozick's closest continuer theory in fact entails regarding Williams's second puzzle case is not that *A* survives through psychological disintegration, acquisition of new psychology, and torture, but simply that *A* ceases to exist, since his closest continuer, i.e. the later *A*-body person, does not have him as a closest predecessor. And this is exactly the description one can give of the case if one accepts my own account of continuant identity and hangs on to the Only *x* and *y* principle. For one can say that the degree of continuity between the earlier *A*-body person and the later *A*-body person is insufficient to constitute personal identity – the only *kind* of continuity, in fact, is bodily, and it is surely entirely plausible to suppose that this by itself can never be adequate to constitute personal identity.

The closest continuer theory and my own account of continuant identity also obviously entail the same description of Williams's first puzzle case, i.e. that A and B switch bodies. So our intuitions about these two cases can provide no reason for preferring Nozick's theory to mine. Rather, I think, the opposite is true, if anything; further reflection on these cases provides an argument *against* the closest continuer theory. For consider the variant on Williams's second puzzle case that we get if we drop the supposition of a causal process of transmission from B to A but leave everything else exactly the same. In this case, then, the later A-body person is not a continuer of the earlier B-body person (for continuity requires causal links, i.e. to say that something is a continuer of x is not just to say that its properties are qualitatively the same as x's or resemble them); and so the earlier B-body person is not a predecessor of the later A-body person. *A fortiori* then it is not a closer predecessor than the earlier A-body person. So it is compatible with the closest continuer theory that A continues to inhabit the A-body throughout all the changes that happen to it in this case, even though he ceases to exist in Williams's second puzzle case. But this, I suggest, is absurd: if there is exactly the same degree of continuity between the later A-body person and the earlier A-body person in both cases, and what happens elsewhere, i.e. to B, is exactly the same, so that the only difference is in the external cause of the later A-body person's psychological state, this cannot determine whether or not A continues or ceases to exist. And indeed Nozick himself implicitly endorses this conclusion, for in his discussion he in fact runs together Williams's second puzzle case and the variant on it I have just suggested (and in fact a second variant in which B is not in the picture at all and the later A-body person's psychological states are identical with those of *no* other actual person). Far from reconciling and justifying our common-sense intuitions, then, it looks as if in this case the closest continuer theory cannot even justify those of its originator.

But the closest continuer theory does provide the materials for a refutation of Williams's argument for a bodily continuity criterion of personal identity, just as Nozick claims. The heart of this argument is a challenge to the defender of a mentalistic criterion of personal identity to draw a line somewhere in the series of cases (i)–(vi) listed in Chapter 10, section 10.4, i.e. to say at what point it becomes incorrect to say that the A-body person is still A after the change described.

The defender of a psychological continuity criterion of personal identity must say that in (vi) the *A*-body person is no longer *A* after the change described, since the *B*-body person is. But, Williams asserts, he cannot deny that *A* survives the change described in (i). Hence he must draw the line somewhere in between, but this, Williams argues, he cannot do.

However, (vi) is simply Williams's first puzzle case, (v) his second, and (iv) the variant on his second case I just distinguished, and, as we have seen, a defender of the closest continuer theory can consistently regard what happens to *A* as different in each case. Far from being unable to draw *any* line between (i) and (vi), then, he can in fact draw two lines: one between (iv) and (v) and one between (v) and (vi). So if the closest continuer theory is correct Williams's argument collapses.

But it collapses anyway, as we have seen in Chapter 10, even if the closest continuer theory is incorrect, and even if the Only *x* and *y* principle is true. For Williams misapplies that principle in arguing that the *A*-body person must still be *A* after the change in (v) if he is still *A* after the change in (iv). Since this is so the fact that the closest continuer theory enables Williams's argument to be blocked is not a consideration in its favour – even for a supporter of a psychological continuity criterion of personal identity.

11.5 Fission

Finally, I turn to the problems of fission, where Nozick again claims superior explanatory power for the closest continuer theory.

According to the closest continuer theory, in a fission case the original person ceases to exist (for a fission case, by definition, is one in which there is a tie for continuity). But, Nozick wishes to say, it would be absurd for the original person in a fission case to adopt the same attitude to what is going to happen to him as he would adopt towards death.

If you are the original in a fission case, Nozick argues, though you do not continue to exist, still *they* do, each of the people who would be you if he alone existed; and they might, without getting in each other's way, fulfil different parts of your incompatible aspirations. It would not be reasonable for you to pay a lot of money to have all but one of these future continuers eliminated in order to avoid ties, even though by doing so you would ensure the future existence of a closest continuer and hence, according to the closest continuer theory, ensure your own future existence. On the other hand, Nozick argues, though the *existence* of a continuer closer than all others is not something to be especially concerned about, the *fate* of such a continuer, when it exists, *is* something one should be especially concerned about – 'especially' in the sense that the degree of one's concern for it ought not to be merely proportional to the degree of closeness of continuity it bears to oneself.

This point of Nozick's was elaborated in Chapter 9, and argued to be correct. My concern for the fate of the person who I believe will, in some situation I anticipate, be me, is a special one, and is not simply explicable as concern for the fate of someone who is continuous with me to a certain degree. Consequently, as argued in Chapter 9, Parfit's claim that what matters in survival is not identity must be wrong if it is taken as a description of what we actually and non-derivatively care about, and not merely as a recommendation of a different system of values. On the other hand, Nozick's intuition also seems correct when he says that it would be unreasonable for someone facing the prospect of fission to be prepared to pay a lot of money to eliminate all but one of the tied continuers, even though, since he is one and they, if they exist, are many, it seems that this is the only way he can ensure his own survival.

So, as Nozick recognizes, there is a puzzle here, and any adequate theory of personal identity will have to provide a solution to it.

Nozick, of course, thinks that the closest continuer theory provides such a solution. To see why he thinks this we have to digress briefly into his views of the structure of philosophical concepts, and consider what he calls 'the best instantiated realization' view of a philosophical concept. Briefly, a concept has this structure if one can explain the satisfaction conditions of the predicate denoting it by a statement of the form: x satisfies 'F' if x satisfies condition C, or if nothing satisfies condition C, it satisfies condition C'. Satisfying condition C is a better way of instantiating the concept than satisfying condition C', but if nothing satisfies C then satisfying C' is good enough. Or there might be a whole series of conditions C, C', C'' . . ., each a better way of satisfying the concept than its successors; then something satisfying, say C''' will instantiate the concept only if nothing satisfies C, C' or C''. Nozick suggests that two concepts which perhaps have such a best instantiated realization structure are *knowledge* and *solidity*. It is a requirement on a belief being knowledge that it varies with the truth of what is believed, but we can imagine possible beings whose beliefs vary with the truth of what is believed over a far wider range of situations than do ours, and this is one reason why we feel that our claims to knowledge are vulnerable to sceptical attack. But it is a bad reason, Nozick points out, if knowledge has a best instantiated realization structure, for though, if this is so, our beliefs would not be knowledge if such beings were actual, given that they are merely possible, our beliefs can qualify as knowledge in virtue of varying with the truth of what is believed to be the extent that they actually do. Though not the best possible examples of knowledge, and not examples of knowledge in other possible worlds, in the actual world they still qualify as knowledge.

Similarly, Nozick suggests, if one accepts a best instantiated realization view of the concept of solidity one can settle the dispute between Eddington and Stebbing over the solidity of tables in favour of Stebbing. If there *were* extended objects with no internal spaces anywhere then they alone would be solid and tables, which, as Eddington pointed out, are largely holes, would not be; but given that there are no such objects, and tables are further along the relevant dimensions of solidity than other things, liquids and gases for example, then tables do count as being solid: though not the best possible examples, they are good enough.

Now we can return to the problem of fission and state Nozick's solution to the puzzle that interests us. Why do we care especially for our closest continuer when it exists, but not care that there be a closest continuer when we know that there will be close enough tied continuers? Nozick's answer is that one's special care is not for oneself as such, but is rather for the best instantiated realization of the concept of oneself. If my closest continuer exists he is the best instantiated realization of the concept of myself and other continuers, who are sufficiently close to be me in the absence of competitors, are not realizations of that concept at all. Consequently, I will care for them only in proportion to their degree of continuity and reserve my special care for my closest continuer. But if there is a tie, so that I have no closest continuer, then a best instantiated realization of the concept of myself is any satisfier of the condition: *continuer of myself than which no other continuer is closer*. All the tied continuers satisfy this condition, so each of them will merit the special care I have only for the best instantiated realization of the concept of myself. I will therefore care for each of them in a way that is not merely proportional to its degree of closeness to me. And I will have no motive for paying a lot of money to eliminate ties, since so long as there is a best instantiated realization of the concept of myself I do not care how good a realization it is. The tied continuers are not as good realizations as a unique closest continuer would be, but they are good enough, and that is all I care about.

This, then, is what Nozick offers as his solution to the puzzle. But the first thing to notice is that it is simply no solution at all. Part of the puzzle as Nozick originally stated it was that one cared especially for one's closest continuer irrespective of its degree of closeness to oneself, but that one's degree of care for any non-closest continuer was merely proportional to its degree of closeness. It is part of his 'solution', however, that one's care for one's tied continuers in a case of fission is *not* merely proportional to their degree of closeness to oneself. So what is being explained has shifted as the explanation has developed, and the original statement of the puzzle has been ignored.

Second, notice that it is in fact wholly misleading of Nozick to bring in the terminology of 'best instantiated realizations' into the statement of his solution to the puzzle. For as he originally explains that notion it is senseless to speak of something being the best instantiated realization of a concept which is empty. But when the concept is that of myself, and the 'best instantiated realizations' of it are merely satisfiers of the condition: *continuer of myself than which no other is closer*, then, as he notes parenthetically, the concept is empty – I no longer exist.

In fact, if Nozick had stated his 'solution' to the puzzle without using this misleading terminology it would have been apparent at once that it was no solution at all, but a mere denial of the problem. For so stated the 'solution' is simply that one has a special degree of care for any continuer of oneself than which no other is closer, but no special degree of care for oneself, i.e. one's closest continuer, as such.

Once again, then, the explanatory power Nozick claims for the closest continuer theory turns out on investigation to be illusory. But the puzzle as Nozick originally stated it still remains, and I now wish to argue that my own account of continuant identity can provide a solution to it.

The essential difference between my account of continuant identity and Nozick's, it will be remembered, is that according to my account every line of sufficiently close continuity represents the history of some entity, irrespective of what is the case elsewhere, whereas Nozick's theory denies this and entails the rejection of the Only x and y principle. It thus follows from my account that each of the tied continuers must have existed before the fission. Now this, of course, puts *some* constraints on the concept of a person: it must be such that each of the persons who existed after the fission existed before. But this still leaves various ways of defining the concept available. We might try the following: a person is a certain collection of person-stages, a collection containing a member – let us call it a 'marker' for the collection – such that all and only the members of the collection are the closest continuers or predecessors of that member when they exist. However, this definition is inadequate to cases of fusion followed by fission, because it does not allow one to say that there is a person involved in such a situation for *each* line of personal continuity, and so does not allow one to survive through the *whole* course of events – which is required by the Only x and y principle. The revision required to deal with this difficulty is as follows. Call what has just been defined a 'person-set'. Then the extension of 'person' can be indicated thus. Any person-set is a person. The union of any two person-sets determined by markers a and b, where a and b are linked by personal continuity, is a person if it contains no simultaneous person-stages. If such a union of two person-sets does contain simultaneous person-stages consider all its sub-classes got by omitting all but one member of any simultaneous group of person-stages. Any such sub-class all of whose members are related pairwise by personal continuity is a person. Nothing else is a person.

On this definition three people are involved in a fission case (assuming just two tied continuers): two of them survive the fission and one does not. On the other hand, when there are several continuers but no tie for closeness the number of people involved is simply identical with the number of continuers, and this, I think, seems right. Now it seems reasonable to suppose that if this is our concept of a person the reference of 'I' on a particular occasion of utterance will be that person for whom the person-stage tokening 'I' is a marker. If so, when I look forward to the prospect of my own fission I must acknowledge that I look forward to an event after which I will not exist, even though each of the survivors of the fission will be able to say truly on looking back on the fission: 'I existed before that happened.'

It is now easy to provide an explanation of one of the two intuitions which constitute our puzzle. Given that I am especially concerned about my own fate, but care for those of my continuers who are not me only in proportion to how closely they continue to me, as Nozick plausibly suggests, then, of course, I will not care especially for the fate of my tied continuers when I face the prospect of fission, and, of course, anyone whose fate I do care about especially will be me. But, then, why will it be irrational for me, facing the prospect of fission, to pay out a lot of money to have all but one of my tied continuers eliminated? If the fission takes place I will not survive, if it does not, if there is no tie, I will survive. I care especially about my own fate. So how *can* it be irrational for me to pay out the money? This is the other half of the puzzle.

But let us compare the two situations between which I am choosing. In one of them I do not pay out the money, the fission takes place and I cease to exist. Let us suppose this is what actually happens. What might have happened instead? Well, the money might have been paid out and all but one of the tied continuers eliminated. Would I then have lived any longer? No. For the person who in this situation survives beyond the point at which fission takes place in the actual situation is *that* one of the tied continuers in the actual situation who has not been eliminated, and he is not me. If I exist in this possible situation at all I live not a moment longer than I do in the actual situation and in fact do not even qualify as a person. Nor does anyone in this situation live any longer than he does in the actual situation. Nor are there any people in this situation who are not in the actual situation, but are longer-lived than certain people in the actual situation. The only difference is that as compared with the actual situation this possible situation contains fewer people. And I *would* be totally irrational if I thought that by acting to bring about such a situation I could ensure my own survival.

Let us look at the matter from the other side. Suppose that what actually happens is that I pay out the money, and all but one of the possible tied continuers is eliminated. Then I am that one of the possible tied continuers who actually exists. Reflecting on what would have happened if I had not paid out the money, can I find any justification for my action? Of course not. The possible situation which my action eliminated was not one in which my life was any shorter. For, of course, in that situation *I* survived the fission. Indeed it was not a situation in which anyone's life was any shorter. It differed from the actual situation in one respect only; namely, in containing more people. But I would have to be insane to regard my action as justified on the ground that it eliminated as a possibility a situation which differed in this respect only from the actual one. Thus if I do pay out the money I can then provide no possible justification for doing so; but an action cannot be a rational one which once performed it is impossible to justify.

Given my account of continuant identity, then, a solution can be found to the puzzle about fission which Nozick states but himself fails to solve.

But a final attempt may now be made to defend the claim of the closest continuer theory to superior explanatory power. For it may be said that the real puzzle is *not* the one to which I have just given a solution, but the puzzle Nozick himself solves. That is, the intuitions we actually have about fission are not those I have just explained but those Nozick explains. For when we reflect on the possibility of fission we realize we do *not* care especially just for ourselves, i.e. our closest continuers, but also for those of our continuers than whom there are no closer. Of course, if this is so it has to be acknowledged that Nozick originally misstated the puzzle; but this is a minor criticism given that he did actually provide a solution to it.

The first point I wish to make about this rejoinder is simply that it seems to me to rest on a false premiss. The intuitions we actually have about fission are those for which I have just provided an explanation, and not those which Nozick explains. However, there is no need for me to insist on this point, because the rejoinder fails anyway, whether or not it is correct, for the fact is that *whichever* set of intuitions we actually have, they can be explained in accordance with my account of continuant identity.

To see this point it is necessary to recall that my account of continuant identity is compatible with more than one definition of the concept of a person. With the definition I gave earlier we can, as we saw, solve the puzzle Nozick originally states, the one which, as I have just said, still seems to me to be the real puzzle. I take this to be an argument in favour of that definition. But if one accepts a slightly different definition of the concept of a person one can provide a solution to the other puzzle – the one which the rejoinder takes to be the real one.

Specifically, one can provide such a solution if one accepts David Lewis's (1976) definition according to which a person is a maximal summation of person-stages related pairwise by personal unity, i.e. that relation which obtains between two person-stages whenever one is a sufficiently close continuer of the other. This definition of a person is compatible with my account of continuant identity and incompatible with Nozick's, for it entails that every line of sufficiently close bodily and/or psychological continuity represents the history of some person, irrespective of what happens elsewhere.

Now on this definition the number of people involved in a situation in which I have multiple continuers is invariably identical with the number of those continuers; so there are just two people involved in a fission case in which there are exactly two (tied) continuers, and both of them survive the fission. And it seems reasonable to suppose that if this is our concept of a person the reference of a token of 'I' on a particular occasion of utterance will be that person whose history one traces by following the line of closest continuity from the person-stage doing the tokening. So in the fission situation the reference of 'I' will be indeterminate between the two people involved.

It is now easy to provide an explanation of the two intuitions which constitute what the rejoinder takes to be the real puzzle. First, since neither of the two people involved in the fission ceases to exist at the moment of fission, and it is only between these two people that the reference of 'I' is indeterminate, when I envisage the prospect of my fission I must acknowledge that I am looking forward to an event which it is definitely true that I will survive. So it would be quite absurd for me to think it necessary to pay out a lot of money to have one of the (possible) tied continuers eliminated as a means of ensuring my own survival. Second, since it is only between the two people involved in the fission that the reference of 'I' is indeterminate, a necessary and sufficient condition of its being definitely true that I have a certain property after my fission is that each of the tied continuers has that property. In particular, then, a necessary and sufficient condition of it being definitely true that I am happy after the fission is that each of the tied continuers is happy after the fission. Given that I am especially concerned for my own well-being, in the sense of 'especially' explicated by Nozick, it thus follows that in the same sense I must be especially concerned for the well-being of my tied continuers.

Given Lewis's definition of the concept of a person, then, together with the plausible assumption that I am especially concerned for my own well-being, both the intuitions which the rejoinder on behalf of the closest continuer theory asserts to constitute the real puzzle can be explained in a way that is compatible with my account of continuant identity.

So again it turns out that no cogent argument for the superior explanatory power of the closest continuer theory has been put forward. In fact, I think, we can again see that on closer investigation precisely the opposite is the case. For, of course, the things mentioned in an explanation ought to be different from the thing being explained. Now the explanation which I have just sketched satisfies this condition: in particular it does not simply postulate that I care especially for my tied continuers, but derives this proposition from the assumption that I care especially for myself together with an assumption about the way in which the reference of 'I' is fixed. Nozick's 'explanation', however – when we extract it from the misleading terminology of 'best instantiated realizations' in which he states it – does simply postulate precisely this. So really it is no explanation at all – for if someone wants to know *why* we care especially for our tied continuers, Nozick has no answer.

I conclude that there is nothing the closest continuer theory can explain that my own account of continuant identity cannot explain more plausibly, and that there are some things my account can explain that the closest continuer theory cannot explain. Using this very criteria of theory choice in philosophy that Nozick himself is so insistent upon, then, I submit that my account of continuant identity must be regarded as definitely preferable to the closest continuer theory.

BIBLIOGRAPHY

Alston, W.P. and Bennett, J. (1988) 'Locke on people and substances', *Philosophical Review* 97:25–46.

Brennan, A. (1988) *Conditions of Identity*, Oxford: Clarendon Press.

Brody, B. (1980) *Identity and Essence*, Princeton: Princeton University Press.

Broome, J. (1984) 'Indefiniteness of identity', *Analysis* 44: 6–12.

Butler, J. (1736) 'Of personal identity', First dissertation to *The Analogy of Religion*, reprinted in A. Flew (1964) *Body, Mind and Death*, New York: Macmillan and J. Perry (ed.) (1975) *Personal Identity*, Berkeley and Los Angeles: University of California Press.

Butterfield, J. (1985) 'Spatial and temporal parts', *Philosophical Quarterly* 35: 32–44.

Care, N. and Grimm, R.H. (1969) *Perception and Personal Identity*, Cleveland: Ohio University Press.

Chisholm, R.M. (1969) 'The loose and popular and strict and philosophical senses of identity', in N. Care, and R.H. Grimm (1969) *Perception and Personal Identity*, Cleveland: Ohio University Press.

—— (1970) 'Identity through time', in H.E. Kiefer and M.K. Munitz, (eds) *Language Belief and Metaphysics*, Albany: State University of New York Press.

—— (1976) *Person and Object*, London: Allen & Unwin.

Cook, J. (1968) 'Hume's scepticism with regard to the senses', *American Philosophical Quarterly* 5: 1–17.

Curley, E. (1982) 'Leibniz on Locke on personal identity', in M. Hooker, (ed.) *Leibniz: Critical and Interpretive Essays*, Minneapolis: University of Minnesota Press.

Dummett, M. (1982) 'Realism', *Synthese* 52: 55–112.

Ehring, D. (1987) 'Survival and trivial facts', *Analysis* 47: 50–4.

Evans, G. (1978) 'Vague objects', *Analysis* 38: 208.

—— (1982) *The Varieties of Reference*, Oxford: Clarendon Press.

Flew, A. (1951) 'Locke and the problem of personal identity', *Philosophy* 26: 53–68.

—— (1964) *Body, Mind and Death*, New York: Macmillan.

—— (1986) *Hume: Philosopher of Moral Science*, Oxford: Blackwell.

—— (1987) *The Logic of Mortality,* Oxford: Blackwell.

255

Frege, G. (1950) *The Foundations of Arithmetic*, trans. J.L. Austin, Oxford: Blackwell.

Garrett, D. (1981) 'Hume's self doubts about personal identity', *Philosophical Review* 90: 337–58.

Geach, P.T. (1962) *Reference and Generality*, Ithaca: Cornell University Press.

—— (1965) 'Some problems about time', *Proceedings of the British Academy* vol. 60: 321–36.

—— (1967) 'Identity', *Review of Metaphysics* 21: 3–12.

—— (1971) 'Ontological relativity and relative identity', in M.K. Munitz, (ed.) (1971) *Identity and Individuation*, New York: New York University Press.

—— (1972) *Logic Matters*, Oxford: Blackwell.

—— (1976) 'Names and identity', in S. Guttenplan (ed.) *Mind and Language*, Oxford: Clarendon Press.

Geach, P.T. and Black M. (1952) *Translations from the Philosophical Writings of Gottlob Frege*, Oxford: Blackwell.

Gibbard, A. (1975) 'Contingent identity', *Journal of Philosophical Logic* 4: 187–222.

Glanville, J. (1970) *The Vanity of Dogmatizing*, ed. S. Medcalf, Hove, Sussex: Harvester. First printed London (1661).

Hobbes, T. (1961) 'De Corpore' in *The English Works of Thomas Hobbes*, ed. Sir William Molesworth, London: John Bohn 1839. Reprinted Oxford 1911.

Hume, D. (1978) *A Treatise of Human Nature*, ed. L.A. Selby-Bigge, Oxford: Clarendon Press. First printed 1739.

Johnston, M. (1987) 'Human Beings', *Journal of Philosophy* 84: 59–83.

Kant, I. (1964) *Critique of Pure Reason*, trans. Norman Kemp Smith, London: Macmillan.

Kripke, S. (1971) 'Identity and necessity' in M.K. Munitz, (ed.) *Identity and Individuation*, New York: New York University Press.

—— (1980) *Naming and Necessity*, revised edition, Oxford: Blackwell.

—— (unpublished) 'Lectures on identity'.

Leibniz, G.W. (1953) *Discourse on Metaphysics*, trans. P. Lucas and L. Grint, Manchester: Manchester University Press.

—— (1981) *New Essays on Human Understanding*, trans. and ed. P. Remnant and J. Bennett, Cambridge: Cambridge University Press.

Lewis, C.S. (1967) *Studies in Words*, Cambridge: Cambridge University Press.

Lewis, D. (1968) 'Counterpart theory and quantified modal logic', *Journal of Philosophy* 65: 113–26. Reprinted with added postscript in D. Lewis (1983) *Philosophical Papers*, Oxford: Oxford University Press.

—— (1971) 'Counterparts of persons and their bodies', *Journal of Philosophy* 68: 203–11. Reprinted in D. Lewis (1983) *Philosophical Papers*, Oxford: Oxford University Press.

—— (1976) 'Survival and identity', in A. Rorty (ed.) (1976) *The Identities of Persons*, Berkeley: University of California Press. Reprinted with added postscripts in D. Lewis (1983) *Philosophical Papers*, Oxford: Oxford University Press.

—— (1983) *Philosophical Papers*, vol. 1, Oxford: Oxford University Press.

—— (1986) *On The Plurality of Worlds*, Oxford: Blackwell.

Locke, J. (1823) *The Works of John Locke*, 10 vols, London: Tegg.

—— (1936) *An Early Draft of Locke's Essay together with Excerpts from his Journal*, ed. R.I. Aaron and J. Gibb, Oxford: Clarendon Press.

—— (1961) *An Essay Concerning Human Understanding*, ed. J. Yolton, London: Dent.

Mabbott, J.D. (1973) *John Locke*, London: Macmillan.

Mackie, J. (1976) *Problems from Locke*, Oxford: Clarendon Press.

Madell, G. (1981) *The Identity of Self*, Edinburgh: Edinburgh University Press.

Mellor, H. (1981) *Real Time*, Cambridge: Cambridge University Press.

Munitz, M.K. (ed.) (1971) *Identity and Individuation*, New York: New York University Press.

Nagel, T. (1971) 'Brain bisection and the unity of consciousness', *Synthese* 22: 396–413, also in T. Nagel (1979) *Mortal Questions*, Cambridge: Cambridge University Press.

—— (1979) *Mortal Questions*, Cambridge: Cambridge University Press.

Noonan, H. (1980) *Objects and Identity*, The Hague: Martinus Nijhoff.

—— (1982a) 'Williams on "The self and the future" ', *Analysis* 42: 158–63.

—— (1982b) 'Vague objects', *Analysis* 42: 3–6.

—— (1983) 'Personal identity and bodily continuity', *Analysis* 43: 98–104.

—— (1984) 'Indefinite identity: a reply to Broome', *Analysis* 44: 117–21.

—— (1985a) 'Wiggins, artefact identity and "best candidate theories" ', *Analysis* 45: 4–8.

—— (1985b) 'The Only *x* and *y* principle', *Analysis* 45: 79–83.

—— (1985c) 'A note on temporal parts', *Analysis* 45: 151–2.

—— (1985d) 'The closest continuer theory of identity', *Inquiry* 28: 195–229.

Nozick, R. (1981) *Philosophical Explanations*, Oxford: Clarendon Press.

Parfit, D. (1971) 'Personal identity', *Philosophical Review* 80: 3–27.

—— (1984) *Reasons and Persons*, Oxford: Clarendon Press.

Peacocke, C. (1983) *Sense and Content*, Oxford: Clarendon Press.

Penelhum, T. (1955) 'Hume on personal identity', *Philosophical Review* 64: 571–89.

—— (1970) *Survival and Disembodied Existence*, London: Routledge & Kegan Paul.

Perry, J. (1972) 'Can the self divide?', *Journal of Philosophy* 73: 463–88.

—— (ed.) (1975) *Personal identity*, Berkeley and Los Angeles: University of California Press.

—— (1976) 'Review of Williams's *Problems of the Self*', *Journal of Philosophy* 73: 416–28.

Pike, N. (1967) 'Hume's bundle theory of the self: a limited defence', *American Philosophical Quarterly* 4: 159–65.

Prior, A. (1957) *Time and Modality*, Oxford: Clarendon Press.

—— (1968) *Papers on Time and Tense*, Oxford: Oxford University Press.

Quine, W.V. (1960) *Word and Object*, Cambridge, Mass.: MIT Press.
—— (1961) *From a Logical Point of View*, 2nd edn, New York: Harper Torchbooks.
—— (1976) 'Worlds away', *Journal of Philosophy* 73: 859–63.
—— (1985) 'Events and reification', in E. LePore and B.P. McLaughlin (eds) *Actions and Events*, Oxford: Blackwell.
Reid, T. (1941) *Essays on the Intellectual Powers of Man*, ed. A.D. Woozley, London: Macmillan.
Robinson, D. (1982) 'Reidentifying matter', *Philosophical Review* 91: 317–41.
—— (1985) 'Can amoebae divide without multiplying?' *Australian Journal of Philosophy* 63: 299–319.
Rorty, A. (ed.) (1976) *The Identities of Persons*, Berkeley: University of California Press.
Salmon, N.U. (1982) *Reference and Essence*, Oxford: Blackwell.
Shaffer, J. (1977) 'Personal identity', *Journal of Medicine and Philosophy* 2: 147–61.
Shoemaker, S. (1963) *Self-knowledge and Self-identity*, Ithaca: Cornell University Press.
—— (1969) 'Comments on Chisholm', in N. Care and R.M. Grimm, (1969) *Perception and Personal Identity*, Cleveland: Ohio University Press.
—— (1970) 'Persons and their pasts', *American Philosophical Quarterly* 7: 269–85.
—— (1984) *Identity, Cause and Mind*, Cambridge: Cambridge University Press.
—— (1985) 'Critical notice: Parfit's *Reasons and Persons*', *Mind* 44: 443–53.
—— (1986) 'Introspection and the self', *Midwest Studies in Philosophy* 10: 101–20.
Shoemaker, S. and Swinburne, R.G. (1984) *Personal Identity*, Oxford: Blackwell.
Sperry, R.W. (1968a) 'Mental unity following surgical disconnection of the cerebral hemisphere', *Harvey Lectures*, New York: Academic Press.
—— (1968b) 'Hemisphere deconnection and unity in conscious awareness', *American Psychologist* 23: 723–33.
—— (1977) 'Forebrain commisurotomy and conscious awareness', *Journal of Medicine and Philosophy* 2: 107–25.
Strawson, P.F. (1970) 'Chisholm on identity through time', in H.E. Kiefer and M.K. Munitz, (eds) *Language, Belief and Metaphysics*, Albany: State University of New York Press.
—— (1976) 'Entity and identity', in H.D. Lewis (ed.) *Contemporary British Philosophy*, London: Allen & Unwin.
Swinburne, R.G. (1973–4) 'Personal identity', *Proceedings of the Aristotelian Society* 74: 231–47.
—— (1976) 'Persons and personal identity', in H.D. Lewis (ed.) *Contemporary British Philosophy*, London: Allen & Unwin.
Thompson, J.J. (1983) 'Parthood and identity across time', *Journal of Philosophy* 80: 201–20.

Vesey, G. (1974) *Personal Identity*, London: Macmillan.

Wiggins, D. (1967) *Identity and Spatio-Temporal Continuity*, Oxford: Blackwell.

—— (1968) 'On being in the same place at the same time', *Philosophical Review* 77: 90–5.

—— (1979) 'The concern to survive', *Midwest Studies in Philosophy* 4: 417–22.

—— (1980) *Sameness and Substance*, Oxford: Blackwell.

Williams, B.A.O. (1956–7) 'Personal identity and individuation', *Proceedings of the Aristotelian Society* 57: 229–52. Reprinted in B.A.O. Williams (1973) *Problems of the Self*, Cambridge: Cambridge University Press.

—— (1966) 'Imagination and the self', *Proceedings of the British Academy* 70:105–24. Reprinted in B.A.O. Williams (1973) *Problems of the Self*, Cambridge: Cambridge University Press.

—— (1970) 'The self and the future', *Philosophical Review* 79: 161–80. Reprinted in B.A.O Williams (1973) *Problems of the Self*, Cambridge: Cambridge University Press.

—— (1973) *Problems of the Self*, Cambridge: Cambridge University Press.

Wittgenstein, L. (1953) *Philosophical Investigations*, trans. G.E.M. Anscombe, Oxford: Blackwell.

Index